Michael Montgomery lives near Oxford with his Australian wife. He was educated at Harrow and Hertford College, Oxford, to both of which he won Open Exhibitions. Since his widely-praised travelogue *All Out For Everest*, describing a 2-month overland journey to Kathmandu and an 18-day trek to the Everest Base Camp, he has divided his time between fiction and historical subjects; including the mysterious loss of the World War II cruiser *HMAS Sydney* with all hands (his own father among them) and the central role of Emperor Hirohito in Japan's campaign of imperialist aggression. He has written numerous feature articles and reviews in a wide range of newspapers and magazines, and is currently working on a screenplay centred around the tragic story of Lear's lengthy and ultimately unfulfilled love affair with Gussie Bethell, the daughter of Gladstone's Lord Chancellor.

To Gigi
my original cicerone

Lear's Italy
in the footsteps of
Edward Lear

Compiled and edited
by Michael Montgomery

CADOGAN

Cadogan Guides
Network House, 1 Ariel Way
London W12 7SL
info@cadoganguides.co.uk
www.cadoganguides.com

The Globe Pequot Press
246 Goose Lane, PO Box 480, Guilford,
Connecticut 06437–0480

Printed in Italy by Legoprint
A catalogue record for this book is available
from the British Library
ISBN 1-86011-219-6

Contents

Contents

Introduction

> There was an Old Man of th' Abruzzi,
> So blind that he couldn't his foot see;
> When they said, 'That's your toe,'
> He replied, 'Is it so?'
> That doubtful Old Man of th' Abruzzi.[1]

Edward Lear has been known for generations, the world over, as the author of *The Book of Nonsense*. First published in 1846, it went into nearly 30 impressions in his own lifetime and has never been out of print since. Two years before his death in 1888 John Ruskin, that Olympian arbiter of Victorian taste, declared that 'I really do not know any author to whom I am half so grateful, for my idle self, as Edward Lear. I shall put him first of my hundred authors,'[2] and as recently as 2001 one of the poems, 'The Owl And The Pussy-Cat' was voted Britain's All-Time Children's Favourite Poem.[3]

This celebrity soon overshadowed the fact that Lear had worked all his life as a professional artist. Only 20 years later the editor of a collection of his letters wrote:

> the English and American public of the present day only know Edward Lear through his *Books of Nonsense*. To only a cultivated few, and the survivors of a past generation who possess many of his works, are his pictures existent.[4]

Even more quickly forgotten was his reputation as a travel writer and, in particular, his association with Italy, his adopted home for the last 50 years of his life, apart from the period of revolution before the eventual triumph of Garibaldi's Risorgimento movement.

During these years he managed to explore every furthest corner of that diverse and fascinating country. Travelling for the most part on foot or, at best, on horseback, he was very often the first Englishman ever to have been seen in many of the remoter areas and he was able to correct some of his hosts' hilarious misconceptions about the land of his birth. All this he recorded not only in his art but also in his travelogues, diaries and voluminous letters: he once reckoned to have as many regular correspondents as there are days in the year.

Coloured with the same unique humour that inspired his nonsense writings, Lear's descriptions of Italy and its people give a wonderfully evocative and entertaining picture of a country that was only then beginning to emerge from a haphazard, centuries-old conglomeration of petty feudal fiefdoms into the single but still firmly individualist nation that we know today. Lear's writing also serves to give a moving and penetrating insight into a man who was one of the most remarkable characters of the Victorian era. As with so many of the world's great comedians, all the fun helped to mask a lifelong struggle against adversity – physical disabilities, financial burdens and a series of unconsummated love affairs. It was a cruel irony indeed that the man who gave so much pleasure to countless children was never to be blessed with any of his own.

This was not the fate that seemed to be in store for him when he arrived into the world on 12 May 1812, as the 20th child (the 13th of those who survived their infancy) of a well-to-do London stockbroker, Jeremiah Lear. The extended family lived in a large Georgian house, Bowman's Lodge, in the then fashionable village of Holloway, surrounded by fields and woods overlooking the City. According to a memoir handed down by Edward's niece, they housed no less than 12 carriages in the stables, but this seems fanciful even for such a numerous brood. Edward's own earliest memory was of being bundled up in a blanket from his bed as a three-year-old and taken out to watch the fireworks lighting up the sky in celebration of the news of Wellington's great victory at Waterloo.

This childhood idyll was rudely cut short the following year, however, when Jeremiah was caught out in the post-war bust and was declared a defaulter on the Stock Exchange. Bowman's Lodge was put out on a furnished lease, but this proved less of an economy than it promised, for the Jewish tenants 'always opened the windows in thunderstorms – for the easier entrance of the Messiah, but to [the] greater spoiling of the furniture'.[5] The deficit was eventually cleared with the help of a bank loan of £1,000 and the house was repossessed, but the family was never to recover from the reverse. Those of the children who were now old enough to fend for themselves were dispersed: one son into the Army and another as a missionary to Africa (both later emigrated to the United States), while four of the older girls went into domestic service as governesses or companions, thus reducing it to a nucleus of Edward, Ann (the eldest) and four other sisters.

The impact on the long-suffering Mrs Lear appears, not surprisingly, to have been severe, and the responsibility for her remaining son's upbringing now devolved entirely upon Ann, of whom Lear was later to write that 'she brought me up from the leastest childhood... & what I should have been unless she had been my mother I dare not think'.[6] That on Lear himself was no less traumatic, as one of his very earliest attempts at versifying perhaps testifies:

> Sad was the hour, and luckless the day,
> When first from Bowman's Lodge we bent our way![7]

The pain of this parting continued to haunt him so powerfully that he was almost into his 60s before he could overcome it sufficiently to take possession of a house of his own, while many of his nonsense creations rejoiced in the thought that they had little or nothing to lose in the way of material belongings.

It was shortly afterwards that he began to suffer from the epilepsy which was to plague him for the rest of his life, although he never suffered the climactic seizures that overtook his sister Jane. His form of the complaint was the *petit mal,* which induced seizures akin to brainstorms; they usually gave him premonitions of their coming, and so successful did he become at reading these signals that 60 years later he was able to boast in his diary that 'it is wonderful that these fits have never been discovered – except that partly apprehending them beforehand, I go to my room'.[8] He marked each seizure there with an X and totalled them up at the end of the month: 20 was an average score, although as many as three might occur in a single day.

On top of these and the additional handicaps of weak eyes and lungs, Lear was burdened with another affliction, 'The Morbids', as he called them, or fits of depression; they obviously sprang from his emotional disturbance, for they invariably followed experiences of intense pleasure. He recalled the first of them thus:

> The earliest of all the morbidnesses I can recollect must have been somewhere about 1819, when my father took me to a field near Highgate where was a rural performance of gymnastic clowns, &c. – & a band. The music was good – at least, it attracted me – & the sunset & twilight I remember as if of yesterday. And I can recollect crying half the night after all the small gaiety broke up – & also suffering for days at the memory of the past scene.[9]

Ann was also placed in charge of her brother's education, and he was 11 years old before he enlisted in any formal schooling, but this was one circumstance that caused him little later regret. 21 years older than her charge and, according to the memoir, 'exceptionally handsome', Ann could have been excused if she had made the realisation of her own prospects her first priority. She certainly received at least one proposal of marriage, and this from a baronet, Sir Claudius Hunter, whom 'you were in love with so many years ago', as her brother was to remind her near the end of her life, but whom nonetheless she 'did not, or would not, marry'.[10]

She devoted herself instead to Edward. A sincere Christian, she leavened instruction in the Bible with readings from classical mythology and modern poets. As with so many of her contemporaries, Byron was her particular heart-throb, and the news of his death in 1823 affected them both deeply: 'Do you remember the small yard & passages... when I used to sit there in the cold looking at the stars &, when I heard that Lord Byron was dead, stupefied & crying,'[11] her brother reminded her almost 40 years later. She was also blessed with a generous sense of humour and throughout the constant correspondence that he maintained with her right up to her death his letters are regularly spiced with twittings at her expense.

There was still one room in the house where Lear's earliest memories remained unclouded. This was the 'painting-room', a large downstairs room next to Ann's and the nursery. Their father Jeremiah was himself something of a connoisseur of paintings and he had this room set aside for the education of his daughters in the fashionable art of water-colouring. Sarah, the second oldest, was the most talented among them, and it was under her tutorial eye that Edward allied his own talent with his already consuming interest in natural history to produce his first sketches of birds, flowers and butterflies. 'The happiest in all my life',[12] he described the room half a century later when returning for a last look-round before the house was demolished.

Jeremiah Lear finally retired from the Stock Exchange in 1827, and he decamped to Gravesend with his wife and one daughter, leaving the rest of the family to go their own separate ways. For the rest of his life Edward, who never saw either parent again, complained of having been 'turned out into the world literally without a farthing – & with nought to look to for a living but my own exertions'[13] at the age of 14, but at least Ann had a modest inheritance from her maternal grandmother to fall back on. They took rooms together on the top floor of a tenement in the unprepossessing area of Gray's Inn Road, from where Edward sallied forth daily in search of whatever work he could find with his pen. In his diary he recalled:

> I began to draw, for bread and cheese, about 1827, but only did uncommon queer shop-sketches – selling them for prices varying from ninepence to four shillings: colouring prints, screens, fans; awhile making morbid disease drawings for hospitals and certain doctors of physic.[14]

According to Daniel Fowler, the Canadian painter whom Lear was shortly to become acquainted with, his 'first attempts at earning money were made in offering his little drawings for anything he could get to stagecoach passengers in inn yards'.[15] He was able to supplement this meagre living by giving drawing lessons in the more fashionable parts of London, probably as a result of recommendations from contacts he had made in Sussex through his sister Sarah's marriage to a banker, Charles Street.

The newly-weds had set up home on the South Downs near Arundel, an area that opened up whole new vistas to Lear, not only of landscape, but also of society and his own personality. It was here that he discovered his capacity to amuse: reconciled to the belief that he was never going to find happiness himself, he could at least derive consolation from bringing happiness to others, asking no more than to be considered '3 parts crazy – & wholly affectionate'.[16] He made particular friends with the Drewitts, a family living at nearby Peppering, one of whom, the young Eliza, was the recipient of his earliest known illustrated verses. Another near neighbour was Lord Egremont, the owner of a magnificent collection of Old Masters and the chief patron of J.M.W. Turner, at Petworth Park, where Lear met both the Earl himself and another of the great man's patrons, Walter Ramsden Fawkes, who also happened to be a leading ornithologist. Turner remained Lear's idol for the rest of his life: 'Copy the works of the Almighty first and those of Turner next,' was the advice that he passed on in turn to another aspiring artist in his old age.[17]

During his regular visits to Arundel Lear began to fill a small album with studies of the wildlife, particularly birds, on the Downs, and it was these that now caught the eye of Fawkes's daughter, Mrs Godfrey Wentworth, who was sufficiently impressed to introduce him to the artist Prideaux Selby. Inspired by the recent publication of John Audubon's magisterial *Birds of America*, Selby had begun to work on his own *Illustrations of British Ornithology* in collaboration with the naturalist Sir William Jardine, and he agreed to take Lear on as his assistant. Under Selby's influence Lear's work began to take on a much bolder and more lifelike appearance, and he was soon considered good enough to make several contributions to the second and third volumes.

This success emboldened him to embark on a project of his own for a similar work devoted to a single genus, parrots. Thanks again to Mrs Wentworth, his talent had been brought to the attention of the London Zoological Society, and in June 1830 they gave him permission to draw the specimens in their recently opened London Zoo. Although he was also given the run of the stuffed parrots in the Society's offices in Bruton Street, he always made a point of drawing from life, and his presence in the parrots' cages became almost as much an object of curiosity as the birds themselves.

The attic in Gray's Inn Road soon proved an inadequate workshop. Lear apologised to a fellow artist:

> Should you come to town, I am sorry I cannot offer you a home pro tempore, for unless you occupied the grate as a seat, I see no possibility of your finding any rest consonant with the safety of my Parrots, seeing that, of the 6 chairs I

possess, 5 are at present occupied with lithographic prints. The whole of my exalted upper tenement in fact overflows with them...[18]

Consequently he and Ann moved into new rooms at 61 Albany Street, on the eastern side of Regent's Park; these were not only altogether more convenient in themselves, but they lay only a few minutes' walk away from the Zoo. He chose lithography rather than engravure as his method of reproduction because of the greater fidelity to the original that it permitted, although he confessed that he knew little or nothing of the process. He entrusted the finished drawings to Hullmandel's Press in Great Marlborough Street – where, on some unrecorded date, he once met Turner.

Published in 12 folio volumes and limited to 175 copies sold by private subscription, the book was greeted with gratifying acclaim. 'Sir, I received yesterday with great pleasure the numbers of your beautiful work,' one admirer wrote, 'in my estimation equal to any figure ever painted by Barraband or Audubon, for grace of design, perspective or anatomical accuracy.'[19] Lear had originally intended to produce 14 volumes, but the expense and the tardiness of some of the subscribers appear to have forced him to curtail them. 'I have pretty great difficulty in paying my monthly charges,' he admitted, 'for to pay colourer & printer monthly I am obstinately prepossessed – since I had rather be at the bottom of the River Thames than be one week in debt, be it never so small.'[20]

However, he did not have to wait long for his enterprise to be rewarded. Within a year he was commissioned to contribute illustrations to no less than seven other works, including *The Zoology of the Voyage of* [Charles Darwin's] *H.M.S. Beagle, A History of British Quadrupeds* and *A Century of Birds from the Himalayan Mountains.* The last-named was published by John Gould, the Zoological Society's taxidermist. He was no artist and, as Lear was to write on his death, 'owed everything to his excellent wife [Elizabeth] and myself – without whose help in drawing he had nothing'. This did not, however, prevent him from claiming Lear's work as his own, and the fact that, in contrast to Lear's *Parrots*, the book made a handsome profit must have been doubly galling to his young assistant. In the course of a joint tour of Continental zoos the following summer in search of specimens for Gould's next project, *The*

Birds of Europe, Lear was nevertheless talked into contracting himself to the book's completion: 'At Amsterdam we laid the foundation of many subsequent years of misery,' he later lamented.[21] It was eventually published in 1837 although Gould conceded in its Preface that some of the drawings 'have been made by Mr Lear, whose abilities as an artist are so generally acknowledged that any comments of my own are unnecessary,' he still saw fit to sign them 'by J.& E. Gould', even when they included Lear's own signature.

Relief was at hand, however, as a result of the most important of all the introductions that he had made at the Zoological Society. Its President, Lord Stanley, heir to the 12th Earl of Derby, had already lent Lear some of the birds from his own very extensive private menagerie for inclusion in *Parrots*, and he now invited him up to the family seat of Knowsley, outside Liverpool, to draw its other inmates. 50 years later Lear was able to boast that 'Lord Derby is always employing me in one way or another, as did his father, his grandfather and his great-grandfather. Fancy having worked for 4 Earls of Derby!'[22] He had every reason to express such satisfaction, for it was their patronage that, more than any other, had sustained him in his life's career.

Arriving as a junior employee of the great house, Lear was given quarters 'below stairs' with the other servants, but as he was eating his supper Lord Derby himself appeared,

> gave me a regular <u>shake</u> of the hand & apologised for my having been put where I was. 'I intended of course,' quoth he, 'that you should be <u>one of us</u> – & not dine with the servants. Pray,' he continued, 'finish your supper, & then come & join us in the drawingroom.'[23]

'Up Lear went, and from that moment he took his place in the society that he was likely to find in his lordship's dining-room and that he moved in with ease for the rest of his life,' Fowler later wrote. 'There indeed was partly the secret of his great success in life: he was all things to all people.'[24] This ease left him unabashed even, as we shall see, at the very pinnacle of society.

Lear found that the old Earl (he was nearing 80) possessed a 'joyous temperament, and a love of society and good cheer',[25] and that, in addition to his enthusiasm for horseracing, as the founder of the annual Derby, he was something of a cricket fanatic:

> Morning, noon & night, bats & balls have no sinecure. After breakfast the green — for there is an immense lawn before the house, covered with the most odd gamesters, Sir J. Shelley… & all the children male and female play away till I should think their brains nearly fry.[26]

When it fell to Lear to entertain the children in the evening,

> the lines beginning 'There was an old man from Tobago' were suggested to me by a valued friend as a form of verse lending itself to a limitless variety for rhymes and pictures, and thenceforth the greater part of the original drawings and verses… were struck off with a pen, no assistance ever being given me in any way but that of uproarious delight and welcome at the appearance of every new absurdity.[27]

The verse had first appeared in a collection published in 1822 under the title *Anecdotes and Adventures of Fifteen Gentlemen*, and illustrated by Robert Cruickshank (elder brother of the more famous George). It read in full:

> There was a sick man of Tobago,
> Lived long on rice-gruel and sago;
> But at last, to his bliss,
> The physician said this:
> To a roast leg of mutton you may go.

Precisely when the form took on the name 'limerick' is unclear, but it was certainly Lear who first popularized it — although at this stage he had no eye at all towards publishing his own 'rhymes and pictures'. He eventually collated 128 of them into an album, but it was not until 1846 that they first became available to the public in the first *Book of Nonsense*.

Lear alternated between Knowsley and London (and Gould) for the next five years. The old Earl died in 1834 and his heir at once embarked on a major expansion of the menagerie. A huge new cage was built for the birds and ten acres of woodland were enclosed for the animals, creating, in effect, the country's first 'wildlife park'. Some of the drawings Lear did there were eventually published privately in

1846 under the title *Gleanings from the Menagerie and Aviary at Knowsley Hall*. Even with the aid of spectacles, however, such a mass of detailed work placed a considerable strain on his eyes, and on another visit to Sussex in 1834 he experimented for the first time in the less strenuous art of landscape. He also enrolled at Sass's School of Art, with the idea of entering the Royal Academy Schools, but he stayed only a few months there, possibly realising that he would never be in a position to maintain himself during its 10-year course.

Next year he made a sketching tour of Ireland with the young Arthur Stanley, first cousin of the 13th Earl and later to become a famous Dean of Westminster, and he undertook another the following summer, this time of the Lake District, with J.J. Hornby, a second cousin. Lear wrote to Gould in October:

> The counties of Cumberland & Westmorland are superb indeed, & tho' the weather has been miserable, yet I have contrived to walk pretty well over the whole ground, & to sketch a good deal besides. I hope too I have improved somewhat (hard if I haven't after slaving as I have done) – but you will judge when I get back.

His mind was now made up that it was in landscape that his career lay, for, as he told Gould, 'my eyes are so sadly worse, that no bird under an Ostrich shall I soon be able to see to do.' But what landscape? His eyes were not the only problem: the 'miserable' weather had brought on severe attacks of bronchitis and asthma, which had left him 'half blind' and feeling 'colder than Kamschatka',[28] so that it was out of the question to continue with such a career in England. Fowler had just returned from Italy with glowing reports of the country, and another artist friend, Sir William Knighton, whom Lear had met at Sass's, was about to make the journey there.

Italy it was therefore to be, and in July 1837, accompanied by Fowler and financed by advanced commissions from Lord Derby and his nephew Robert Hornby, Lear set out.

Chapter One
Florence and Rome (1837–8)

Disembarking at Antwerp, the two artists travelled via Brussels to Germany in order to draw the Mosel Valley, but shortly after their arrival Fowler fell sick and returned home, leaving Lear to go on alone. He himself was then detained in Frankfurt for a few days by illness; what else befell him there is not recorded, but whatever it was it engendered in him a lifelong antipathy towards Germans and 'Gerwomen'. His health restored, he turned south for Italy, but it was not until mid-September that he finally gained the St Gotthard Pass and caught a glimpse of the land that he was to think of as home for the rest of his life.

The country fulfilled his very highest hopes. Its beauty was 'quite beyond anything that I had seen,' he exulted to Ann six weeks later. 'It seems strange to see day after day scenes so beautiful, and such variety!' He had only one reservation: 'Nothing can give you an idea of the horror one first feels at Italian village inns; now I am used to it, but at starting I thought the huge cold rooms, stone floors and open windows – and long passages – abominable.' His sufferings at these establishments provide a regular refrain of outraged humour in his subsequent accounts of his Italian travels.

Ann herself had now followed him across the Channel, to Belgium, and he was 'so glad to find [that] you are so comfortable and well. Your account of Bruxelles and its people very much amuse me, and though by your praises of the Beer there I fear you have taken to drinking, I rejoice to hear you like the place so much' – so much, in fact, that she stayed until the following May, seemingly in the hope of an invitation to join him in Italy once he had settled there.

He stopped in Milan just long enough to deposit his baggage, then headed north again to Como 'with only knapsack and sketch book. There I fell in with Sir W[illiam], who used to draw at Sass's with me, Lady, and all the Knighton party, and a famous holiday we had on the beautiful Lake.'

The palatial Villa d'Este did not impress Lear overmuch, however: 'a large place, but with no comfort about it,' he commented, perhaps drawing a subconscious comparison with the family atmosphere of Knowsley, which had meant so much to him. He then took a steamer and 'rushed into the uttermost parts of the lake 50 miles off', where 'the enormous Alps, Jiggy-Jaggy' inspired him to further superlatives. Chiavenna, on the Swiss border, he found awfully grand:

> some time ago (in 1680), part of the mountain under which it stands fell down plump and killed 500 persons – a whole village. After getting some sketches of it, I was glad to proceed Southward again, along the east side of the lake – a plan of which I place below – to Colico. I tried to stop at Novate but could not, as all they had to eat was mutton and goat's flesh, half putrid, garlic – and dreadfully sour wine, and although Colico is not overcomfortable, it was a good deal better.

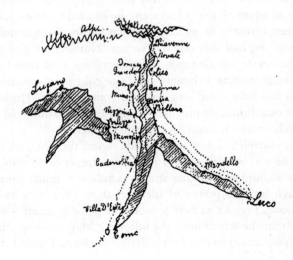

The inn at Bellano was better still, and he stayed there for three days before going on to Lecco:

> a sweet town – a bustling little port, and the boats on Como, which have red, blue or white sails, are like so many large butterflies. After staying 2 days here, back again I rushed to Colico, and then crossed again to Domaso once more, where I stayed prowling about Gravedona for 2 or 3 days, and then walked to Cadenabbia – Dongo – Musso – and Rezzonico [which] are all lovely, and by sunset exquisite, for the Alps are then perfectly pink.

> From Cadenabbia, as the weather continued lovely, off I scouted to Lugano, a lake partly in Switzerland and partly in Austrian Lombardy; if possible it is more beautiful than Como, though very different, for the hills are quite perpendicular to the water, so that you must go in a boat, as there is no road. Up to the top of these mountains there are thick woods, so that as it was now late, all was a mass of crimson and yellow foliage.

The city of Lugano itself struck him as 'a sort of Paradise' – not least for wealthier Italians seeking, then as now, a haven from tax inspectors and the uncertainties of domestic politics.

> However, I had not much time for this lake, so back I trotted to Como, which had now become a sort of old friend. Unluckily I could not sketch it all as I wished, for on the 21st of Oct. the cold set in so violently that I thought it wiser to go South and accordingly walked from Cadenabbia to the town of Como that day... And so on the 22nd I left my dear lake of Como, with a folio full of sketches, and having enjoyed my fortnight beyond description, back I went to Milan once more.[1]

One of his commissions from Lord Derby was to make a note of anything that might make an interesting addition to the Knowsley menagerie, and in a letter to him Lear reported seeing

> a sort of Bird shop, but among several Amazon Parrots & canaries, one Passerine Owl was the only respectable bird – but that was in a bad condition. I should have mentioned that all through Switzerland I diligently enquired for chamois & mar-

mots, but found none. Of the former I heard afterwards of one for sale when I had left the country, but usually the Swiss do not like to part with these things, which they keep as pets…

To return to Milan – & to indulge in a little more horror, the skinning of frogs there (a very popular dish) is a very odious operation: the market women sit talking in circles, each with her tub of froggies, & nipping their feet off with little scissors & most adroitly turning off their skins like gloves from an incision they make in the back, they put the poor little victims in baskets, where, in the spirit of Munchausenism, they caper & leap about ad libitum as if nothing had happened. Bah! But the Milanese have a weakness for clippings & cuttings: not a cat but hath lost all or part of her tail, the reason, according to the owners, for which embellishing with cuts is that they will never forsake the house in which they have lost that useful member.

Many years later Lear would enjoy the uninterrupted company of just such a cat himself.

Grimalkin is better treated in more northern Lombardy, for about Chiavenna I was amused delightfully by every cat having her ears bored, & little bows or tassells of blue or pink ribband depending therefrom! I used to like to watch the large bats on Lake Como: they are very fine fellows, & indulge in beetle catching every twilight, though I never could secure any.[2]

On his arrival in Milan he had found the Knightons just about to leave for Florence, and so he booked a place on the next *vetturino* – 'a good deal like a hackney coach,' he told Ann – with another of their party. The week-long journey across Lombardy – 'as flat as a pancake; you see nothing but millions of poplars for whole days together' – was monotonous until they entered the Ducal State of Modena; not only was the city 'more lively than usual', but 'after this, passports and customhouses become innumerable as there are so many petty States':

Towards evening we arrived at Bologna in the Pope's dominions, whose empire is as full of beggars as Russell Square used to be. Two most curious towers are in this town – immensely high but quite as if they would fall – one is 8 and the other 4 feet out of the perpendicular. Arcades on each side of the streets give the city rather a look of gloom.

Back on the road again, Lear considered that the Passo di Futa, at a mere 3,000 feet, was hardly to be compared with the St Gotthard:

though oxen were necessary to draw up the carriages. You may imagine how beautiful the road looked, with a string of 8 coaches being so pulled up and all the passengers walking. So much for the loneliness of mountain passes! At the place we lunched, 32 people [the Knightons included] – all English – sat down together... and after a walk (while the vetturino crawled) of 20 miles, we came quite over the Appenines, and, in the most beautiful valley I ever saw, there was Florence!

The city of the Medici was

much more magnificent than I looked for. It is all paved, and the houses are enormous and gloomy – like Newgate or the Mansion House – great, arched windows and lofty, narrow streets. As for the Arno, with its 4 bridges – it is quite beautiful ... The Piazza Granduca [now della Signoria] is over-whelmingly grand – such huge buildings – and gigantic statues – all by first masters such as Michael Angelo etc. etc... The galleries – the pictures – the endless churches – the Zebra Cathedral of black and white marble... It is all a hurly-burly of beauty and wonder.[3]

There were feasts too for more than the eyes: 'The hot roasted chesnuts here are delightful. I eat them perpetual – for to think, for a halfpenny in value one gets about 40 fine, smoking ones!!'[4] Another source of satisfaction to him was the size of the expatriate community: after meeting the 300-strong congregation at the English Church, he was able to recruit four pupils for lessons in water-colouring. There was only one disappointment, he told Lord Derby:

At Florence, the Grand Duke has (or thinks he has) a live Zoological collection – though the inhabitants, an ostrich, a chamois, sundry goats & an infirm wild boar, looked piteously forlorn & dirty. At Pisa (which I did not go to), there are

several (2 or 300 I believe) camels: they have long existed, &
multiply there; also I think at Leghorn – I do not know why
they have not more widely spread throughout Italy.

Indeed, he had to report that:

in spite of all my researches I have seen very little new in the
way of living creatures on my journey here: neither shall I
add much to zoological lore in any way. Of little birds there
is a great paucity throughout the Continent – such a constant warfare is carried out against the little wretches; neither
robins – sparrows – thrushes or any other of the pretty fellows that we have so many of, can feel very comfortable in
countries where thousands of them are shot for daily food.
[They still are, as anyone who has been showered with pel-
lets beside their holiday pool can confirm.]

I saw a mantis also by the lake [Como] one day, & had it
been procurable should have saved it for Knowsley; but it
was a maternal mantis & not at all fit for flattening between
the leaves of a book. On the road between Milan & Florence,
we killed 2 tarantulae & 1 scorpion: these with myriads of
large locusts in Swiss vallies, & stupendous fleas everywhere
conclude my entomological observations.[5]

He had intended staying in Florence for the next six weeks, but
with a sudden drop in the temperature and the news that Rome was
now free of cholera he decided to move on, telling Ann to address any
letters to the Poste Restante there.

His next letter to her will have an all too familiar ring for others
who have suffered the vagaries of the Italian postal system:

My dear Ann, I only received your letter yesterday, although
it has been at the Post Office these 10 days; but they are sadly
careless here, and told me there were none for me. I was getting quite into a fidget about you, though I knew the ways
of this part of the world in matters of post delivery.

Tuscany had rather belied his expectations, consisting of:

miles of hills and plains of mud – vineyards and olive trees –

and here and there a village… Radifocani – an enormous mountain, visible for two days' journey – is the boundary of the Pope's dominion, and on descending the other side one begins to see the sort of country Rome is placed in – lines and lines of blue mountains stretching into the sky, and plains that look as if they extended to Jerusalem. On the 4th day, you pass a beautiful lake – Bolsena – like a flat blue mirror and then hills after hills bring you slowly to the waste, dreary desert of the Roman Campagna… The effect is very wild and melancholy – for you see no towns – only the dome of St. Peter's – and you wonder at such a vast tract of unpeopled waste.

His first sight of the Eternal City was also something of a let-down:

It is all modern, and the English and French hotels are all together, fine, square buildings etc. etc. – but all the old part is a good way off. However, glad enough we were to arrive! It seemed the end of a long journey from last July.

With the help of William Theed, a fellow passenger and artist (he later acquired fame as the sculptor of the 'Africa' frieze on the Albert Memorial) and an old Roman hand, Lear soon found suitable lodgings ('for which I only give 10 dollars a month – not £2-10-0 – I should not have got them so cheap had not Mr. Theed known the landlady well, who is a very respectable woman') at 39 Via del Babuino near the Spanish Steps, then as now the recognised quarter of foreign artists. It did not take him long to fall into step with their way of life:

At 8 I go to the café, where all the artists breakfast, and have 2 cups of coffee and 2 toasted rolls – for 6 1/2d. – and then I either see sights – make calls – draw out of doors – or, if wet, have models indoors till 4. Then most of the artists walk on the Pincian Mount (a beautiful garden overlooking all Rome, and from which such sunsets are seen!) and at 5 we dine very capitally at a Trattoria or eating house, immediately after which Sir. W. Knighton and I walk to the Academy – whence after 2 hours we return home. This is my present routine, but there are such multitudes of things to see in Rome that one does not get settled in a hurry, and bye and bye I shall get more into the way of painting more at home, for I have 2 or 3 water coloured drawings ordered already, <u>so I shall not starve</u>…

Rome is beginning to look gay and the streets as full as Regent St. almost – but this is only at a time such as Christmas or Easter, for usually there is a great dulness observable. The people lounge and sit and swing about and the better orders saunter (for 20 mad bulls would not stir an Italian out of a slow walk!) and everything but Art and artists seem stagnant… The shops are not very good – everything is less forward at Rome, by half a century, than at Florence. Nobody seems to care about anything; it is all stagnation – 30 years back there were no carpets or chimneys!! The church for the English is a large room, holding perhaps 2 or 3 hundred…

How the variety of costumes would delight you! As for priests – they are innumerable – white – black – piebald – scarlet – cinnamon – purple; round hats – shovel hats – cocked hats – hoods and caps – cardinals with their 3 footmen (for cardinals <u>never</u> walk) – white friars with masks, bishops and Monsignori with lilac and red stockings – and indeed thousands and thousands of every description of religious orders. Just now the town is full of Neapolitan pipers, called Pifferari, who come at Xmas, to play the Virgin: they have tall black hats, with peacock's feathers in them – blue or brown cloaks – red waistcoats, and sheepskin's and cord breeches – and they puff at enormous droney bagpipes all day long to the shrines so constantly seen.

The last, but not the least, of the novelties was the change in climate, which was 'exquisite. You have no idea <u>how well I have been</u>; what will you say tonight (20th of Dec.) being the first I have wanted a fire through? I assure you all of last week was like June.' On the other hand, he promised his sister that he 'would leave directly' if cholera re-emerged.

Another surprise was the small number of the structures of Ancient Rome that were still intact, being 'all more or less mixed with modern buildings'. However, he thought the Arches of Titus, Severus and Constantine

the most perfect things – the Coliseum, and some of the gates – and the Pantheon – and by some lights, the melancholy and grandeur of these huge remains are very awful. But as to the <u>extent</u> of the ruins of Rome, no one who does not see them can form an idea; the palaces and baths of the Emperors – some filled up into convents – some covering acres of ground with masses of ancient walls – the long lines of aqueducts and tombs on the desolate and beautiful Campagna – and (in the enormous palaces of the modern Capitol and Vatican) the thousands of busts and statues! – judge how bewildered one's noddle becomes! For my part, I am taking things very quietly, and like better to poke about over and over again in the Forum than to hurry with the stream of sight seers all day long.[6]

In the evenings, however, his social life was becoming increasingly active, expanding beyond the initial dinner invitations from fellow artists:

There are constantly very grand balls here, so that one may be very gay if one pleases. At Torlone's, the rich bankers, the other night nearly all Rome was present: cardinals – priests – Russians – English – French & Germans – all the world, in fact. But I am pretty well sick of these things. When I come home at night with my key I often think of Gray's Inn Road & Albany St! How you used to swear! Such oaths!!! Don't you recollect?, he twitted his 'dear great-grandmother', signing himself 'Your affect. young buffalo, Edward Lear'.[7]

The absence of any female company to replace Ann led him to suggest that she should come to Rome, since 'other folks have sisters and wives and mothers here, so I don't see why I should not too,'[8] but his next letter was more noncommittal: 'If ever plans should be so concocted, I should contrive to meet you either at Marseilles or Genoa – but until I hear from Mr. Hornby, who talks of coming abroad this summer, I do not know on what spring arrangements I may decide.' The idea was to be revived at regular intervals over the years, but it never came to fruition; he was torn, it seems, between the consciousness of his debt to her and the realisation that she would not easily fit into the more sophisticated circles in which he was now moving.

He had also by now got the measure of the city's physical environment:

It is not large at all (although the extent walled in is), but, being built <u>all</u> on little hills like so many Ludgate Hills and Mount Pleasants you see it generally all at once from the high parts, & then it is most exquisite; long lines of architecture with magnificent pines beyond give a grandeur you have no idea of; I think the Pincian walk is the loveliest in the world, & the sunsets are wonderful! Perhaps Rome may be about as big as Bath...

Concerning the Campagna, the country is covered like the South Downs – a browny green verdure; there are very few houses – huts here and there – but enormous flocks of sheep are fed on it – guarded by <u>horribly fierce dogs</u> [a recurring phobia of Lear's] which it is not safe to go near; they never attack you though if you don't approach the sheep. There are bits of ruins all over this wonderful plain, & 2 or 3 lines of astonishing aqueducts, all ruins; the ancient tombs & the old Roman roads are just as they were, in some places. One doesn't meet peasants as you seem to think, for it is loneliness itself; foxes & hawks, tortoises & porcupines are the only inmates. I never go out (for I am speaking of 5 or 6 miles beyond the walls) without 1 or more companions – not that it is unsafe, but still it is more comfortable to be in a party...

This perhaps will give you some idea of the Campagna; the trees are the large umbrella-like pines so common here; you must remember that the aqueducts in the distance are 70 or 80 feet high!! Then the mountains beyond are quite blue, & the ground all sorts of lovely colours from the clearness of the atmosphere. However, it is impossible to give any good idea of the most amazing wildness & beauty of these plains.[9]

To Lord Derby he confessed:

my zoological notes are at a most deplorably low ebb: my visions of Bustards & porcupines have faded away... Speaking of bustards, the following anecdote will shew your lordship that Zoological lore flourishes vigorously here: at a dinner, (some person having shot a bittern in the morning) I heard a confused discussion about bitterns – bustards – & buzzards, and finally a Mr. Somebody was appealed to, who settled this point by stating confidently that the 3 terms were precisely synonymous!! I have amused myself by sending Lady Coventry (for it was at her house) sketches of the injured birds in question.

I think that the Zoological Society should have a pair of Buffaloes – though by no means are they fit for Knowsley – piggylooking, hideous spectacles they are! – melancholy objects, but very useful: they bring up marble & stone from the river, & you may always see them in the Forum; in the vast marshes by the Tiber they abound in great herds, and are there very dangerous & fierce. The Campagna dogs – sheepdogs – also are subject to very unpleasant ebullitions of ill temper, & it is not at all safe to approach sheep when the shepherds are not with them: 10 or 12 of these brutes (the <u>dogs</u> not the shepherds) devoured a priest some time back…

The flowers & plants in all these places are delightful; &, if your Lordship likes, I will make a dry collection of those found at the Coliseum: cyclamens often grow wild, & on top of Augustus's palace (where there is a terrace with the most glorious views), the wallflowers & violets have been blooming all through the winter, & the aloes & Indian figs are in high abundance… It is all very beautiful & interesting & wonderful here – but it is not England, & I am stupid enough to get into very homesick fits sometimes; I ought to be thankful however that my health is so much better than it ever was. For improvement – I say little as yet: I try hard enough & if improvement in art must necessarily follow, I shall be sure to have it; but I think sometimes, one bird drawing was worth 2 landscapes – I go on hoping nevertheless.[10]

In his next letter to Ann, dated 29 March, he returned to the theme of the improvement in his health:

Two or three days ago I had one of my spring bilious attacks, sickness and dysentry – the only moment's illness for the whole months since I left Frankfurt – but Dr. Gloas (a Scotchman) soon set me right again: I kept in bed two days – but I had a levee of visitors and enquiries; my landlady made capital broth and was very maternal, and Lady Knighton sent gruels and all sorts of things. On the whole the banting has done me a great deal of good; I was much too fat. (I cannot tell you my landlady's name – very likely she has none at all; the Romans don't care about names – surnames particularly; all the curiosity and gossip of our country is unknown… All strangers they call only 'Forestieri' – unless they have lived many years in Rome, and then they say 'Signor Riccardo Scultore' – 'Sign. Giovanni Pittore' – or 'Sign. Giorgio Inglesi', but they never take the trouble to learn surnames. The common people are designated in the same way by their trades: 'Demetrio the butcher' – 'Alessandro the baker' etc. etc.)

The Goulds are going to Van Diemen's Land to catch kangaroos; Victor Audubon [the son of the celebrated American bird illustrator] too wrote the other day, and they are in Scotland, but are shortly to return to America – such little trips one takes nowadays,

he added – but made no mention of her joining him this time. He went on to describe how he and Sir William Knighton had taken part in the Shrove Tuesday Carnival:

We two entered completely into the uproar, and having disguised ourselves as women of Albano (fancy me with a red bodice and green skirt – with a white scioccatura which is the name of the beautiful headdress the common women wear, like this – besides a black mask!!) we hired a coach and pelted away famously. But on the last evening is the best fun of all. Directly after the horse race dusk begins, and by degrees every door and window all down the long and narrow Corso becomes illuminated with candles called 'mocoli'. The houses being of such vast height, the effect is wonderfully beautiful. Besides this, the thousands of foot passengers each carry a 'mocolo' – some short and others on long sticks – and every coach (and the carriages are by hundreds) is crowded with masks each with a light or 2. The fun is for everybody to extinguish everybody's candle, yet keep his own alight, and you have no idea what a scene it is! Nothing is heard but an immense cry of 'senza mocolo' and it is as like magic as anything you can fancy. As the coaches go creeping along, it is delightful to steal up behind and with a handkerchief darken a whole party! But everything is done goodnaturedly, and no disturbance ever occurs... At a given hour the lights are all put out, and after another ball the Carnival is over by midnight. I confess I was extremely sorry, and wish there were another, for it was such a very merry time.

He told Ann that he was now going to have to wait until Easter and then go further afield for any more such entertainment:

Soon after Easter I mean to go to Naples, with an artist [and nephew of a Royal Academician] of the name of Uwins – a quiet, good tempered, sensible fellow; had he not been so, I should have gone with anybody rather than alone, for I know how unpleasant it is to be quite without society. Uwins knows all the Neapolitan ground well, which is an advantage. I do not mean to stay long at Naples, because I know I shall dislike it, since it is universally reckoned the noisiest place in the world – but we shall go to Amalfi, and Sorrento – and in the hot summertime to the beautiful islands of Ischia and Procida, which are said to be Paradise. I am sometimes melancholy at having seen and being about to see so much loveliness, for I think England will look very queer and dummy bye and bye.[11]

He wrote again before setting out in early May to give an account of the postponed visit to Tivoli, which was to become a frequent retreat during his subsequent years in the capital. Once across the Campagna,

you see Tivoli perched on a rock a great way up. By degrees the buildings become more distinct & you see quantities of Cypress trees – so black – sprinkled about the town... You now pass a vast tract of ruins – Cypresses etc. – towers etc. – these are the remains of the Emperor Hadrian's villa, but I

did not see them as I ought to have done. Then you commence a long pull up to the town through the most beautiful olive wood! – such trees! – & every now & then you see
bits of the ancient villas – all that is left of once vast buildings – now only a few arches with the curious Roman brick
work... And as you get higher & higher, such a view as you
cannot imagine is seen all over the Campagna with Rome 18
miles off quite on the horizon.

The town itself, 'a nasty dirty narrow filthy place', had little to com-
mend it – likewise the inn,

a beastly place – as you may judge when I tell you there are
16 dogs, 10 cats & all sorts of poultry all over the house! One
soon gets accustomed however to this – & the dinners are
very nice – nice fish & omelettes particularly. Nevertheless 4
of the dogs ate up a large meat pie we had taken, the first day.
In the inn yard is a beautiful ruin of the Sybil's temple – very
old, & standing on a great precipice; for Tivoli, as I said,
stands on a ledge of rock which projects like a tongue into a
long valley – & as the river comes to Tivoli, it is obliged to
tumble (with such a noise) down the rock before it gets to
the valley below, & it is over this chasm that the temple
stands. Much of this river is detained for mills, & it falls in
20 or 30 cascades all down the rock to different parts of the
valley – so that such a squashing of water as there is at Tivoli
was never heard! Below this temple are most lovely gardens!
which wind down to the very bottom of the chasm – where
there are caverns & cascades & rocks – & alleys – & ruins of
immense villas more than I can describe to you.

In contrast to its Como namesake, he considered the Villa d'Este

a scene worth walking to Italy from England, if one could see
nothing else. It has struck me more than anything since I left
home... The house is very grand & simple in form but it is
its situation that so bewilders one. I could not believe that I
was awake at first. It is raised quite above all Tivoli, at the top
of an <u>extremely</u> steep hill – <u>all</u> of which is turned into one
exquisite garden. You come on to the upper terrace and you

Villa D'Este.

are struck dumb; the most enormous trees – pines & Cypresses are beneath you; long walks of gravel, grass & box formally cut; fountains by hundreds of thousands – terraces; flights of stairs from the villa to the bottom of the hill – & to crown all – the whole Campagna beyond. You proceed down these flights of stairs & wonder that you have been so deceived on arriving, at the Cypress trees – which look like giants; they are the largest in the world. From the end of the long valleys you look back – & it is really like magic…

So now I have done with Tivoli. I told you I returned in time for Holy Week – but I did not like its ceremonies at all; I hate crowds & bustle. The grandest of all is on Thursday at noon when the Pope comes into the great gallery of St. Peter's & the Piazza is full of people kneeling while he blesses them. The illumination is also <u>wonderful</u>. About dusk men (400) are slung by ropes (!!!) all over the dome & colonnades of St. Peter's – where they put little paper lamps in regular places – till the evening grows darker – every line, column & window becomes gradually marked by dots of light! It has the exact appearance of a transparent church – with light seen through pricked holes. Imagine a dark sky & my ink dots all light! – about 9 o'clock, by an astonishing series of signals, the whole fabric blazes with hundreds of torches; immense iron basins

full of oil & shavings are suspended <u>between</u> the little lamps,
& these all at once burst out into light! I can only compare it
to a stupendous diamond crown in the dark night. It is the
most beautiful thing in the world of its sort.

True to his anti-clerical instincts, he declined to describe the Week's
other events,

& only pass to the winding up of all the celebrated fire-works
at the Castel S. Angelo. This renowned affair is really also
beyond belief. This grand castle is over the Tiber & joins a
bridge, so that when lighted up by the glare of the immense
blaze – it is superb to a degree. With a terrific explosion at 9
o'clock off go the most unaccountable mass of rockets!!!! You
would think all Rome had gone off in one rocket! & as soon as
that is over – all the castle is a blue blaze of sparkling festoons,
trophies, mottoes, etc. etc. This is succeeded by <u>thousands</u> of
squibs & Catherine wheels – blue lights – & eccentric rockets
of uncouth sorts – running fire spitting spouting spurting –
cascades of sparks – columns of yellow balls – globes of crimson sputtering stars – & all this goes fizzing & bouncing about
for half an hour!! – till you are nearly deaf & blind & astonished beyond all measure !!!!!!! I'm afraid you will laugh at my
very bad illustrations, but I think they will amuse you.

Since the Holy week everybody has been leaving Rome – for
Naples & other places, & now it is very dull indeed – for
those who like gaiety. Did I tell you that my friend Sir
William Knighton is going to be married? To a Scotch lady.

(Years later Lear wrote of this lady that 'she made him give up all
art & artists as wulgar.')

He returns next winter. There are numbers of nice people
here too, but to describe is tedious. Mr. Acland who goes
with me [and Uwins] tomorrow is a friend of the Hornby's.[12]

Four years later the same Mr Acland, the son of Sir Thomas
Acland, Bt, accompanied Lear on his first tour of Sicily.

Chapter Two
The Campagna and Naples (1838)

Lear, Acland and Uwins set out by the cooler, inland route – not without some misgivings on Lear's part. As he told Ann:

> having packed up everything and given up my very comfortable lodgings, I was very sorry to leave Rome – for in all the world there can be no place which retains so strong a hold on the memory and imagination. However, it is consolation that one may return to it next winter. I wish you could be there too – but that cannot be.

At their first stop, Tivoli again, they had the misfortune to find that their arrival coincided with another religious celebration: 'The odious part of the matter was this: a whole hill was bored full of holes (in a manner peculiar to Italy), and gunpowder – like cannons – was let off for 3 hours in a running detounade enough to deafen you.' His ears were still ringing the following morning when, at the very next village, Castel Madonna, they ran into yet another festa: 'it seemed a sort of fate that I should again have been doomed to bang bang from cannon all day long,' he reflected ruefully.

Lunchtime found them at Vico Varo, 'a beautiful town on a rock in a valley full of trees', but this too flattered to deceive on closer inspection:

> Lovely as these Italian towns appear, they are universally filthy within, and as we at last arrived tired and hungry, we actually found that Vico Varo, though containing three convents and two cathedrals, did not possess one single inn! These notes of this journey will convey to you a good idea of Italian travelling in a rough way – for it is only by actually

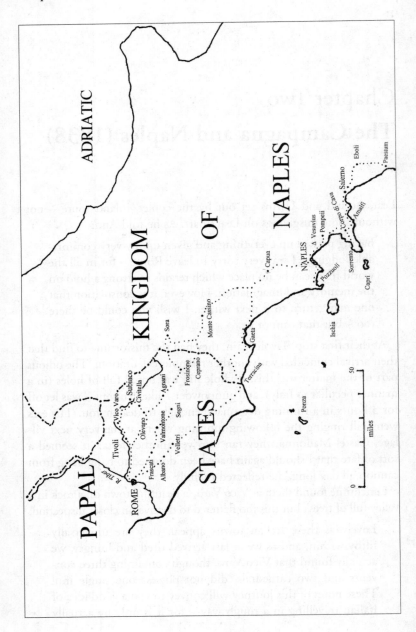

visiting a country that one understands it – books are nothing. The stuff talked about Banditti and treachery etc etc. is
absurd – and I as yet have never found matters worse in Italy
than in England. I would much rather sleep in the wildest
hot-house here than on Hounslow Heath.

Any modern traveller fallen among the banditti of Heathrow (as it
was later renamed) might heartily endorse this last observation.

Well!! However hungry or tired we were, we were obliged to
go through Varo Vico without eating – though we soon
found a little Osteria (or public house) on the other side.
Here we had some hard boiled eggs and wine – and, you recollect how I used to like eggs – I am here laughed at very
much because I eat 7 eggs to everybody else's 3.

The day's greatest disappointment was still to come, however:

On we went towards the convent of San Cosimato – where
they receive travellers for the night – for there are no inns
there. As the monks, however, were all asleep, we went down
into the valley by the river to sketch till they woke… and
then [at 6 o'clock] we went up to the Friars. Imagine our
extreme disgust and surprise when, at that time of the
evening, with heavy knapsacks and after walking 14 miles,
they told us they could not receive us!! We knew the rooms
could not have been all occupied as they said – but however
we could not make them relent.

The travellers decided that there was nothing for it but to trudge
on another four miles to the next village, La Speggia. With few land-
marks to guide them, they began to regret the decision:

It is difficult in the out-of-the-way places in Italy to find
one's way – you may ask, but the excessive care for nothing-
ness or indifference of the people is so very odd that you are
seldom the wiser. 'How far is it to La Speggia?' 'Is it a town,
or a village?' 'Are there inns there?' were our frequent
enquiries, but [in return] 'Who knows?' 'How can anybody
tell?' 'I don't live here.' 'Maybe there are, or maybe not.'
'Inns? Of course.' 'Many, many.' – & such vague answers

(after which they go on working) were all the replies we could get. This was not agreeable as it was growing dark.

At last, however, we reached La Speggia – & glad we were, for there were 16 or 17 miles more to Subiaco – & we knew that not a house was on the road. La Speggia itself was 3 houses!!!

One of these was an inn consisting of a single room, to be shared not only with the resident family of six, but also with a donkey, horse, hens, six dogs and five cats. Fortified by 'some very good wine', however, they determined to make the best of it:

You must not judge from this that we were crowded: all rooms in Italy are immense, & the largest drawing-room in Grosvenor Square is pigmy to a country inn parlour here. We got some macaroni-rice soup & an old boiled fowl, & some eggs – & I assure you we made a good dinner. What is very strange here is that, however wretched the appearance of the inn, they universally give you better food than you could look for.

Sleep, on the other hand, was another matter:

…tho' there was no fear of robbery, yet the fleas were astonishing!!!!!!!!!!!!!!!!!!!!!!!! You have no idea of the quantity of these fleas – in England you would be shocked to catch 5 in a morning: here, 100 are nearer the mark. The only way to get rid of them is this, which I adopt very frequently: strip entirely & then shake out your clothes well & then walk up & down the room barefooted – presently the creatures settle all over your feet like mites on a cheese, & you may then kill them by dozens.

Hardly surprisingly, they were on the road again by dawn, accompanied by the locals on their way to work in the fields:

The women walk quite upright, & the mothers carry their very young children in a pretty wicker cradle on their head too – spinning or knitting as they walk. The children of a year or 2 old are stuck about the bigger children – being swaddled in the curious manner used all over Italy – just like large caterpillars they look when the bandages are of striped cloth. I am sure I always laugh at them heartily.

They were still in good spirits when they reached Subiaco,

which is reckoned the finest place near Rome; it is piled up on a pyramidal rock, in a beautiful valley full of trees as usual... A more picturesque place never was; though its poverty & filth are excessive. Many of the artists of all nations residing at Rome pass the summer here, so there is a sort of inn & table d'hote at which there is plenty of society.[1]

They had good reason, then, to linger for some days there, and when they did set out again it was minus Acland:

The valley we passed I do think the most lovely I ever saw – Claude's pictures give you an exact idea of such spots. On every side were hills crowned with towns & bye & bye we wound up through magnificent oak forests to Rona St. Stefano, a miserable little town. These people are wondrously poor, though quite beautifully dressed – the amount of two pence halfpenny procured us as much wine as we could drink, & gave 3 people charity besides!! From this place we wound down through equally grand scenery – beechwoods, convents etc. etc. till another tremendous rock staircase brought us to Civitella, the highest village in those parts. Immense walls of solid stone without cement – like Stonehenge – are scattered round it – older by many hundreds of years than the Romans & supposed to be of Pelasgian building.

Lear described Olevano, their next stop, as being:

topped by a fine old castle – & the view over all the neighbouring mountains & the Campagna of Rome (for it is about 25 miles off) is most glorious. Tuesday 15th & Wed. 16th were sadly wet & gloomy, though we sketched at times – but the children of Olevano (tho' not so vile as those of Tivoli) are very annoying: as soon as you appear, every living creature cries out 'Sir Angre' (which means Signor Anglais, I suppose), 'Date me mezzo biocco'!! – & they surround you

by the dozens when you sketch; the people at Olevano &
some other neighbouring places have no costume, & are
dirty & dowdy.

Thereafter their route took them through Gennazano, 'a sort of
Paradise', Palliano, 'a nasty, dirty, disagreeable town', and Anagni:

Here the dresses begin again to be beautiful & perhaps are
more striking than any in Italy – as yet – that I have seen.
Without their aprons, the women are a good deal like
Hindoos – for they carry such weights (jars, wood, etc.) on
their heads from their youth that their shape is perfect.

Of Ferantino, Lear wrote similarly: 'Here I do think the people are
more astonishing than ever. They carry their cradles with their babies
on their heads in the most beautiful manner.' As for Frossinone, 'the
noise the frogs made was wonderful! Imagine a legion of ducks all
speaking at once.'

At Ceperano, 'the last place in the Pope's territory',[2] the main thoroughfare through the Kingdom of Naples turned south for the coast,
but they decided to continue on the more direct road inland to Sora:

The country round is just like Switzerland, which greatly
surprised me, as I had no idea there were mountains so far
south always covered with snow. We were also obliged to
cross some very ugly swollen torrents too, which I did on ass
back. The peasantry of Sora are quite delightful, so kind &
polite; there is no begging – no want – no apparent poverty;
pigs & spinning wheels & fat rollypoly babies abound – & I
do think the Golden Age seems to have never left this beautiful place.

Three more days brought them to San Germano, which was

also in Paradise: just above it rises an old castle, & far above
castle or town on a tremendous precipice is the famous
Monte Cassino – or convent of San Benedetto, still the
largest & richest in all Italy. You wind up to it, for 2 or 3
hours, the view you may suppose wonderful; but the extreme
extent of the convent is more surprising still. Its church is
really a glitter of carvings & gildings; the French robbed it of

its jewels – but its library of 60,000 manuscripts of great age is yet invaluable. There are 70 or 100 monks, & the building contains picture galleries, gardens, etc. etc. etc. – till one grows sick of seeing so much.

Having devoted another day to admiring its contents (since further ravaged by the German occupation and subsequent Allied bombardment in 1944), they resumed their approach to Naples.

Lear's worst forebodings of the city were rapidly fulfilled:

Not being by an interesting road we hired a caricola, or cart, & rode thither. You have heard of the cheating of Neapolitans: here I begin to understand it: they are truly & really most outrageous thieves! At first it is most disgusting to battle every farthing – but it is dreadfully necessary. Fancy me – who am always so shockingly indolent about money – positively roused into a rage about these odious people! They asked us for our fare to Naples – 8 piastres; we offered (like fools) 4, which they snapped at so instantly that we saw our error too late – the truth was, we ought to have gone for 2!!! Well: we paid our coin by way of earnest at starting; unluckily, it was a coin containing 5 grana more than a piastre. Now, as we knew already that we had been cheated out of 2 piastres, we were resolved not to lose those 5 grana – at least, I was. A queer vehicle is a caricola

a caricoli.

The driver stands behind & drives over your head usually the Neapolitans stick 8 or 10 or 12 people on to these cars – & drive like maniacs: I stare with wonder! We drove through most lovely & woody country for upwards of 30 miles, & then we reached Capua, a large city – having first seen Vesuvius far off.

Here our driver would not go any further – but said anoth-

er man would. This latter would insist on the 5 grana extra
– & also on carrying 3 other people & on having one horse
only. Had we granted one demand, 20 others would have
followed – so I think I will be immutable. Accordingly I
ordered our knapsacks out & set off on foot, which brought
our good man of Naples round – & we were actually starting again when he poked up behind 4 dirty companions. I
stopped the horse, & he, with the energy of these strange
people, played the most wonderful tricks: he kneeled – he
rolled – he rushed up & down – scrunched his hat all to bits
– tore his hair – yelled – swore – cried – & after all seeing I
was quite firm, finished by saying 'Very well then, let us go'!
– & set off as good as possible. So I had my way after all. But
this is only one example: they are always mad – always quar-
relling or capering about: queer animals.

A week later Lear felt sufficient recovered from the assault on his senses to 'describe Naples, so I shall try if I can to give you an idea of it':

Well, this city is a very large one – & quite full of people –
not like Rome, half deserted – but composed of houses 8 stories high all brimfull. 60,000 people died of the Cholera – but
they say no one can tell the difference; it is reputed the noisiest city in the world, [so] judge how I – who hate noise –
must like it! First, there is not a good-looking building in the
place; all the churches & public places are tawdry & vulgar –
all the streets are of white-washed houses with flat roofs – like
Clapham Common villas grown very tall, & with their roofs
cut off; Venetian blinds & everything French prevails also.

Just to give you an idea, I will describe one drive nearly
through the town – as if it were, from Westminster to
Cheapside. I begin with the Toledo, the Corso of Naples.
This is a really noble street of immense length & width, but
otherwise not remarkable – except for the wonderful bustle
& noise in it – morning, noon & night; one can hardly
believe the whole population are not stark mad – raving.
They yell & shout – nobody in Naples speaks – in a manner
quite superhuman. They allow themselves no repose. If you

empty all the streets of all the capitals of Europe into one, then turn in some thousand oxen – sheep – goats – monks – priests – processions – cars – mules – naked children & bare-legged mariners – you may form some idea of the Toledo! Once I walked up it, but would not again for a great deal, as I was nearly deaf & run over (almost) 20 times before I came out of it. It is a dreadful place – yet at 8 o'clock people lounge & eat ices at every doorplace, although the noise is like all the thunder in the world. I should not forget that the Royal family are continually scampering up & down – in 2 carriages & 4 without [i.e., outside] riders – troops of soldiers & kettle-drums. My ears will always ache at the word Toledo.

At the end of this street you come to some large piazzas – all ugly enough – & full of military with which all Naples is thronged; here you leave right & left large quays – docks – squares & streets, & so you proceed to a large semicircle in which is the Royal Palace opposite to a large church very like an apple pie. Here the kettle drums & music & shrieking become agonising, but the worst is not yet. A little further you come full on the sea – Vesuvius – & the whole opposite coast, whose mountains are superb. But at this spot – Santa Lucia, the fish market – you become so stunned & bewildered, that you don't know if you are dead or alive; it is like a horrid dream, when all the world is shrieking at you. As you pass, every woman screams out 'will you sit?' 'will you drink?' 'will you give me something?' 'anything?' 'a grana?' 'Signor, Signor, Signor, Water – Water – Fish – meat – muscles [sic] – oysters – baskets – eggs – roses – apples cherries?' – while every man steps before you overwhelming you with the most tremendous shouts of 'Come along, Sir – come: a boat! a boat! instantly – now – this minute – this minute! to Capri – to Vesuvius – to Sorrento – to wherever you please – a boat boat boat boat!!!' It is no use to speak – you must only walk on. All Neapolitans speak with a wonderful quickness & curtail half each word: for instance, a Roman would say 'Volete una barca'; here it is only 'Vol' 'n' barc"!! & 'N'r' for 'Signor', always. The people generally might as well talk

Greek, for it is impossible to comprehend them.

Barring only the advent of cars and cigarettes, and the brooding presence of the Camorra, it seems that little has changed in Naples over the past 150 years.

The travellers then fled for a day's inspection of the ancient remains at Pozzuoli:

> By the little map you will see it is on the west side of Naples in what is called the Bay of Baiae, once most famous for vast cities & for all the rich Romans having villas there as at Tivoli. Having reached the end of the Chiaija [promenade], you find yourself at the foot of a great hill, through which you go by an astonishing grotto or tunnel called the Grotto of Pamillippo; as it was regarded as an antiquity in the time of the earliest Romans, nobody knows how it was made. It is of vast height & cut out of the solid rock – nearly – of a mile long!... It is only lighted by a few small lamps, & it is near-ly dark, & from the closeness of the air & the screams of the drivers – horrible – one is glad to get out of it.

Today one is gladder still, now that there is the added ingredient of carbon monoxide.

A dull road leads to Pozzuoli – the ancient Pestioli – built on rocks jutting out into the sea. The foundation of every house is one of antiquity – & temples & mosaics – old pavements – & ruins of all sorts meet you at every turn. You see a little figure 2 in the map? This forms the Bay of Baiae – &

immense ruins now extend under water all over it; it is supposed all to have been dry land once, but [was] covered by
an earthquake. Masses of ruins are seen here & there sticking
up out of the sea. As you progress round the bay, you arrive
at a large hill – like a South Down – which tumbled up – the
nasty thing – one night in 1538 – during an earthquake.
Beyond are the lakes of Avernus etc. etc.– & all the scenes of
Virgil's Aeneid highly interesting to a classic – but not over
beautiful to look at… The whole bay is now nearly a desert
owing to the bad air, which renders it dangerous after the
end of June; bad air, 'Malaria', means ague. Returning to
Pozzuoli – just above the town is a large volcano, now
extinct; it is a nasty thing – the crater is like a little valley, all
of hard sulphur – here & there it is all hot & smoking &
bubbles, bubbles!

The effect on his lungs was such that even Lear was grateful to
retreat again to Naples. They arrived back just in time to witness the
Festa of Madonna del Arco:

All the people were in cars – most furiously driving some
cows – asses – horses, or a mixture of all. Nothing could better display Neapolitan character: not a creature but was as if
outrageously mad, dressed as a complete scarecrow.

I should tell you that for 3 days previously crowds thronged
to do penance at the church – & having wound up everything (talk of Juggernaut) by crawling so many times on their
stomachs & LICKING THE DUST, some certificate is
given them, & then they rush home as I was describing.
Every man & woman is twisted all over with beads – chesnuts – nuts & all sorts of trumpery: feathers – 5 or 6 hats one
over another – turbans – tinsel scrolls of painted paper etc.,
& each carrying a trophy or portrait of the Madonna, with
huge branches & several baskets & spoons – why, I could not
learn! Imagine some thousands of such complete New
Zealand maniacs each more ridiculous than I can describe &
all shouting like madmen! Through a whirlwind of dust we
at last reached the church, round which is a great fair of

cows, pigs & horses – strange medley! Inside, unluckily, the best crawling was over – but I had the satisfaction to see one fat woman crawl all the way from the door to the altar – on her stomach – like a great frog swimming!!! Her white dress was none the cleaner for the operation.[3]

Two days later the travellers were shaking some of the dust off on the road south again. Leaving inspection of Pompeii and Herculaneum for the return journey, they pressed on to the tiny village of Corpo di Cava, on the lower slopes of Monte Pertuso. Lear wrote in his next letter to Ann that the contrast it offered could not have been more welcome: 'Nothing can be so delightful as the quiet of this place after Naples – the birds singing in the morning, & the exquisite air.' He described its environs as

> a sort of Devonshire – all rich vallies – but with larger hills… immense rocks & solitary hollows. Salvator Rosa studied for many years among the woods of La Cava, & you see numbers of the actual rocks so common in his paintings; one or two especially are particularly grand… All along most of the paths are fountains of most delightful water & the wild flowers are really superb – red lilies – larkspur – roses – myrtles – & thousands of other plants cultivated by us grow here wild on all the rocks, & the butterflies & all sorts of insects are beautiful. The population are quite the best in these parts, & are a very quiet, civil, nice set of people. If ever you come to Italy you shall certainly stay at Corpo di Cava.

Thoroughly restored in mind and body, they headed south again,

> first to Vietri & then by the sea shore to Salerno, a large sea port (that is, for this part of Italy), but you must not fancy it is like Portsmouth or Liverpool, for all that… After about 20 miles you ascend a hill & perhaps see the finest plain & mountains it is possible to find. As far as you can see extends an immense park of oak (belonging to the King's summer palace of Persano), & where there is not wood, fields of corn & vast tracts of myrtle are instead. Beyond this runs that grand chain of mountains – Postilione – which you see from Corpo di Cava, & to your right the whole Gulf of Salerno is

visible, with mountains dwindling away to the horizon. Further on you come upon Eboli – not a handsome town – but from such a superb situation, I think at sunrise, quite wonderful. The moon was where I have placed it.

Well, at Eboli we got rooms at a huge convent – now an inn – full of long galleries & doors, & spent the day in looking about us. Next morning about 4, we started in a car for Pesto [Paestum], the object of our expedition. To get there you cross this immense plain, which as you approach the sea grows very desolate & lonely. The peasants have an unhealthy & melancholy air, for after June it is so dreadfully unwholesome an atmosphere that strangers cannot stay in it, & the few poor wretches who live on in it are always ill [from malaria].

At last you spy the three temples of Pesto – once a magnificent Greek town, & of such antiquity that nobody knows anything about them: the Emperor Augustus went to see them as ruins in his time, so judge they are no chickens. Notwithstanding this they are nearly perfect, being of such wonderfully strong architecture – although the rest of the city is reduced to nought; the vast walls are still to be traced – with an amphitheatre, etc. etc. – but only the temples are left whole [for which, of course, they also have to thank the malaria].

One – of Neptune – has all the outside pillars standing, & everything is as it was 2,000 years ago; the other 2 are minus their insides or part of them. To describe these monstrous yet exquisitely beautiful buildings would be impossible: they are of the simplest, earliest architecture, & all I can say is that they leave stronger impressions on the mind than anything I

Looking toward the mountains.

ever saw. Myrtle & heath & fern grow about them – vipers
too are rather unpleasantly common – hundreds of jackdaws
build in their summits. One is of a rich yellow, the other 2
of white marble – & this with the blue sea, sky & mountains
make a wonderful landscape. After sketching & wandering
about for the whole day, we returned by evening to Eboli.

Next morning a most laughable circumstance occurred. I
think I told you that all these people – these odious
Neapolitans – ask you 10 carlines for what is valued at 2, so
one is obliged to be always squabbling – & it is very annoying. Well, the people at the inn at Eboli asked us 50 carlines
for 2 days' keep, & we knew that 30 was too much; however, we said you shall have 30 – you nasty cheats! So Uwins
put down 15; I thought he had paid for me – he thought I
had paid for myself – so we took up our hats leaving the
landlady only 15. Of course she got into a fury – as well she
might – but we, thinking she had 30 & was only making a
noise (as they always do) for 50 – were quite deaf – & insisted on going; however, she seized upon me, & calling to a servant to shut the outer doors, a pretty storm ensued. Still
believing it was the 50 on which the matter depended, I got
up a most particularly outrageous passion – I don't think you
ever saw me in one – but I really inform you I am very awful.
I at any rate stormed & acted so well, that not only the
frightened landlady let go her hold, but the very menservants
were scared – so we rushed the door, & out we went. The
tempest was not allayed, however, for the landlady came
screaming after me, calling out Police! Police! – but, as these
things are so common in Italy – & as nobody knew if she or
we were right or wrong – nobody heeded her, & by dint of
walking we at last got clear of the town.

About 7 miles out we discovered our mistake – that we had
actually by our own oversight cheated & bullied a
Neapolitan landlady out of 15 carlines!!!!! So I was obliged,
having the longest legs, to trudge back instantly to Eboli,
where I paid the disputed sum. On my entering the house,
the whole family called out 'Ah! we thought it was a mistake!'

– & we were soon reconciled. Only the landlady said (after giving this advice) 'My son (filio mio), another time don't be so furious – although I was quite wrong, for I was also furious – [but] what a shocking thing that such an honest young man should be a dreadful Protestant!'

Lear was still evidently infected by the humour of the incident when he dispatched the letter to his sister a week later, signing himself 'Your pernicious, periwinkle, piggywiggy'.[4]

After another week's relaxation at Corpo di Cava and a brief foray into the Sorrento peninsular, they set off back to Naples via Pompeii. He wrote to Ann about the excavations there:

> Nothing ever impressed me nearly so much… It is one thing to say it is very strange to see a city 2,000 years old just risen, as it were, from the grave, & another thing to walk in the city itself – to see everything fresh as it was in the past ages – & be convinced that all you have read of falls far short of the reality. For my part, I think Pompeii alone worth a journey from England.
>
> A sideboard, on which are the marks of glasses set down while wet – a hole in which a lamp was found, the top of which was, & is, all over fresh soot – the wine jars in the cellars of Diomedes, all turned down for the vintage – the stocks in the public prison, in which the bones of the prisoners were still found fixed – the rings at the mangers of the Inn Stables where were also the skeletons of horses – the juggling apparatus of the priests of Isis, when they used to give the oracles – the newly painted signs & the names of the shopkeepers written on the walls, just as you see them now all over Italy – the theatres exactly as they formerly were – the baker's shops and the druggist's etc. etc. – the thousands of articles found & which are all preserved in the Naples museum – the exquisite paintings in all the chambers of the better class of houses, & the beautiful mosaics on all the floors – these, & myriads of other remarkable wonders, are almost, if one had not seen them, beyond belief, & leave a feeling quite strange on any thinking mind [that is, for anyone lucky enough to time their arrival to coincide with the museum's capricious opening hours].

What surprised me very much at Pompeii was the extreme
beauty of its situation – which I never heard spoken of: the
sea & the mountains from it are enchantment. Vesuvius also
is most grand – & from the perfect amphitheatre (where
everybody was at the time the eruption broke forth) it is very
majestic. Imagine the front series of circles to be the first vast
stone steps of an amphitheatre & then think of a wide plain
betwixt it & Vesuvius, & you may suppose the sublimity of
the view. Altogether, Pompeii was the greatest delight that I
ever remember to have passed.

His pleasure was interrupted, he told Ann, by a brief headache
brought on by the glare of the midday sun reflected from the stone
streets, but in a letter to John Gould, written after the latter's return
from Australia, he confessed to having suffered rather more seriously:

I was taken very ill, & owing to the too fine & sulphurous
nature of the air my cough returned & also spitting of blood,
& had I not left the neighbourhood of that filthy old mountain Vesuvius I might have died.[5]

After a few more days sketching in Naples the travellers departed
for Rome, taking the coastal route north for the sake of variety:

2 hours before sunset we reached Moladi Gaeta – a sort of
Paradise – famous for the goodness of its air – for its fine fish
– & for its beautiful women – as well as its exquisite views.
Most unfortunately, I was prevented from enjoying anything:
for in getting out of the vettura, I threw down a sack, to which
I attribute my being covered with swarms of fleas – as nobody
else in the vettura suffered as I did. I attempted to draw, but
was obliged to give it up & undress – & I actually caught 43
fleas before I was quite undressed!!!! I put their bodies all in a
row to prove what seemed so immense a number.

As they advanced, the fleas were replaced by mosquitoes, and they
wasted no time in regaining the relative safety of the Papal States at
Terracina. Then, as now, the town was a favourite seaside resort for
the population of Rome, being

stocked with palm trees so as to look quite oriental; it was hereabouts that so many robberies once used to take place: famous brigands abounded about it – you know there is an opera 'The Brigand' or 'The Man Of Terracina'. Immediately on leaving it commences the Pontine Marshes – in other words, part of that enormous plain called near Rome 'The Campagna'. These marshes – marshes no longer, since they are drained all over – are uninhabitable during summer from Malaria – otherwise ague – & indeed, after great rains, are even now impassable from overflowed canals. For my part, I could never have guessed they were marshes: I should have soon as thought them puddings, or lobsters.

What do you think the 'Pontine Marshes' are like? Why, one straight road – one everlasting avenue, like an arrow – for 40 miles – all the way bordered by the most beautiful trees imaginable; beyond are vast plains & fine mountains. I never saw such an avenue in my life: you see a little round hole at the end like a pin's head – hour after hour till you grow sick. Uwins & I walked a long way – & counted 9 vipers & one snake. I had a most narrow escape from one: walking on, I heard Uwins scream out – which, he being taciturn, surprised me very much; I had trodden on one of these creatures – as they bask in the sun – but on its head! Had I trodden on his tail, I must have been bitten.

The rest of the journey passed uneventfully, apart from 'the most terrific thunderstorm' near Gensano, and 'very soon, on the 30th [August], we arrived once more at my darling city – & it had cleared up and was all as lovely as ever. So ends my journeying – I hope for a long time to come, for I am beginning to find "the rolling stone gathers no moss" – I think a quiet, stationary life more suitable to study.'[6]

Banished now were all his doubts about staying on and his thoughts of returning to England after this year of exile. It was another three years before he saw his native land again, and then he took good care that he was back in Rome again before the onset of winter.

Chapter Three
The Alban Hills and Sicily (1838–42)

Lear was disconcerted to find that Rome was already well-filled ahead of the coming winter season. He later reported to Gould that the city was 'more crammed than it has been since the days of Titus, & people slept in ovens & pigstyes for want of lodgings,'[1] and to Ann he wrote that:

> lodgings are very dear: I could not get my old ones as she asked double – the old hussey: the Italians have no idea of anything but self: one would have thought an old customer would have been better treated. This has all been the better for me, however, for I have luckily got extremely nice rooms – not quite so large – but cheaper & in a far better situation, close by the beautiful Pincian Gardens.

Another compensation was that he found the artists' colony 'well & as kind & as good as ever: a more amiable set of people do not exist'. Although Uwins had soon decided to return to England, '& for a while I missed him dreadfully,'[2] the loss was offset by the arrival of Sir Digby Wyatt (who went on to become the first Slade Professor of Fine Arts at Cambridge) and Frederick Thrupp (future sculptor of Wordsworth's bust in Westminster Abbey). A fortnight later these two accompanied him on another expedition to Tivoli and Vico Varo.

Then, on 2 October, Lear was off again with Penry Williams, the colony's doyen, to explore the Alban Hill and its environs. Lear greatly admired Williams's landscapes of the surrounding countryside and, in particular, his depictions of Italian peasantry, some of which he later used in his own first travelogue, but he ultimately came to regret that this admiration closed him off from the influence of other artists. He continued to his sister:

> The principal towns on this mountain are Albano (where the Pope has a villa, Castel Gandolfo) – Nerni – Gensano – l'Ariccia – Civita la Vigna – Velletri – and Frascati – all perfectly beautiful… Of these, Frascati is the favourite Oct. residence of the Roman grandees, and the villas there are surprisingly delightful. You see the town from Rome, and you rise through the Campagna gradually to it. This sketch will give you some idea of the places:

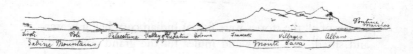

> The other towns are on the opposite side. The Latin valley is that by which we walked to Naples in the spring – only on the left hand side. We only stayed one night at Frascati – but I cannot tell you the beauty of the views from it, as you see the whole Campagna – the sea – and Rome like a map below. There is beautiful wine at Frascati.

That opinion, first voiced by Horace, still holds good 2,000 years later, as Frascati remains one of the favourite Italian whites.

> On the third we set off, passing by Collona – now a ruined town – through magnificent country, and reached Val Montone about noon. This is one of the most elegant Campagna towns and very curious: it is in a deep dell in the Latin valley, but rises on a mound crowned with a superb church and castle – though the town itself is wretchedly poor. Like all these places, it belongs to one prince – and has a baronial building as big as itself, and as much neglected. We went over this grand palace – which is perhaps more like Somerset House than anything else – only of marble and with staircases and rooms of the greatest splendour. Never inhabited, this – like hundreds of other Italian glories – is all decay; all the

Val Montone.

rooms of all the stories were full of Indian corn being beaten and sifted, and horses and mules fill the grand courtyards below… From the windows of this Doria Palazzo – at Val Montone – the view is sublime, as you see all down the valley – to [within] forty miles of Naples – so distant can the eye reach in this atmosphere. Palaestrina – Olevano – Palliano – Ascagni – Ferentino – Frossinone – Ceperano – and San Germano (the route of the Roman Via Casalina, which he and Uwins had mostly followed three months earlier).

The next day we walked from Val Montone (returning at dusk) to Monte Forlino, a strange town on the right of the Latin valley – built like a large pack of cards against the side of a precipice; the people were once celebrated as Brigands – and are not now over respectable, since on the gate of the town are five heads of Banditti in iron cages – placed as a warning. At Somino – on the marsh road – there are yet 25 human heads; this seems very shocking, but was really an excellent plan of the Pope Pius (7th. or 8th.) who caught brigands most industriously and thus cured the country of these pests. One celebrated bandit – Zasperoni – surrendered himself with his whole tribe on condition of being saved alive, and they are now all living in prison at Civita Vecchia; I can't tell you how many people he is said to have killed…

On the 5th we left Val Montone, being desirous of seeing

Segni – a very curious town, and one where hardly no travellers go, as it is not of very good reputation – one would not
go there alone, but Williams having been so long in Italy
speaks like a native. Segni is a long way down the valley –
nearly opposite Anagni – and it is built on a vast height, to
which the pull up is most fatiguing. The town has been six
times destroyed in different ages, being of such vast antiquity that no date can be given to it. It is surrounded by the
most perfect Cyclopean walls in Italy – except those of Aletri,
which I have not seen. These walls I think I told you I had
seen some of at Tivoli or Anagni, but those are Etruscan or
Pelasgic – much more recent. They are of huge stones irreg-
ularly placed – of ten or twelve feet in size – but so strangely fitted that they will last as long as the world, for they are
as strong now as 4,000 years ago… The shepherds with their
goats sit on top of them like the sketch.

Although the surrounding country was 'most beautifully picturesque – covered with the grandest forests of enormous chesnut trees
– and with long ranges of mountains wherever you turn your eyes,'
the town itself did not seem to have advanced much over the centuries, being

> a dreadful obscure place – and there was no inn but a filthy
> osteria which I <u>shall never forget</u>; no sooner were we in bed,
> than bugs dropped from the ceiling by dozens, and fleas were
> insupportable. On leaving this nasty place, the vile landlady
> insisted on double the amount we ought to pay – having the
> impudence to say 'the English are like quails, who come very
> seldom – when they do, we make the most of them.' As she
> was a ferocious creature, and backed by disagreeable men, we
> did not think it safe to make a disturbance, so we paid her;
> but we were even with her, for, having hired a mule to cross
> the valley, we sent it home again minus the payment the
> shocking old creature had asked – so I don't care if I never see
> Segni again…

On the 7th. we left it, and came quite across the valley to my
old delight, Olevano – after Tivoli, my favourite place –

indeed, in many respects being much more beautiful, being greatly superior in grandeur and mountain solemnity. We passed two days very pleasantly here – several artists being there also – and the vintage being at its height. It seems absurd, but if you say to a peasant 'I wish you would give me a few grapes, I am thirsty' he brings you 6 or 8 immense ripe bunches – and goes away, never taking any money for it!! In such profusion are these vast vineyards that you may ramble on picking whatever you please of all sorts; and I can assure you it is a most beautiful thing to see the branches down to the ground full of purple and green clusters. Those large, long grapes which we see in the grocer's shops in England are called Pizzitelli, and are very common and refreshing.[3]

Thirst, indeed, was not a problem, as heavy rain then set in, prompting Williams to return to Rome. Lear hung on for a further two days before he too gave up in despair – only for the rain at once to give way again to unbroken sunshine. By way of compensation, however, he found the city fast filling up with potential customers; Knighton commissioned an oil for £25, others some pencil drawings for £10, and there were some pupils in prospect.

'Everything considered – health and study etc. – I should certainly like to live in Rome,'[4] Lear told Ann two weeks later. He again discouraged the idea of her joining him there. His remark to Gould that, 'though I be not yet arrived at that keystone of hope, matrimony, I anticipate firmly the chance of a Mrs. Lear in 40 years hence at least'[5] might suggest that he had an additional motive for deterring Ann, although he wrote less optimistically of such a prospect to Fanny Coombe: 'I am but too certain of living alone throughout life – a fate for which my sensitive mind ill enough prepares me.'[6] After going on to describe a carnival attended by the city's entire population, he observed that 'no quarrel or disorder ever takes place, and one cannot but reflect sadly on the gin drinking and the vulgar sports of the lower English – the Copenhagen Fields etc. etc.'[7]

There is now, unfortunately, a six-year lacuna in Lear's surviving letters to Ann. The record of his activities up to July 1842 is largely confined to his far more irregular correspondence with Gould, Fanny and Lord Derby. Thus it was to Gould that he wrote: 'What with pupils (of which I had numbers) & friends – & drawings indoors & sketchings out of doors – the spring came before one knew where one was.' He had earlier described himself in the same letter as having been 'over head & ears in employment' during the winter:

> You will lift up your hands & eyes & legs & possibly fall quite off your chair when I tell you that I was enabled to send some of my earnings to my mother & sisters & to put by £100 besides for the use of the summer!!! – don't go into a fit.

> In May – 1839 – all the world having forsaken the old lady of Babylon – I went a walking tour towards Florence – & was much pleased thereby – after which, I went to a little town at the top of an high hill, where I have remained – in company with sundry other artists – until yesterday evening, when I returned here for the winter campaign.[8]

It is not clear that Lear ever got as far as Florence – indeed, the absence of any description of the city argues against such a presumption. However, the 'little town' he mentions can certainly be identified as Civitella (the modern Bellegra). Among the artists he met there was the newly-wed Samuel Palmer, who was with his wife Hannah (herself the daughter of another leading water-colourist, John Linnell) and a Dane, Wilhelm Marstrand (later to be the Director of the Copenhagen Academy of Art). Civitella became Lear's preferred place of retreat from Rome, as it did for others of the colony, and he later looked back on his time there as being among the high points of his life. Hannah Palmer described an artists' ball there at which 'Lear played very well on the flute,'[9] and in his diary he himself wrote of the 'Civitella days of olé, when one sat from noon to 3 listening to songs'.[10] It was not only fellow artists with whom he struck up relationships: after reminiscing about a 'Donna' whom he met four years later in the Abruzzi, he wondered what had become of 'you, – of Civitella days? Where are you and your babe? A dream world…'[11]

Civitella also became the subject of many of his pictures, including his largest oil (more than six feet wide). He told Gould that he had first dabbled in oils the previous year, without much enthusiasm, but

> this summer however I have pursued it again with a little more success – but am as yet of course a beginner, tho' I hope

ultimately to paint some thing or other. It takes a long while to make a painter – even with a good artist's education – but <u>without</u> one it tires the patience of Job; it is a great thing if one does not go backward. Meanwhile I am extremely happy – as the hedgehog said when he rolled himself through a thistlebush...

Do tell me if there is art at all in Sydney (except portrait painting which I conclude flourishes all over the world) – & what sort of people you are among. An Italian asked me the other day 'if New Holland were not peopled entirely by the worst criminals sent from home & if they had not returned one & all to a savage state & run the country naked & bare like Adam & Eve?' I said I imagined not, but I could not convince him that there might be some civilisation in the Antipodes.[12]

One of those who kept Lear 'over head & ears in employment' was Lady Susan Percy, a niece of the Duke and Duchess of Northumberland who, as subscribers to *The Family of Parrots*, had been among his earliest patrons. She often accompanied him on his forays into the Campagna and after her death, in 1847, he described her as 'my kind friend – the first I ever had in Rome'.[13] On 22 December 1840 he wrote to her as follows:

Mr. Lear begs Lady Susan Percy will do him the favour to accept the accompanying little scratches on 'shocking paper', which if they are no use in recalling some very nice excursions, may at least serve as a way of wishing her Ladyship a happy Christmas & New Year. Mr. Lear encloses a very insane copy of verses for Miss Percy – & if they are sendable, he begs Lady Susan will fill up the rest of the paper – that at any rate it may be in some degree worth its postage.[14]

He returned to Civitella the following summer to work up his first full-scale oil for Lord Stanley. Marstrand was evidently there also, because he did a pencil sketch of Lear that is dated 10 July 1840.

By the end of the summer Lear had built up a sufficiently representative portfolio of watercolours and sketches to consider the possibility of reproducing them in book form. This necessarily entailed a return to London, which would also have the advantage of salving his conscience towards Ann – it was now nearly four years since he had last seen her. He wrote to Gould in February 1841:

> What I shall do in England I have no idea, [except] run about on railroads – & eat beef-steaks. I am & have been, as you have justly heard, going on very well – which is more than ever I had a right to expect, in spite of your good opinion of me. I am very glad I took to Landscape – it suits my taste so exactly – & though I am but a mere beginner as yet, still I do hope by study & staying here to make a decent picture before I die. No early education in art – late attention, & bad eyes – are all against me, but renewed health & the assistance of more kind friends than any mortal ever had I hope will prove the heaviest side of the balance.

He returned again, however, to the recurring topic of his loneliness:

> I wish to goodness I could get a wife! You have no idea how sick I am of living alone!! Please make a memorandum of any Lady under 28 who has a little money – can live in Rome – & knows how to cut pencils & make puddings…
>
> Do you know that foolish & furious old bigot [Charles] Waterton has been here these 2 winters? He walked the last 20 miles to Rome BAREFOOT (fact), & was in bed 6 weeks: he is very much run after by all silly people, & has entirely demolished all Zoological artists (yourself & Audubon inclusive) for evermore…

(Waterton was an eccentric naturalist who during his time in Rome scaled St Peter's and left his socks on the lightning conductor.) Lear concluded: 'I hope you will be in town this summer. I hope too you will come to the Florence meeting – & so to Rome - & that you will bring Mrs. Gould also', and he sent her his 'very best remembrances'.[15]

No record survives of what passed between brother and sister when they were eventually reunited. However, the rooms in Southampton Row that Ann had kept on, in the hope that he would set up home with her again, were then given up and the two of them moved into separate lodgings. She appears to have resigned herself to his wish for independence, devoting the last 20 years of her life instead to the beneficiaries of various charities.

In August Lear was invited back to Knowsley by Lord Derby, and it was while he was there that he learned of Elizabeth Gould's death. He wrote to Gould:

> I cannot tell you what grief the tidings I received have given me. I do not know what to say to you... I should much like [it] if you will let me have some little sketch – nothing of value to you – done by Mrs. Gould, as a memorial of a person I esteemed and respected so greatly.[16]

After continuing on to Scotland at the invitation of Lord Breadalbane, a Fellow of the Royal Society, Lear returned to London in September to supervise Hullmandel's production of the lithographs that he had worked up from his Italian portfolio for publication in December, under the imprint of Thomas McLean. Twenty-five in all, they appeared under the title *Views of Rome and its Environs: Drawn from Nature and on Stone.* Only five were of the city itself, the majority being devoted to his favourite boltholes in the hills, such as Tivoli, Subiaco, Olevano, Val Montone and, of course, Civitella. The 300 copies of this collection were available by private subscription only, but what the subscribers may have lacked in quantity they made up for in quality. In addition to Queen Victoria, Prince Albert and the Queen Dowager, they included a good number of the dukes and earls of England – not to mention a certain C.S. Dickens, Esq.

John Murray's *Handbook for Travellers in Central Italy, including the Papal States, Rome and the Cities of Etruria*, which was published a year later, declared of Lear that 'a series of lithographic drawings, lately published in London, from his sketches show his skill in Roman landscape composition', and described him as 'an English Artist of great promise'.[17] His future as an artist, both in Rome, where he arrived back just before Christmas, and London, was now secure. Nevertheless, he complained to Lord Derby the following June (1842) that:

> The Roman season was very dull & stupid this year. Everybody was at Naples, for the Roman lodging-keepers

have outwitted themselves by doubling their prices. The Society also was not as good as usual, & there were but two Lions (Lady Charlotte Bury & Mrs. Trollope [mother of Anthony and a prolific author herself]) – a small quantity for winter consumption.[18]

The faithful Lady Susan Percy had also evidently still been on hand, however, for in February he had sent her a note with eight pen-and-ink 'representations of frightful facts which occurred 3 or 4 hours ago' when he had lost his hat out walking in a high wind.[19] The letter continued:

So towards March – as I was rather idle & very homesick – I thought a tour round Sicily would take up a month's time very improvingly, & accordingly I set off with one of Sir T. Acland's younger sons – & a nephew of Sir Stamford Raffles. And although from a most wonderful combination of delays & ill fortunes my one month's tour stretched into one of 10 weeks – to the great loss of my time & money – yet I am thankful now that I made it, since I look to returning at some future day to various spots in the island of which I should like to make pictures.

He did indeed return five years later, when he also wrote of the island at rather greater length than he did in this letter. The following is the only other passage from the latter that seems worth quoting here:

Just above Taormina on a perpendicular rock of vast height is a town called Molia, where we had heard that all the babies were tethered to doorposts by strings around their waists for fear of their falling down the precipice; so we made an excursion there, to see for all or any such babies, but – after diligent search – none were to be found; only – just as we were giving up the scrutiny – lo! one solitary piggywiggy, tied by its body & fallen just 3 feet over the edge of the rock – being the full length of its cord! From Taormina we came to Messina, & thence to Naples, & so to Rome once more, where I arrived the 26th May.[20]

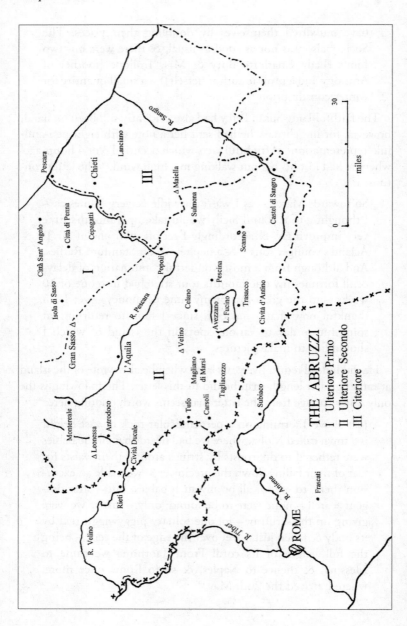

THE ABRUZZI
I Ulteriore Primo
II Ulteriore Secondo
III Citeriore

Chapter Four
The Abruzzi (July-August 1843)

Among the English community that had made Lear welcome on his first arrival in Rome was the Knight family. As he later reported to Ann, the five daughters were unfortunately of a somewhat delicate caste: 'Miss Isabella whom you ask after is always on a sofa, neither better nor worse, but her eldest sister is fast declining in consumption,'[1] though another sister succeeded in marrying no less than the Duke of Sermoneta. Their brother Charles, however, enjoyed a more robust constitution, being an experienced rider and the owner of a pedigree Arab, and he now suggested a joint expedition on horseback into the mountains of the Abruzzi. Lear was keen to mine the area for fresh landscapes, but he nursed a phobia of horses that was only marginally less powerful than his fear of dogs. Knight, however, proved a more than competent tutor, for his pupil was soon boasting to Gould that 'I am <u>unexpectedly</u> become a tolerable horseman.'[2]

I changed his position for the sake of variety.

Along with his drawing materials Lear packed a notebook in which to record their experiences, in the hope, to be amply fulfilled, of producing an illustrated travelogue.

Eventually published in 1846, under the title *Illustrated Excursions in Italy*, it opens on 26 July 1843:

> It was not without experiencing many delays that we were at last enabled to begin our long-proposed tour in the Abruzzi, or three Northern provinces of the kingdom of Naples. The plan arranged was first, that we should gain a general idea of our ground on horseback, and afterwards that I should proceed alone on foot to sketch and examine details. C.K. lent me his Arab (by name Gridiron), he riding the iron-gray; and, having sent my luggage to Rieti, we started from Frascati, with our valigie strapped before our saddles, on as brilliant a morning as one could desire for the beginning of a long journey.

After two days covering old ground along the ancient Via Valeria to Subiaco, they left the Papal States at the hamlet of Pianura di Cavaliere,

> which abounds in game and is greatly frequented by sportsmen. [Holiday-makers there, beware!] A short boundary question ensued on reaching the Neapolitan frontier, where, however, we were scarcely detained by some very civil officials; so on we cantered, fording a stream below Poggio-Cinolfo, and soon arriving at Carsoli, hidden from the plain in a little nook of its own. A ruined bridge below and a shattered castle above give a more picturesque than comfortable air to the modern town, which contains eight or nine thousand inhabitants, and is successor to, though not on the same site as, the ancient Carseoli; within, dirty narrow streets, only redeemed here and there by a bit of Gothic door or window, raise no favourable idea of the present condition of this once respectable abode of the Equi, where they sacrificed foxes to Ceres and where the Romans imprisoned Bituitus, king of Thrace.
>
> It was nearly noon: so we put up our horses and, having satisfied the authorities as to our passports and permessi for our steeds, we adjourned to a wretched Locanda, where the Oste

flattered us with hopes of something to eat, bidding us to wait in a closet, very nearly filled up by a large bed, a cracked spinette and an inclined table with uncertain legs; but when the repast was brought, both eatables and drinkables were such that, though pretty well used to uncommon food, we were compelled to be content with bread and water; and, leaving our dinner in the charming chamber, where 'cold and unhonoured, its relics were laid,' we strolled by the willow-edged Turano, a stream which rises near Carsoli, till our horses were ready to start. This was the first place where we encountered that horrible beverage, called Vino Cotto, which is wine boiled when new to make it keep; and, in spite of its nastiness, is drunk all over the Abruzzi by the common people. I have tasted some, kept for many years, that was little inferior to good Marsala, but when new, it is filthy beyond imagination.

About two, we set off again, by a pathway through a rising valley. Beyond Carsoli, there is no road for carriages into the Abruzzi; bare rocks were on our left, and on our right high hills, covered, as far as [the] eye could reach, with forests of oak, looking black and untrodden enough to shelter a world of bears and wolves… Beyond this, we toiled onward through this long stony pass, and all our hopes were fixed on Rocca di Cerri, a village at the top of the hill; on arriving at which, we confessed to being well repaid for our labour, by the view over the sublime Marsica. On our left, the snowy peaks of Velino, more than seven thousand feet in height, were gloomy beneath threatening clouds, and a wild confusion of misty mountains closed that side of the scene. Far below, in bright sunshine, a long streak of the blue Lake of Fucino, with its beautiful plain, dotted and spangled with woods and villages; and beyond the Lake up rose the strangely-formed mountain of Celano, with many a high range of faint, blue hills, while the dark-castled rocks and formidable pass of Tagliacozzo were at our feet. Having admired all this, we descended by a steep serpentine path, and were soon at the level of the Castle of Tagliacozzo, which guards the entrance to the plain below.

I have never seen anything more majestic than the approach to Tagliacozzo. It is a precipitous ravine, almost artificial in appearance; and, by some, indeed, considered as having been partly formed by the Romans, for the transit of the Via Valeria. A monastery, with a Calvario, or range of shrines, stands at the entrance of this extraordinary gorge, the portals of which are, on [the] one hand, huge crags, crested with a ruined castle; on the other, perpendicular precipices; between them is placed the town, receding step by step to the plain below, while the picture is completed by the three peaks of the towering mountain of Velino, entirely filling up the opening of the ravine.

Although they had a letter of introduction to the local don, they decided to press on 'because we were not so well provided with dress as a visit to so grandiose a Palazzo as the Casa Mastroddi might render desirable. So down we went, by a street strongly resembling a stair-case, to the plain below.' At Avezzano, their goal for the night,

[a] fine castle, built by the Colonna in the fifteenth century, stands well at the entrance of the town, and is a good specimen of a baronial residence. We asked for some inn or Locanda, but these are wanting in Abruzzo; and unluckily we had to seek our night's quarters in a place to which we had not brought a letter of introduction. One house, a Casa Corradini, was indicated as likely to receive us, and so we entered the town in search of it...

We sate sometime on our horses, waiting for the Padrone of our lodgings that were to be, and meanwhile, were highly amused by one of those torrents of pigs, common to Italian country towns, when the sable tribe, for black they are all, return at night to supper. Most of these towns being upon hills, the swine are obliged to go up, and therefore arrive in a state of placid expectation; but at Avezzano, they all have to come <u>down</u> hill, and so rush into the piazza in an uncontrollable frenzy. How we did laugh, to the diversion of half the rabble of the town, who had come to gaze on us, as the immense current of grunters burst from the long street into the market-place, with a wonderful hubbub, and ran shrieking away through all the lanes of the place.

When the pig-storm was over, and we had seen to our steeds, we made the most of the short remaining light and hurried to our lodgings, where three ineffably polite females showed us into a large, raftered room of a bewildering aspect, with much furniture and a great assortment of old clothes, and strewed with articles of female dress, intermixed rather oddly with fowls of all sizes, fluttering about in every direction, over and under two very misshapen beds. All this, added to the walls having a speckly appearance which, to the initiated, denotes the presence of certain flat entomological visitors, did not promise much repose; nor did the pensive chirping of an afflicted, one-winged chicken, upon whom one of our landladies lavished the most touching caresses, at all strengthen our admiration of the dormitory we had selected.

Meantime, while one of our hostesses reduced our chamber to order, we assisted the other two (one of whom was very handsome, but alarmingly fierce), to pluck and roast some pigeons, which eventually produced us no bad supper; for wine, alas! the horrible vino cotto was a most unsatisfactory substitute. As for our horses, fortunately for them, they were far better lodged than their masters…

There was no lock to our door. All night long, two or three frantic hens kept tearing round the room, and would by no means be expelled: the afflicted chicken with a broken wing scrambled about the floor without intermission: vermin of two species (politely called B flats and F sharps*) worried us beyond endurance: a perpetual chorus of pigeons thrilled over our heads, and an accompaniment of pigs resounded from below. So we were very glad when morning appeared.

Thus ended our first day and night in the Abruzzi.

July 28th. By sunrise we had taken our coffee and bread, and were on our horses; our day's programme being to see the Emissario [an Ancient Roman drainage tunnel built by the

Emperor Claudius to create an aquatic equivalent of the Colosseum], and then to coast the Lake. *

Lear was more impressed by the latter:

A herd of white goats blinking and sneezing lazily in the early sun; their goatherd piping on a little reed; two or three large falcons soaring above the Lake; the watchful cormorant sitting motionless on its shining surface; and a host of merry flies sporting in the fragrant air – these were the only signs of life in the very spot where the thrones of Claudius and his Empress were placed on the crowd-blackened hill; a few distant fishing-boats dotted the Lake where, eighteen centuries ago, the cries of combat rent the air, and the glitter of contending galleys [in simulated naval battles] delighted the Roman multitude. The solitary character of the place is most striking; no link between the gay populous past, and the lonely present; no work of any intermediate century breaks its desolate and poetical feeling. I could willingly have lingered there for hours, for I can recall no scene at once so impressive and beautiful.

Eventually tearing themselves away, they arrived at Transacco in time for lunch and,

on asking for a Locanda, we were directed to the first family of the town, the De' Gasparis, who had resided there for several centuries; to whose house we went, and asked boldly for aid for ourselves and horses. This was cheerfully given, though we were strangers, and without any letter of recommendation: Don Serafino (everybody is called Don throughout the Neapolitan states, a remnant of old Spanish customs) doing the honours of his establishment, a small but decent dwelling, with great friendliness.

After a dull and hungry hour of converse with some younger sons of our host, mostly on the subject of hunting, &c., we were taken, with many apologies for its being fast-day, into another room, where a repast was already on the table. The father De' Gasparis did not appear, but his six sons supplied

[* and impolitely, B..... fleas and F...... mosquitoes]

his place; and, to say [the] truth, the hospitality of this worthy family was rather oppressive, for there was no end of dinner, and the way in which they continually loaded our plates seriously threatened apoplexy. The macaroni, a word used in the Abruzzi to express long slices of paste (usually in summer dressed with Pomi d'oro or Tomatoes), was what we could least fight off; and, since Benjamin's days, nothing was ever seen like the supplies we groaned under. 'Bisogno mangiare!' 'e un piatto nazionale!' exclaimed the six brothers if we paused in the work set before us. 'Non possiamo piu!' said we. 'Mangiate! Mangiate! Sempre mangiate!' said they.

Fruit and excellent coffee having closed our refreshment, and rather relieved us from the terror we felt at the continual exhortation 'mangiare', K. and I, [in] spite of our friends' earnest entreaties not to brave the sun, wandered forth to explore the land.

As they headed back to Avezzano, however, the sun gave way to a tropical storm and they entered the town 'pretty well soaked, driving before us an immense troop of unhappy donkeys, who had lost all command of their intellects at our first rapid approach, and rushed wildly before us all the way home'. At their lodgings

We found our landladies in a state of distress at the death of the before-mentioned invalid chicken, who had committed suicide in a tub of water. This did not, however, disturb our peace so much as the summons of an inspector of police to his office, on the ground of our passports not being in order; but, as we considered them to be quite right (setting aside the fact of our being wet through, and that our supper was waiting), we politely requested him to come to us instead; which eventually he did, and signed our passports on looking at some of our introductory letters. A distinct 'Carta di Passo' is, however, requisite for every separate province of the kingdom of Naples for those who travel out of the high-road – a circumstance they had not informed us of at Carsoli; and, although we were not to blame for our involuntary ignorance, the inspector was no less in the right.

After these events we retired to bed, and were charmed for another night by the sportive proceedings of fowls, fleas, bugs, pigeons, and pigs, as before.

They awoke to brilliant sunshine once more and, leaving the lake behind at the fortress town of Celano, they began the ascent to the mountain pass of Forca Carusa via

Goriano Siculi (or Goriano Sicco), a little town containing seven hundred inhabitants. It stands on a tranquil valley, where we were glad to stable our horses, and refresh ourselves on raw ham, bread, and an omelette, at a little Osteria. No one, until after much travelling in Italy, can be aware of the universality of omelettes: omelettes plain, with tomatoes, with artichokes, or with garlic; not a bad dish, if well contrived, but rather tiresome by over-repetition…

At the summit, a vast and new scene was opened to us. We had passed out of the land of the Marsi, and were entering that of the ancient Peligni, separated from their neighbours of old by high mountain-walls, over which the stupendous Maiella reigned pre-eminent. A beautiful place, indeed, is the vale or plain of Solmona, twelve Neapolitan miles in length, and three or four wide; almost every spot in it cultivated with vines, and corn, olives, and garden-fruit, for which, especially melons, the district is famous. Solmona, the Sulmo of antiquity, stands at one of the extremities of the vale…

A ruined church, a rent wall, a leaning house, or a tower out of drawing, speak the earthquakes which have so frequently desolated this interesting spot, well known as the birth-place of Ovid, and still, after many sieges and other calamitous vicissitudes, a fine city. We admired its well-paved streets and numerous shops (half of which seemed confectioners', for the confectionery of Solmona is famous all over Italy), its cafes, palazzi, and churches, as we passed along the principal thoroughfare, and made our way to the great deserted convent, or hospital, now used as the inn. The interior, however, of that refuge was so uninviting, that we resolved to go on eight or nine miles further to Popoli, only

resting our horses for an hour; a duty which we accom-
plished for them in a vast stable, full of mules, the jingling of
whose bells was distracting; meanwhile, we rambled over the
city, and indulged in Limonata at various cafés.

They found Popoli, which they reached shortly after dark,

a bustling, narrow-streeted, dirty town, containing 3800
inhabitants, situated at the junction of the three roads leading to Aquila, Solmona, and Chieti, and therefore called the
key of the Abruzzi. Happily it contained an inn, where we
found no very bad accommodation.

Leaving the horses to a well-deserved rest, they spent the next day
exploring the remains of Corfinium, the ancient capital of the Peligni
tribe who had led the revolt against Rome's aggressive expansion in
the 3rd century BC, before making an early start for the 21-mile journey to Chieti, the capital of Abruzzi Citeriore. Their progress was
slowed, however, by Knight's horse casting a shoe and by

apparently endless windings of monotonous, though good,
carriage-road; the ascent to this ancient city (formerly Teate of
the Marrucini) is truly 'un vero Calvario'. The view from the
summit of the hill is extensive and magnificent in the extreme;
yet, excepting perhaps the group of mountains about the Gran
Sasso – that which terminates the fine chain bounding the
plain to the right – the whole scene has little attraction for a
landscape-painter, from its extreme panoramic vastness. To the
left, the huge Maiella stands almost alone; and beyond, plains
of undulating clay ridges, clad with vineyards, and spotted
with countless towns and villages, stretch southward as far as
[the] eye can reach, and eastward to the broad blue Adriatic...

We found an inn, the Aquila d'Oro, a strange straggling place,
with one immense bedroom containing six beds; a common
occurrence in these parts of Italy, where they have no idea of
anyone being so fastidious as to dislike sharing a sleeping-
room with chance passengers. What is worse, they will not let
you pay for the whole, which one would willingly do; for that,
say they, would be unjust to after-comers, who have a right to

hire unoccupied beds. Fortunately, we were the only strangers in the Locanda, so we slept in our six beds accordingly; a repose we were not sorry to have after an early dinner.

Thus refreshed, they set off at dawn for Pescara and the coast of the Adriatic, only to find it 'a most dull little town'. Staying only for a quick dip in the sea, they were soon heading back again to Chieti for another night in their Emperor-size bed. A full day's journey 'of a most treadmill-like nature' over a succession of ridges and valleys then brought them to Città di Penna in the foothills of the Gran Sasso, at over nine thousand feet the Abruzzi's highest peak.

In vain, on entering the town, we enquired for a Locanda, an Osteria, a stable; all Città di Penna seemed guiltless of such common-place conveniences. Nor were we at all better off, when, sending our introductory letter, we received an answer, that such a house would shelter us, and such a stable our horses; a reception so different to that afforded us by our Marsican friends, that we were not a little surprised. And, having sought the stable, it was so cold and damp, that one of our horses was instantly taken ill; and, as we could not persuade anybody to bring in food for them, we adjourned once more to the market-place, where we waited long, in vain, for any assistance: this man had a stable, but had lost the key; another had some hay, but was gone to a neighbouring town; and thus, these and other equally apropos suggestions were all we had to amuse us till the arrival of Don Andrea Giardini, the Mayor or Syndic of the town, to whom meanwhile I had applied.

Charming little Syndic of Syndics! Did you not instantly bring forth your own groom, open your stables, and cause the unlucky Gridiron and Iron-gray to be refreshed forthwith? And shall we not always remember you with a hearty goodwill – the sole oasis in that barren haunt of apathy and inhospitality?

It was now, however, too late in the evening to change the nasty lodgings we had gone to on the recommendation of our new acquaintance; and most particularly filthy ones they were. Sleep, from the little we saw of our room, was not to be expected; and, to add to our sorrows, the police declared our passports out of all order (not being Carte di Passo for the province), although signed by the Governor of Chieti himself.

This entailed a diversion to Città Sant'Angelo to obtain the necessary papers, and it was not until the following afternoon that they were back again on their planned route. The long slog up the mountain was not made any easier by Gridiron suddenly falling lame, but at the summit they were rewarded by a breathtaking view stretching all the way to the Apennines:

> Immensely below us was the deep valley to which our course was to be directed; and there, about the second hour of the night, we arrived well tired with our long day's journey. Villa Santa Lucia, a poor village, but our home for the night, did not look especially inviting; neither did the house of Don Domenico Nunzio, to whose care we had been recommended by our anonymous friend at Città di Penna.
>
> Yet this, though dark and small, was not nearly so unpleasant an abode as our first at Città di Penna, inasmuch as the poor people who received us here offered all they had with the greatest cheerfulness; nor were the rooms so irretrievably filthy. But what a stable! How often, on opening the door, did startled hens dash wildly against the candle and leave us in darkness! How often, when we had effected an entrance, did misguided calves, and eccentric goats, pigs, and asses, rush against us to our utter discomfort! And, having settled our steeds, how queer a place was shown us for our supper and sleeping-room! A sort of granary, holding one diminutive bed, and a table to match; all the rest of the space being choked up with sacks, barrels, baskets, hams, &c., &c. But the apologies made for all these inconveniences were profuse, and attention was shewn far more than could have been expected: so we congratulated ourselves on being once more in the province of Aquila, whose bounds are defined by the mountain-wall we had so recently climbed.
>
> Having tossed up who should have the bed, it fell to me, and directly afterwards fell under me, because it had but three legs, and one of those but feeble. As for K., he took up his quarters

upon the small table, and we talked and slept as much as we
might, till day broke; when a sound of Choc! choc! choc! per-
vaded the room, and forthwith numbers of little chanticleers
rushed from all corners, and, mounting the table, were astonished to find their accustomed crowing-place already occupied.

The further descent the following day proved no less arduous, and
even when they hit the high road to Aquila they were still faced with
'twelve or fourteen miles of dust, and ineffable stupidity…'

It would be difficult to enter the precincts of Aquila without
feelings of interest and curiosity… The cold look of desertion
in its well-paved streets struck us forcibly as we passed through
them; and we acknowledged that its title, 'la Roma degli
Abruzzi', was well merited by its character of departed
grandeur – its fine palaces, gloomy and uninhabited; its splendid convents and churches, and its extensive walls enclosing
vineyards where once were flourishing quarters of the town. A
scanty population, and the total absence of bustle in so large a
place, increased its resemblance to the eternal city.

They had been given a letter of introduction to the city's
Intendente, but on presenting themselves they were informed that he
was away taking the thermal baths at Antrodoco. Their disappointment, however, was quickly dispelled by the discovery of 'a really
good inn: "Il Sole" might do credit to any place in southern Europe,
and in its spacious chambers we were right glad to repose'.

The road up to the next pass was, in Lear's judgement, 'greatly inferior in grandeur and beauty to many passes in Cumberland', but,
once across it,

you go down by a most zig-zag route (supposed to represent a
carriage-road) to the valley, where the torrent, whose course
you have been accompanying, joins the river Velino, and where
it has pleased the founders of Antrodoco to place their town,
mainly because it is protected by a rock, the castle on which
commands three formidable passes. From the last few turns of
the spiral descent, where a vast rock overhangs the road, there
is a very grand view of the town at the foot of immense and
gloomy hills; but it was so nearly dark on our arrival that we

could only gaze with awe into the solemn abyss, where an indistinct mass of towers and roofs was alone discernible.

The single osteria in the place was no more inviting, but they were just resigning themselves to a supper of 'two wooden-looking slices of ham and one egg' – everything else, the inn-keeper explained, had been consumed by the visitors to the baths – when an invitation arrived from Prince Giardinelli, the Intendente, to dine with him. He turned out to be

a lively little man of friendly manners, who spoke English. Near him was a sweet little girl, his only child, of about ten years of age; and about the room were various uffiziali attached to his suite, and sundry personaggi of the town, who were paying their evening devoirs. These by degrees subsided, and we were left with the Governor and Donna Caterina, who, after a long hour in which I was more than half asleep, took us into a room where was a table, plate, covers, &c.

And what did we not see when those covers were removed! A positive plain English-looking roast leg of mutton, in all its simplicity and good odour! And two dishes, one of simple mealy boiled potatoes, the other ditto baked! Add to this a bottle of excellent Champagne – and imagine our feelings! (The secret of these amazing luxuries was, that the Prince and his cook had both been in England.)

Not content with that, the Prince regaled them in the morning with 'a regular English breakfast' and insisted that they accompanied him in his carriage while the horses were sent on ahead.

The valley of the Velino is much wider beyond the little town of Paterno (believed to be the ancient Cutilia), and the flat waste near the river is full of the most curious mineral springs, forming numerous little lakes. Some are hot, some cold, some sulphureous, some charged with iron, &c.; and I cannot say but that I wished them all anywhere else, as we were presented with several glasses of their contents, only varying in degrees of nastiness. When this impromptu refreshment was over, we took leave of our host, who returned to Antrodoco, while we rode on slowly to Città Ducale.

Founded on the remains of a pre-Roman site and regularly shaken over the years by subsequent earthquakes, the town wore a curiously patchwork appearance, the only building of any note being the Palazzo occupied by the local governor:

> Its interior was spacious in the extreme; and, having present-ed our letters, we were received most graciously by Don Francesco Console, the Sottointendente, in an endless suite of lofty rooms, containing royal arms, and royal busts, and royal portraits in profusion.

> The repast which followed, though a very good dinner, was rather wearisome, owing to our host being very full of elab-orate compliments, which our English wits could not fully appreciate: we were very well pleased nevertheless, for our good-natured entertainer did his best, according to his coun-try's fashion; and what more could anyone expect?

By the next evening the pair were back again on Papal territory, at Rieti. Here Knight had planned to leave Lear for a few days' sketch-ing and continue on to rejoin his family at Frascati, but the following day he was struck down with sunstroke and it was not until the 11th that they finally parted company. Rieti in the meantime fulfilled Lear's best hopes:

> From various villas or vineyards, situated on the sides of the wooded hills which entirely surround the plain, magnificent views of the city may be obtained. That from the Villa Pomane is, perhaps, the finest; though the Villa Potenziani commands a more extensive prospect. I thought I had scarce-ly ever beheld any lovelier scene than the towers of Rieti and its quiet world of vineyard, as I saw it the last evening of my stay. The Marchese Vecchiarelli had given a little entertain-ment on the Cypress Terrace, beyond the Casino; and as we sat at supper by the brilliant light of the full moon, slanting between the trunks of the aged trees, the city at our feet, and the majestic mountain of Leonessa forming the most glori-ous background possible, imagination could hardly have pic-tured a more perfect scene of Italian villeggiatura.[3]

Chapter Five
The Abruzzi (August–September 1843)

Once again Lear felt the lack of company very keenly. He wrote the next day:

> Having no longer a companion to share the ups and downs of a rambling life, I could not look forward to my second series of explorings with great pleasure. To be sure, it is better to be alone than in company with a grumbler, or a caviller about farthings, or one who is upset by little difficulties, or – what is worse, perhaps, than all – one who regards all things with total apathy. But as my late co-mate had none of these ill conditions, and was moreover of an imperturbably good temper, and fully capable of enjoying every variety of wandering, come in what shape it might, I confess to having been somewhat dreary at first.

Retracing his steps to Città Ducale, he was still less than inspired – 'Dulness and Civita Ducale are, indeed, synonymous... Two months of the Abruzzi after this fashion will be more than enough... Eggs again for supper!' At Antrodoco the next day, however, he was cheered to catch up again with Prince Giardinelli, who had now moved into his summer residence there, and who

> very good-naturedly assigned me a lodging, and particularly invited me to be present at the centesimo, or fête, of Tagliacozzo, on the 29th.

After having hunted out my luggage, well-nigh lost in the

confusion attending the migration of the Intendente and his suite, and having arranged with a Don somebody Todeschini to take a room in his house (a rambling place, full of break-neck stairs and abrupt corners, let out to the 'various bathers'), I adjourned to supper in my host's house – a sort of pension, where was a great mingling of odd people. The only way to be comfortable was to adapt oneself to circum-stances, so I did as everybody else did after supper – namely, sang songs and played on the guitar perpetually, and was consequently pestered for 'un'aria Inglese' every five minutes afterwards during my stay. Two widows from Aquila were incessant in their requests for 'Ye banks and braes'; but 'Alice Gray' had the greatest number of votes. Thus the evening went by merrily enough; and if there was not much refine-ment in the society, at least good-nature and high spirits were not wanting.

August 13th. The cool valley of Antrodoco is in deep shade till late in the morning. I was sauntering by the brawling river, when a little boy passed me carrying a dead fox. 'It is delightful food,' said he, 'either boiled or roast.'

After two more days of sketching Lear decided to join the Prince's expedition to Tagliacozzo.

August 16th, 1843. An hour before daylight being the time named for our starting, we assembled in the market-place, although two hours after the sun was fully risen we were still unprepared to set off. Great was the tumult in the narrow street where the Intendente had lodged: the arrangement of his luggage – the soothing and menacing of eccentric mules and perverse horses – the collecting together [of] all his Excellency's suite of domestics – the simultaneous drinking of coffee at the last moment – and the noisy adieux of the Antrodochesi spectators. How many saddles were found to be inverted, just as they should have been on their bearers' backs! How much string was required to tie on irregular arti-cles of baggage! And how many times all the horses, mules, asses, luggage, grooms, guides, and spectators were involved in the wildest confusion, by some sudden freak of one or two ungovernable quadrupeds! These are matters only to be guessed at by those who have [not] sojourned in Italy.

At length we were in order: the Secretary and the Judge on very forlorn-looking mules; the cook and all the male house-hold, with most elaborate accompaniments of food and utensils, on creatures of every description; and the Maestro do Cavalleria, with a mounted groom leading Prince Giardinelli's gray horse, and two others on little animals as ugly as vicious (with no tails, and eyes a long way out of their heads), dignified by the title of Pomeranian ponies, and intended for the use of Donna Caterina [the Prince's young daughter]. As for me, I had a very decent black horse, with a most uneasy saddle, the stirrups appertaining to which gave way in about a quarter of an hour, and rolled hopelessly down the ravine. Behind came the gend'armes, with guides and baggage-mules; and a highly-picturesque cavalcade we were. However, our appointments might want the full digni-ty to be looked for in a Governor's establishment. Slowly we wound up the pass as far as Rocca di Corno.

Their hosts for the night were the Placidi family,

a very striking group, composed of a most venerable old lady, 98 years of age, whose long white hair fell on her shoulders, and two sons, both upwards of 70, and in appearance as old as their mother, who called them 'my mannikins' and 'little boys'. By these good people we were taken to the Palazzo Placidi – a huge rambling old house, with gloomy, dirty state rooms, full of ancient furniture arranged round the walls, damask sofas and leather chairs, and tables with gilded legs, none of them apparently having been in use since the days of the early Siculi Kings…

Nothing could be more hospitable or well supplied than the supper-table, which we were glad to join. Donna Serafina de' Placidi was a wondrous old lady, in full possession of all her faculties, and conversing while she knitted with great assiduity. A chaotic-looking chamber was shown me as mine for the night, containing a vast bed, with crimson velvet about it enough for three such; on which I was glad to repose in my cloak, seeing that its comfort and propriety were wholly external.

Tagliacozzo was reached the following noon, and the whole party was put up at the Palazzo Mastroddi. Lear wrote that he

> found a great change in its appearance from that which it bore at my visit in July. The green before the town was covered with people preparing for the fair held there, and the houses were all more or less decorated in honour of this great fiesta of the Madonna (called la Madonna dell' Oriente, from a picture of the Virgin, supposed to be of Eastern workmanship), which is held but once in a century, and consequently with great pomp and expenditure. All round the Piazza a temporary colonnade had been built; and in the centre a very pretty Gothic chapel of ornamented wood, in which the painting of the Madonna was placed, no church in Tagliacozzo being of sufficient size to accommodate the multitude expected.

He was allotted 'a quiet little bed-room, whose snugness and perfect nicety contrasted favourably with the unclean magnificence of my last night's abode'. He was woken the next morning at dawn with a cup of coffee brought to his room, before descending to take more coffee with his hostess in the great Loggia. The crowded Piazza outside was already a babel of chatter, augmented with the din of rival bands.

> To one whose greatest horror is noise, this sort of life was not a little wearying; but having been informed that not to leave the house during the festa would be considered as the greatest insult to the family, I felt obliged to remain, and resigned me to my fête accordingly.

Lunch, albeit at a table laid for 60, came as something of a relief, especially since, as the only foreigner present, he found himself seated at the ladies' end. Afterwards yet more coffee was taken in the Loggia,

> before everybody sallied forth to the promenade outside the town, where platforms were erected to observe the horse-

races, which shortly took place, and about which great interest was shown. The winning horse was taken up to the chapel of the Madonna dell' Oriente, and led to the steps of the altar, by way, I suppose, of expressing that a spirit of thankfulness may be graceful and proper upon all occasions.

And after the race, a fire-balloon should have ascended; but somehow or other there was a reigning destiny adverse to balloons, for the first caught fire, and blazed away before it left earth; the second stuck in a tree, where it shared the same fate; and the largest ran erroneously among chimney-pots, and was consumed on the house-tops, to the great disgust of the Tagliacozzesi.

Now followed an invitation from Madame Mancini, or some one else who possessed a house in the Piazza, in order to see the girandola or fireworks; so away we went (the Intendente leading the way), and ate ices in the draped galleries overlooking the square. This was about Ave Maria [8 o'clock], or later, and I can never forget the scene it displayed; the dense crowd of people, some four or five thousand, were at once on their knees, and burst forth as if one voice were singing the evening chant to the Virgin, the echoes of which rang back from the black rocks of the Pass, with a solemnity of deep melody, the more soothingly beautiful after the past hours of hubbub.

Crack – bounce – whizz! the scene was changed in a twinkling by the flash and explosion of all kinds of fireworks; rockets flying hither and thither, serpents rushing and fizzing all round the colonnades, and that which should have been the fountain blazing away in streams of fire.

The final event of the day was a performance at the Opera, but greater entertainment was enjoyed between the acts,

> laughing at the strange dresses of some of the personages from the neighbouring towns, who displayed fashions unchanged, said the Tagliacozzesi, since the last century's

festa. One charming old lady, with a rose-coloured satin bonnet, at least four feet in diameter, and a blue and yellow fan to match, was the delight of the whole audience.

The entire programme was re-enacted over the following two days as well, but the final display of pyrotechnics capped everything that had gone before:

During the last act of 'Il Barbiere', a breathless individual rushed into the theatre, and yelled out the fatal word 'Fire!' Great was the confusion, and on gaining the narrow street, the scene was terrible: an immense body of flame was rising behind the old Ducal Palace, and dense volumes of smoke obscured the moon. The fire had not yet reached the building, but must inevitably do so unless speedily checked, as the offices of the Institution immediately communicated with an extensive magazine (or fenile) of straw, whose contents had been burning internally for some time before the flames burst forth, and led to the alarm being given.

To rescue the children was the first object, and great good feeling and promptitude were manifested on all sides. As soon as the terrified females – most of them carried straight from their beds to various adjacent houses – were out of danger, and the furniture moved to the street, everyone did his best towards the extinction of the fire – no easy matter, since no water was within reach; and the only method adopted was to unroof part of the fenile nearest the Palazzo, and smother the flames as far was possible with continual baskets of earth, until the rooms joining the premises to the burning barn could be destroyed, to prevent the further spread of the conflagration. This was a long operation, though many men were immediately pressed into the service, and commenced the work of demolition with rapidity. Meanwhile we were all marshalled into companies, and set to work in a garden to fill tubs and baskets with earth, which were handed, when full, to the top of the wall of the unroofed fenile, where lines of men threw their contents out on the burning fuel.

The exact amount of good resulting to the common cause

from my individual exertions was small: for having grubbed
and clawed away at the ground until I had filled a very handsome tub, I turned round hastily to carry it to its destination
– but not being aware that the ladies' garden was formed ter-
race-wise, and being too blind to perceive it, I fell down a
height of about six feet, into the centre of a bed of broccoli,
where all my carefully-filled tub was bouleversé on to my
respectable person.

Happily, after the burning barn was isolated, by all communication between it and the surrounding buildings being
destroyed, the danger to the town was diminished, though
the showers of falling sparks throughout the night gave great
cause for uneasiness. I could hardly help thinking, that the
origin of all this might be sought for in the fireworks of the
evening; but I found that the Tagliacozzesi were rather scan-
dalized at such an idea. And thus ended the great festa of
Tagliacozzo in 1843.

After moving on to Magliano for a rather more relaxing night in
the Palazzo Masciarelli, in which 'I could have fancied myself in old
England,' he was back again in Avezzano, where he spent another two
days trying to capture the fickle light on the waters of Lake Fucino.
His next stop-over, in the house of the don of Città d'Antino, where
everything was 'much as you might find them at any country gentleman's in our own country,' again brought back memories. Better still,
there was

a most delightful garden, attached to the house, and com-
manding the whole of the vast Swiss-looking valley of
Roveto. Nothing could be more unexpected or charming
than this well-kept villa, in so wild a spot; and I could easily
believe that for months, nay years, the family do not go
beyond their own grounds. In truth, the toil of ascent to
these eyrie homes must make it infinitely desirable that they
should contain all things to satisfy the wants of their owners.
A nook in the garden contained a solitary wild boar, lately
taken in the woods near the house, who seemed no wise reconciled to the garden luxuries of his new home.

I was anxious to obtain a faithful representation of Città D'Antino, but was scarcely able to do so, when a terrific thunder-storm, whose warning clouds had clothed the scene with inconceivable grandeur, drove me to the Palazzo Ferrante, where, till evening, I was amused by the good performance on the piano-forte of Don Manfredi Ferrante, whom I found on my return to the house. At supper, our party was further increased by Donna Maria Ferrante, and one daughter, who, though far from being so handsome as her sister Donna Constanza Coletti, was yet extremely pretty. The mistress of the mansion was still as remarkable for the beauty of her face as for her agreeable manners. The lady-like quiet self-possession and simple friendliness of these Abruzzese females, of the higher orders, much delighted me, and I fancied I saw the fac similes of the dames of our own country, in the fourteenth and fifteenth centuries.

The next day Lear proceeded to Celano,

a place I longed much to examine; and the Sotto-intendente of the Distretto, Don Romeo Indelicato (as odd a name as any one may discover), had obligingly furnished me with a letter to one of the principal families of the town, the Tabassi... We had seated ourselves to supper the first evening of my arrival, when I felt myself suddenly shaken forward in my chair, till my nose nearly touched the table: some novel domestic arrangement of a servant behind, shaking everybody into his seat, said I to myself – but the moment after all the family rose, and various people, screaming 'Terramoto!' ran wildly into the room. Celano, and indeed the whole province of Abruzzo Ulteriore Secondo is very subject to earthquakes, and during my stay in the neighbourhood there were four shocks, which I soon learned to recognise as such.

This alarming experience notwithstanding, he stayed on for another four days, mostly spent still attempting to capture the atmosphere of Lake Fucino and its surrounds. On the fifth he crossed over to Trasacco, where he found the whole town in agitation at the horrible news just arrived, that Don Tita Masciarelli's coachman had murdered the housekeeper at Paterno; that the murderer, who had been committed to the prison of Celano, had strangled himself almost immediately on being left alone, so that no further light could be thrown on the tragedy, which created a great sensation throughout the Marsica, where murders are exceedingly unfrequent.

Not surprisingly, he made an early start the next morning for Pescina,

a large town, containing three thousand inhabitants, strikingly situated on the side of a wild ravine or gorge, through which the little river Giovenco flows to the Lake. Its houses are piled one above the other very picturesquely, and most of them have pigeon-holes attached (the pigeons of Pescina are exceedingly numerous: the refuse of their houses is used as a manure for hemp and fetches fifteen carlini the sack). A ruined castle crowns the whole picture.

His evening meal, at the table of another branch of the Tabassi family, was again interrupted by an earth tremor, 'but no damage resulted; and the bells of Pescina rang the usual alarm on these occasions, namely, three "tocs" of the Campana'. He was taking no chances, however, and set off for Scanno at dawn. He made a diversion en route

to a village called San Sebastiano,where a French company have established an iron-foundry, to the agent of which Don Stefano Tabassi had given me a letter – not that it was an interesting subject to me, but everybody said I ought to see it. Indeed, most of the poor people about here seemed much excited about these iron-works; but as a company of speculators have lately settled themselves near the Maiella, with the intention of extracting sugar from potatoes, the simple peasantry make an odd jumble of the two different crops. 'Do you know what produces sugar from iron?' said one, and 'Do you know the company which makes iron with potatoes?' was the question of another (for a stranger is so rare an occurrence in these wild districts, that he is sure to be set down as one of the iron-workers, or sugar makers).

At San Sebastiano I fell in with Monsr. Richardon, the over-seer of the new works, who informed me that his principal was absent, but invited me very heartily to join his luncheon (to which he was then returning) and thereby I passed an hour very agreeably. Two or three of his lively countrymen had lately arrived from France, and entertained us by their horror of sundry omissions of cleanliness on the part of the aborigines of San Sebastiano, to which the older colonists seemed well broken in; but Monsr. Richardon recalled to their memory some village in Brittany, where, so far from soup plates being only washed occasionally, the inhabitants substituted shallow holes cut in the wooden dinner-table, which communicated by channels with a perpetual tureen in the centre, into which the soup was poured, and diverged therefrom into each guest's plate or trough, to the great sav-ing of trouble and earthenware.

After luncheon I followed my host to the new establishment, which is planted by a beautiful stream of water below a neighbouring village, the name of which I cannot recollect. The scene was really curious; nearly two hundred peasants were at work on the rising buildings: oxen dragging timber, hammers sounding, and all this bustle of activity greatly con-trasting with the desolate solitude of the valley around. The iron ore is obtained in the neighbouring mountain of Lecco, and the Frenchmen expect the whole of their foundry will be completed in another year.

He did not return, however, to ascertain the success or otherwise of this early and unlikely example of French venture capitalism.

Next, Lear approached Scanno, beside the lake of the same name,

one of the perfectly beautiful spots in nature, and the more for being in so desert[ed] a place. Its dark waters slumber below bare mountains of great height, and their general effect might recall Wastwater in Cumberland, but that every craggy hill was of wider and grander form; and that the gold-en hues of an Italian September evening gave it a brilliancy rarely known in our own north.

In the town itself the chief interest lay in the womenfolk,

> whose dress is extremely peculiar, and suggests an Oriental
> origin, particularly when (as is not unusually the case with the
> older females) a white hand-kerchief is bound round the
> lower part of the face, concealing all but the eyes and nose. In
> former days, the material of the Scannese dress was scarlet
> cloth richly ornamented with green velvet, gold lace, &c., the
> shoes of worked blue satin, and the shoulder-straps of massive
> silver, a luxury of vestments now only posessed by the very
> few. At present, both the skirts and boddice are of black or
> dark-blue cloth, the former being extremely full, and the
> waist very short; the apron is of scarlet or crimson stuff.
>
> The head-dress is very striking: a white handkerchief is sur-
> mounted by a falling cap of dark cloth, among the poorer
> orders; but of worked purple satin with the rich, and this
> again is bound round, turbanwise, by a white or primrose-
> coloured fillet, striped with various colours, though, except-
> ing on festa days, the poor do not wear this additional band.
> The hair is plaited very beautifully with riband; and the ear-
> rings, buttons, neck-laces, and chains are of silver, and in rich
> families, often exceedingly costly.
>
> It is the prettiest thing in the world to see the children, who
> have beautiful faces, and are all turbaned, even as little
> babies. As for the women, they are decidedly the most beau-
> tiful race I saw in the Abruzzi – their fresh and clear com-
> plexion, fine hair, good features, and sweet expression, are
> delightful; and owing to their occupation being almost
> entirely that of spinning wool, their faces have a delicacy,
> which their countrywomen who work in the fields cannot
> lay claim to.

After this his hosts for the evening were a distinct disappointment:

> Our party at supper consisted of the master of the house, his
> sister, and their uncle. When I asked if their mother was
> coming, 'She's busy' was the answer. As for the sister, she
> never said a word; no, not one; and I should have thought
> she was dumb if she had not arisen after a very slight meal,

and first saying 'Prosit' (the Latin 'Prosit' is frequently used, among the middle and lower classes in some parts of Italy, by persons rising from the table; or when passing through a room where others are at meals. It is also addressed to persons when sneezing) with a loud voice, went out of the room. The uncle kept talking about the everlasting Thames Tunnel till I was bored to extinction. [The tunnel, from Wapping to Rotherhithe, had been opened the previous year: Lear had already found it to be a topic of endless fascination in Italy.)]

After another supper, an unappetizing menu of tench, barbel and bream (it being a Friday), and another vain attempt to draw out the 'hopelessly mute' sister, he decided to cut his losses.

The two-day journey to his next objective, Sulmona, lay through the spectacular Foce (Gorge) of Sagittario, and he was obliged to stop midway for the night at Villalago. He arrived to find

half the population (who are very poor and not extremely prepossessing in appearance) were thronging round a small church, whose open doors displayed two large naked figures in the midst of flames representing purgatory... I could not help thinking that I had got into rather an odd place.

This impression was confirmed by his billet for the night, where 'the uncleanliness of both house and owners was something uncommon,' and he decided that a chair rather than a bed offered the best prospect of sleep.

September 12th. Long before sunrise I was on my way down the Foce with a man and luggage-mule, and my step was not less light from any regrets at leaving Villalago. Beyond the Stretti di San Luigi the pass becomes every moment more appalling and sublime, in one part widening out into a broad vale over which on a precipitous rock a little village, Castro di Valva, seems to hang suspended and tottering; but closer to Anversa (the castle of which is seen at the opening of the gorge) the stupendous rocks which enclose the path are really beyond imagining. It is a relief to escape from this cold prison, to the bright open hill beyond...

In the afternoon I walked to Cocullo, a small town remarkable only for its possession of a relic – a tooth of S. Domenico – on account of which numerous pilgrims flock thither continually. Any person who is bitten by a snake or mad dog, be he either in Naples or Rome, loses no time in setting off to the shrine of S. Domenico, in Cocullo; and there is an annual festa in the town, at which the number of snake-charmers is very great; the floor of the church, I have been told by many persons, exhibiting swarms of reptiles crawling over it. I was not fortunate enough to see this display, but I have no doubt of the fact.

By the time that he was convinced of this he found that the sun had already set. It was not until two days later that he was satisfied that his pencil had done the scene justice, and another week before he felt that it had done Sulmona likewise.

Lear's next stop, Castel di Sangro, marked the border with the province of Abruzzo Ulteriore Secondo. The weather in the mountains had now turned distinctly cold, and rather than risk being trapped by an imminent snowfall he made a hurried descent to the 'delicious sunshine and warmth' of the coastal plain around Lanciano. From there it was a relatively easy hike to Chieti and the all-weather route back to Rome:

> The padrone of the Locanda to which I went dared not receive me without my passport being first examined, so I was obliged to present me at the house of the Sindaco, who was sitting in a room full of people, before which assembly I had to give an account of myself. These people cannot imagine one's motives for travelling to be simply the love of seeing new places, &c.; and the more one strives to convince them that it is so, the more certain are they that one has other designs. 'Where are you going!' they scream out, if one goes but a foot's length out of the highway to seek a point for drawing.

His pass finally secured and his interest in the town already exhausted, he was soon back on the road along the fertile but monotonous shore of the Adriatic (made no less so today by its endless succession of package holiday resorts).

Chieti seemed as difficult of access as on August 1st, and I
resolved during the ascent not to enter it, but skirting its
walls, descended into the valley of the Pescara, which I
reached late in the afternoon, and after long waiting (for the
ferry was occupied by a succession of large market parties),
crossed the river into the Province of Abruzzo Ulteriore
Primo, and took the route to the left. Four or five miles
brought us to Cepagatta, an inconsiderable town; and two
more to a quiet little vale of oaks, above which the church
tower of Abadessa peeped humbly forth. While ascending to
the town I was struck by the appearance of what I thought a
group of Turks, but who were really women of Abadessa in
their costume, which they have preserved, though the
Albanese men dress like ourselves in dark cloth, &c.

Lear also observed that their features still betrayed Abadessa's ori-
gins as an Ancient Greek colony. Of the five daughters of his host for
the evening, he considered the eldest to be

the only handsome female I saw in the whole settlement; for
though the Greek nose and forehead were very observably
marked in the face of almost every individual, yet none were
strictly beautiful, perhaps because their doing all the work,
while the men carry on the life of sportsmen, does not contribute to the delicacy of their complexion…

During supper, whenever the children spoke Albanese, they
caught a reproof and sometimes a thump from Don
Constantino. In the course of the evening a blind young man
came in 'to see the Englishman,' and eventually sang twenty
interminable verses of a Greek song about the battle of
Navarino. When the family separated for repose, Don
Constantino and a very old and hideous female domestic followed me into my chamber, the latter of whom proffered her
services to 'undress me', which offer I respectfully declined,
though she again entered to tuck all the sheets round the
bed, an operation I could not prevent as the doors of all the
rooms were open, but was thankful when it was concluded.

He duly made an early escape from her attentions in the morning, only to be greeted at Città di Penna by an equally unwelcome surprise:

> 'Your companion is dead,' said the foolish D. Giuseppe Michelloni, the son of my landlord – an abrupt announcement, which startled me not a little: and in order to ascertain the truth, I went at once to the Baron Aliprandi, at whose house I was told I should find our old friend D. Andrea Giardini. I was right glad to see the little Syndic again; and I learned from the Baron (who, with the Baroness and a large poodle, were the equally uninteresting inhabitants of a prodigiously grand Palazzo) that a foreigner was said to have fallen down the cascade of Terni, and therefore he 'supponeva' it must be my friend, by which lively supposition (and there was no better foundation for the report) my mind was very much relieved, and I returned to my supper at Michelloni's with a cheerful mind. But the spacious room we enjoyed at our first visit was now hired by an avvocato; and although the good people of the house insisted on my occupying one of their own apartments, it was by no means so comfortable, there being a hole in the door, by which a variety of cats ran in and out all night long, while two turtles remained stationary on the top of the bed, moaning dismally.

The onset of rain put an abrupt end to his sketching the next day and drove him inside a neighbouring palazzo, where another surprise – but this time an agreeable one – awaited him, in the shape of a collection of miniatures of the entire Stuart royal line of England, together with 'a long pedigree of the Norths of Grantley in Nottinghamshire'. Tempting as it might have been to link their presence in Italy with Byron's regular disposal of family heirlooms from Newstead during his peregrinations in Italy a generation earlier, it was apparently explained as having been passed down from the last Stuart pretender, Henry, Cardinal York (younger brother of Bonnie Prince Charlie), after his appointment as Bishop of Frascati.

With rain again threatening the following morning, Lear set out for Isola in the foothills of the Gran Sasso, and was, 'after drawing the town, most glad to take shelter by a good wood-fire, for the evening was bitterly cold'.

An old woman, Donna Lionora (who like many I had observed in the course of the day, was a goitreuse) cooked me some beans and a roast fowl; but the habitation was so dirty and wretched that one had need have had a long journey to provoke any appetite. While I was sitting near the chimney (it had the additional charm of being a very smoky one), I was startled by the entrance of several large pigs, who passed very much at their ease through the kitchen – if so it were called – and walked into the apartment beyond, destined for my sleeping room. 'Do you know that the pigs are in there?' said I to the amiable Lionora. 'Yes, they've gone there to sleep,' quoth she, nowise moved by the intelligence. They shan't sleep there while I'm in the house, thought I; so I routed them out with small ceremony, and thereby gave great cause for amazement to the whole of the family. 'He's mad,' suggested some of the villagers sotto voce. 'All the English are mad,' responded an old man, with an air of wisdom, 'the whole lot of them are mad,' an assertion he clearly proved on the ground that the only Englishman who had ever been known to visit Isola (several years previously) had committed four frightful extravagances, any of which was sufficient to deprive him of all claim to rationality, viz.: he frequently drank water instead of wine; he more than once paid more money for an article than it was worth; he persisted in walking even when he had hired a horse; and he always washed himself – 'Yes, even twice a day!', the relation of which climax of absurdity was received with looks of incredulity or pity by his audience.

October 1st. The Gran Sasso was perfectly clear, but his furrowed sides were covered with brilliant snow. No mules were to be had, for they had all gone to Aquila, to carry wine; but Don Lionardo Madonna informed me that there should be one at my service by eventide, and that if I set off after midnight I could accomplish the journey to Aquila in about thirteen or fourteen hours of diligent walking...

This he duly achieved. On his arrival he was relieved to find a letter from Knight assuring him that he 'happily had arrived safely at

Tivoli, instead of having fallen down the Caduta delle Marmore'. From Aquila he followed the same route to Rieti as he had in August, except for a leisurely diversion to Montereale and Tufo,

> where the Coletti family gave me as hearty a welcome as one could wish for... The Coletti are the only Abruzzesi I met who make any approach to a breakfast (and, after my stay with them, they always called it 'colazione Inglese'), sitting round a table to a repast of dry toast and café au lait.

> *October 17th.* The weather had become cold and gloomy at best, and although I should have liked to have made drawings throughout the Cicolano, and in the neighbourhood of Carsoli, yet the season was becoming too far advanced, and, to tell the truth, I was rather tired of wandering alone; so I took leave of my kind friends the Coletti, with much regret, and set out towards Rome...

> The romance of three months' wandering was finished. To the classic or antiquarian the ground I had gone over is rich in interest. To the landscape painter certain portions possess great beauty; but the greater part of the scenery is on too large a scale, and of too barren a character, to be available for the pencil, while much can boast of only cheerfulness of cultivation as a compensation for downright ugliness. But apart from the agreeable variety of impressions so many new scenes had left on my mind, the number of really hospitable and kind people with whom I had become acquainted will ever be remembered by me with great pleasure; and should I never revisit this part of Italy, I shall not cease to cherish the memories of my stay in the three provinces of Abruzzo.[1]

Chapter Six
Rome (1844–6)

On 26 September 1844 Lear set out again for the Abruzzi, to cover what little he had missed the previous year that seemed worth including in his projected *Illustrated Excursions in Italy*. He recorded little of note this time, except the following:

> At Città Ducale a three-parts drunken carabinière prevented my entering, insisting on knowing my name, which I not only told him, but politely showed him my passport, which was one from the Foreign Office in 1837, with 'Viscount Palmerston' printed thereon in large letters, 'Lear' being small, and written.

> 'That's not true,' said the man of war, who seemed happy to be able to cavil, 'You're not Lear! You're Palmerston!'

> 'No I am not,' said I, 'my name's Lear.'

> But the irascible official was not to be so easily checked, though, knowing the power of these worthies, I took care to mollify his anger as much as might be.

> 'What's written is written. Look, Palmerston is written here, and so you are Palmerstoni!'

[His excitement stemmed from the support that the British Foreign Secretary had expressed for the revolutionary movement in Italy, which was eventually to lead to the Risorgimento.]

> You great fool! I thought; but I made two bows, and said placidly, 'Take me to the Sott' Intendente, my dear sir, as he knows me very well.'

'This is even worse,' said the angry man, 'having you incon-venience His Excellency!. Come, come with me at once: I'm clapping you in jail.'

Some have greatness thrust upon them. In spite of all expos-tulations, Viscount Palmerston it was settled I should be. There was nothing to be done, so I was trotted ignomin-iously all down the High Street, the carabinière shouting out to everybody at door and window, 'I've nabbed Palmerstoni!'

Luckily, Don Francesco Console was taking a walk and met us, whereon followed a scene of apologies to me and snub-bing for the military, who retreated discomfited.

So I reached Rieti by dark, instead of going to prison.[1]

Some weeks earlier Lear had learned of the death of his mother. It was in the light of this news that he had written to his sister on 27 August to suggest that,

> all things considered, the present winter will be as good as any for you to pass in Rome... first, although no war will probably break out <u>as yet</u>, two or more years will possibly upset everything; and secondly, as I shall return to England in April, you could accompany me. As far as Paris and Lyons (I hear there is a railroad to Lyons – a great comfort) and Marseilles, you would be well enough as to travelling, having been used so to do alone. At Marseilles you must take your place (<u>first cabin or class</u>) in a steamer to Cività Vecchia... and then I would meet you and bring you on to Rome...
>
> I hope you will dress <u>very nicely</u> (although we shall both be in deep mourning), and I advise you to get <u>good walking boots and shoes</u>, etc., etc. at Paris; lay in a good stock, for shoes here are <u>good for nothing</u> – but you must scrape the souls or wear them as the Douane here seizes shoes... do not forget to bring good <u>warm clothing</u>, and if you want any handsome, plain shawl or dress in Paris (not odd-looking, my dear old sister!) buy it, and keep it as a present from me. You know that I am very much known here, and live in the 'highest respectability' – and so you <u>must not</u> be too dowdy.

Do not forget a thick veil – for cold winds. We shall dine at home, etc., and I shall be as much with you as I can, considering my great occupation and the quantity of people who come to me…[2]

Once again, however, it was not to be, for Ann replied that she did not yet feel up to making such a journey on her own. (One may perhaps conjecture that she had found his concern for her appearance, about which he had so often twitted her in the past, even more intimidating.) He wrote back:

Your letter of the 12th Sept. has just come, and has caused me great disappointment, though I am compelled to own all your say is quite right, and on second thoughts I allowed myself to write and expect too heartily – but you know it is my way. <u>I shall now bring you back</u> when I return from England [as he anticipated he would the following year].

On the whole I am apt to think – nay, I am sure – you have decided quite rightly, however, for the long night journey might have knocked you up, and then the sea would have upset you. I am very sorry, though – for I have been looking forward to your coming and speculating much on our lives…

I am over head and ears in painting, having begun almost all my last year's orders – against coming to England. My large six-foot painting progresses slowly. Lord Ward passed through the other day, and gave me some fresh commissions… Depend upon it, you shall be very comfortable whenever you come.[3]

His earlier claim to be living in the 'highest respectability' was thus no mere boast. Lady Susan Percy continued to be a regular port of call, as demonstrated by the following letter, which begins 'My dear Lady Susan', an unusually intimate form of address for the time:

I was so glad you took my note as it was meant – I could not have come this evening, because I dine late at Capt. Harper's & am engaged afterwards. But I will call or write early tomorrow to ask you to fix some other evening.

Meanwhile I leave the 3 drawings inside this for your amusement. They are highly affecting. Pray read the verses first. I

Present tense. Ind. mood.
So sono — 'High 'Ham.

have been extremely wretched lately having built a cupboard (trianglewise) for the better reception & concealment of a ham which I attack clandestinely at midday – but the horrid thing will not fit it, so the knuckle obtrudes itself on the public gaze most painfully. Your knife & fork are in constant use, for it is an immense joint.

Believe me, ever your Ladyship's sincerely, Edward Lear.[4]

This 'kind friend, the first that I ever had in Rome', was sadly to die in two years' time, but Lear now made another aristocratic connection that lasted him the rest of his life. Aged 22, Chichester Fortescue was a distant cousin of Lord Clermont, from whom he and his elder brother had inherited a considerable estate in Ireland, but not the title. In 1843 he had won a Studentship to Christ Church, Oxford, where he took a First in Classics and won the Chancellor's English Essay Prize. He was also invited to stand for All Souls, an offer he refused because it entailed surrendering his Studentship. His brother was much irked by the loss of the title, but considered that his health was not up to the career in politics required to reclaim it; the duty thus devolved on the somewhat reluctant Chichester, who was now using what time was left to him before the next election (in 1847) to catch up on the Grand Tour.

Setting out from England on 1 February 1845 with his friend Cornwall Simeon, he reached Rome in mid-March and was soon doing the rounds of the studios of the English colony. His diary mentions a dinner with Lady Susan Percy and the Miss Knights, and it was doubtless on their recommendation that on 14 April he called at Lear's, 'where we stayed some time looking over drawings – I like what I have seen of him very much'.

They met again at the English church the following Sunday and afterwards took a walk together 'until near dinner time'. When, four days later, Simeon arranged an outing to Tivoli with some other acquaintances, Fortescue preferred to go sketching with Lear in the opposite direction. He confided afterwards: 'I like very much what I have seen of Lear; he is a good, clever, agreeable man – very friendly & <u>getonable</u> with.' Indeed, it seems that Fortescue was the more forward of the two in cementing the friendship, rather than vice versa, as has sometimes been uncharitably alleged. On the very next day he recorded that 'Simeon and I started for Veii in a fiacre and overtook Lear at the Torre Comacchia, a little this side of La Storta. We drove on [together] to near Isola Farnese,' where they had a minor adventure. Caught in a sudden thunderstorm,

> Lear & I ran on to the osteria at Isola, Simeon stayed behind under a rock. After eating our dinner and waiting some time, we grew uneasy about Simeon and set out in the rain to look for him. We found the little 'Fosso' which we had stepped across an hour before so swollen that we did not like to cross it, & Simeon, who had been delayed by the same cause, was obliged to wade... Lear and I had intended to walk home by the valley of the Cremera, but were deterred by the swollen floods.

For the next three weeks they were almost daily companions. On 1 May the three of them and a Mr Chester took a carriage to Palestrina, where they stayed overnight. The following day Lear walked on ahead with Fortescue to St Vetturino in order to draw a view that the latter considered to be

> perhaps the most beautiful piece of landscape we saw in the two days... After this we soon got into the olive groves below Tivoli, and waited at the foot of the hill while Lear rode up and fetched the carriage. We were to have gone to the Vatican by torchlight with Twopenny's party, but were late. These were two very enjoyable days – Lear a delightful com-

panion, full of <u>nonsense</u>, puns, riddles, everything in the shape of fun, and <u>brimming</u> with intense appreciation of nature, as well as history. I don't know when I have met anyone to whom I took so great a liking.

When a similar expedition to Soracte was planned, the discovery that Lear would be unable to join them reduced Fortescue to 'a rather disgusted and gloomy state of mind,' as did Lear's departure for England as planned a week later:

> I am very sorry he is gone. We seemed to suit each other capitally, and became friends in no time. Among other qualifications, he is one of those men of real feeling it is so delightful to meet in this cold-hearted world. Simeon and myself both miss him very much.[5]

Lear gave some parting advice on the other sights worth seeing that he had not had time to show them, and the notes that they subsequently exchanged on these initiated a regular correspondence which they were to maintain for the next 40 years. It would be posthumously published, in two substantial volumes, by Fortescue's niece, Lady Constance Strachey.

The earliest of Lear's letters to Fortescue that survives was written on 11 October from Knowsley (where he had gone to prepare the publication not only of *Illustrated Excursions in Italy*, but also of *Gleanings from the Menagerie and Aviary at Knowsley Hall*, a collection of 17 lithographs on a scale similar to that of the earlier *Parrots*).

> I wish to know how you liked Solmona & Aquila & Antrodoco. I do hope to see you at Oxford [where Fortescue was now returning for his final year], as I shall visit that city in November… I am also very busy about the 'Libro Anonimo' [*Illustrated Excursions*]. Its first volume is to be Abruzzi & Amalfi, 50 or 60 lith.[ographic] drawings & as many woodcuts & letter press: it gives me great labour & I advance very slowly because there is so much friend-seeing. I am going up to town in about 10 days or a fortnight, & my address then is 27 Duke St., St. James'.

> Is Lady Ormonde well? I wish you wd. give my respects if you see her ladyship, & say that I am so busy about this work

I have not yet commenced her picture. If my first volume succeeds, I shall put forth another wherein <u>our</u> tours will be…[6]

Dedicated, naturally enough, to Lord Derby, the book was published by Thomas McLean in April 1846. Its appearance was to elevate Lear to the very peak of the 'highest respectability' – no less than to the sovereign herself. As we have seen, Victoria had already been among the subscribers to *Views in Rome and its Environs,* and this latest production must have still more impressed her, for she summoned its author to Osborne House, her summer residence on the Isle of Wight, to give her a course of 12 lessons in watercolouring. An entry in her diary for 15 July reads: 'Had a drawing lesson from Mr Lear, who sketched before me and teaches remarkably well.'[7] At the end of the month the Queen returned to London, and the course was completed at Buckingham Palace and Windsor Castle. Never one to be overawed, whatever the company he found himself in, Lear himself was fond of relating the following anecdote, as recorded by Lady Strachey:

> Lear had a habit of standing on the hearthrug. When at Windsor he was in the room with the Queen, and as was his wont, he had somehow managed to migrate to his favourite place. He observed that whenever he took up this position, the Lord-in-Waiting or Private Secretary who was in attendance kept luring him away, either under pretext of looking at a picture or some object of interest. After each interlude he made again for the hearthrug, and the same thing was repeated. It was only afterwards that he discovered that to stand where he had done was not etiquette.[8]

In the same vein, he confided to Fortescue that 'I don't know if it is proper to call a sovereign a duck, but I cannot help thinking H.M. a dear and absolute duck.'[9]

However, it was another of Lear's publications that year that has done the most to preserve his name for posterity. *A Book of Nonsense* had already appeared in February, again under McLean's imprint, either as a result of the encouragement of the Stanley grandchildren on his return to Knowsley or as a means of defraying the initial costs of his other books. It comprised 72 limericks culled from a larger collection that he had set down in an album at Knowsley 10 years earlier, the first of which read as follows:

> There was an Old Derry down Derry,
> Who loved to see little folks merry;
> So he made them a book,
> And with laughter they shook,
> At the fun of that Derry down Derry.

Although published anonymously, the book's authorship was hardly intended to be a secret, for the second volume of *Illustrated Excursions in Italy*, published in July, contains an advertisement for it. The hold that it established over the current generation of children and their successors was such that less than 20 years after the end of Lear's career as an artist Lady Strachey wrote that 'the English and American public of the present day only know Edward Lear through his "Books of Nonsense"'.[10]

With all three publications successfully launched, he hastened to escape another winter in England, crossing the Channel on 7 December. He was not in time, however, to anticipate its onset in Italy. He wrote to Ann from Genoa on the 22nd:

> This is the 3rd. letter I have begun to you while on this journey, which just at present does not seem particularly likely to come to a conclusion. For we started on Saturday the 19th by that vile Neapolitan boat the 'Maria Christina' – and as yet we are no farther than 24 hours voyage from Marseilles. We got here on Sunday evening, after a beautiful night, and day's sail – but, instead of setting off again last night, we were told that 'something in the vessel wanted mending,' a common excuse which these odious people [employ] when they find that they can gain passengers by delay. And today the weather is really bad, so that we cannot start even if we would. Consequently we are all very cross and annoyed, and for aught I see, may stay here a fortnight, for the expense of travelling across by Florence is too great to think of.

It was in Florence, nonetheless, that he added the next instalment, on Christmas Day:

Worse and worse! I go crawling on like an old snail and can hardly help laughing at the absurd time this journey takes, although the expense is no laughing matter at all. On Friday the 22nd (when I wrote the paragraph above) the weather grew better towards the evening, so we sailed from Genoa. But the night was very tempestuous, and we were horribly tossed to and fro – not that I knew very much about it, for I was in bed, and never got up at all. The morning – about 8 – saw us safely however in the harbour of Leghorn, but at 12 o'clock a frightful south wind rose, so that it was impossible to leave the port; and we even landed with difficulty, on account of the heavy surf. Leghorn is a nasty place, with bad inns, and no earthly amusement – and now it was more disagreeable than ever, from the uncertainty of getting away, and the bad weather. I never saw anything like the high wind of the evening: it took people up like feathers and blew them away – puff! I saw 3 women whirled along and over and over like a pack of cards. Much damage was done in the harbour, and the waves were so high we could not get to the steamer even to take away our night things, so everybody managed as best they could.

Five more days passed before he was able to complete the story of this odyssey:

The morning of the 23rd was nearly as windy at Leghorn as it had been the previous evening, and I began to get very impatient – for the south wind might last a week. So I decided at last to go to Rome by land, and so, getting my things on shore, and sacrificing my 30 francs paid to C. Vecchia, I left Leghorn by the Diligence [public coach] to Florence at 1 p.m. A very nice railroad takes you as far as Ponte Dera, and so I got to Florence by midnight, and was housed in Schneiduff's comfortable hotel, where a supper of soup and turkey much revived me. Xmas Day was very fine, and I went to our church, walking afterwards in the Boboli Gardens, which are wonderfully beautiful...

On the evening of Saturday the 26th I set off with the courier to Perugia – my only plan, for there were no places for many days in the Siena couriers. We had pouring rain all night, but it was fine when we reached Perugia next day (Sunday) at 3. Here I got some food and set off by Diligence to Foligno, which I reached at 9 – just as the Diligence to Rome was setting off, and in which I immediately took a place, and started off directly – for fear of snow or worse weather coming. As it was, we had a fearful night: the snow fell fast as we reached the Apennines, and the passage of Monte Somma was a difficult matter, even with 14 horses and 8 oxen. By 10 on Monday the 28th we reached Terni, and the weather was then lovely. We passed Narni, Otricoli and C. Castellana, and reached Rome – to my great joy – about 5 a.m. of Dec. 29th…

The winter has been hitherto <u>most dreadful</u> in Rome, and the inundation of the Tiber very sad; at present it is very fine but cold. Everybody exclaims at my well-looks and says that I have come back half as big again as I went. My old landlady is quite delighted with her presents, and thanks you for them very much. I have hardly time to write, so many people are calling to congratulate me on my return.[11]

In his next letters, however, he was rather less joyful about his adopted home:

I must confess that Rome looks filthier and duller than ever after England, and if I were to tell the truth, I should very willingly be transported back to England forthwith…[12] I am sorry to tell you my old landlady is getting very deaf, and (impolitely speaking) rather stupid – poor thing; in a word, old age is coming upon her, and she is unable to be quite as clean or as attentive as of old. I shall endeavour, however, to remain in her lodgings while I stay in Rome.[13]

He was also missing his old cat. As he explained to Ann in a later letter:

that educated tabby was a victim to vanity before I left Rome in 1845… a friend of mine took her up in his arms and showed her herself in the mirror, upon which she whizzed out of the door & into the street & was never more heard of… Old Signora Giovanina has got one, but it is such a fright, though very amiable; it is of a pale carrot colour, with a head like a frog – such a beast.[14]

A month later the weather was still no better:

I never knew such a wretched season here. It is impossible to go out to walk – and bad enough to go out even to dinner or for the evening. If it continues to rain so, I really fear there will be a second inundation before long. Today [February 6th] is the first of the Carnival, but of course there is nothing going on – it is all mud and water.

His consolation was the fresh demand for his work that his successes in England – in particular, the royal commission – had engendered, although he cautioned his sister against boasting about it, for fear that 'such success may give rise to complaints from those who are more skilful & yet have little to do'. He also warned her against exaggerated hopes of financial return:

For all this, I get but little, for these pictures are of small price. At present, owing to my expensive journey out and clothing, and carriage of packages hither, I am very poor. I reckon that I may get £100, or perhaps £120 this year, & that is what I certainly cannot save much out of. You must remember that I work only up to May – & that the summer does not count. Still, that is far cheaper than what I could live for in London, where £300 does not seem an overplus. We must therefore be grateful on account of my publications, whatever trouble they gave me (& what is done without trouble?), for through them I laid by a whole £100. And when we consider that eyesight is not of long duration, laying by now is really a necessary duty. This year, however, I shall not be able so to do, as you perceive. Meanwhile I have given 10 dollars to the Irish [Potato Famine victims] & 3 to the church here, & I hope as I live – if I live – to be able to spare more in proportion every year.

In this he would be as good as his word, throughout his life erring, if anything, on the side of over-generosity towards his many and even more penurious relatives, not least the two undeserving brothers who had emigrated to Texas. Ann too was much given to good works and in his next letter Lear enquired about some of those for whom she collected the necessities of life: 'How is the blind man? & the blanketty coally people?'

He also reported that the 'frog-like' cat had vanished in its turn: 'I have therefore taken a tabby kitten, which is not ugly, but very shy. However, as I mean to educate her carefully, she will, I dare say, become rational bye & bye. She eats macaroni already – but not if it be more than an inch long. Her name is Birecchino.' In a postscript written three days later he added that she ' behaves herself very well. I have given her a wooden easel peg to play with, which amuses her innocent mind, but she has contracted a naughty habit of playing with the window curtains, which I do not at all approve, as she tears them all to pieces.'[15]

The weather was again the dominant theme of his next letter:

It has been gradually improving, though it is still very unsettled. Excuse me for saying that you have been very lavish of late in your double letters. Triffles – Opperations – Widdows; thank you very kindly, but I am well satisfied with one of those consonants at a time!

Sunday, 28th Feb. [1847] You need not boast of your snow indeed! It has snowed here since last evening, & is actually nearly a foot deep already, though it is now falling fast. It is really too odious, this winter. The weather soon had one of its usual relapses, & yesterday was, though bitterly cold, the only fine day for some time past. Luckily, I walked out some 5 miles on the Campagna, or I should lose the use of my legs. You have no idea how filthy the streets are today; it is like a river of mud & ice…

In another postscript two days later he wrote that 'the snow is still on the roofs. Such a winter surely never was seen here!!'

His plans for the future months were also beginning to take more concrete shape:

I much wish to pass the spring & summer in Sicily if I can… It would be a thousand pities being once here to neglect professional advantages which may be most useful if ever I live in England in after days…[16]

By the end of March he was at last able to report that the weather had taken a turn for the better, but his disillusionment with Rome continued nonetheless:

> Please God I will return & live some time in England. I hope to be more comfortable in London – when I trust you will live with me. We shall be very cosy & antique. I shall be 40 or 41 – you 60 or 61 [in five or six years' time]. We must have an old cat, & some china; & so we shall go on smoothly.

Yet, as he admitted in the next sentence, such a pipedream was 'all nonsense'. He added that he was thinking of touring Calabria as well as Sicily, with the idea of producing another illustrated travelogue, for 'I have just heard that Fortescue – with whom I was often in excursions in 1845 – is coming, & if he will go with me into Calabria I shall go certainly.'[17]

Lear's next letter, of 11 April, contained 'so melancholy a piece of news' that his impatience to head south could only have quickened still further:

> Lady Susan is dead. She was so good & amiable a creature that those even who knew her but slightly regret her death, but to me, & the few who saw her constantly year after year, her loss is a most serious one. On Tuesday evening she called here to ask me if I would go into the country on Thursday or Friday; I was not at home, which I now greatly regret. On the Wed. morning I wrote to say I was engaged on Friday, but would go either on Thursday or Saturday – but before I could send my note, a friend came in & told me of her death within [the last] two hours. She rose, as well as usual; dressed, & dismissed her maid, telling her to call her when breakfast was ready. She was then feeding her canary birds. A few minutes after, another servant heard the cage fall & the birds all scream, & going toward the room to see what occasioned this, poor dear Lady Susan was found perfectly dead... A kinder, gentler, & more excellent creature, & one more full of taste & talent, never lived.[18]

It was not this, however, but a much larger event that, 11 months later, finally prompted him to seek a new home.

Chapter Seven
Sicily (June–July 1847)

On 29 April 1847 Lear informed his sister that

> I set off for Naples tomorrow, but I do not know if I cross to
> Messina or Palermo, or if I go first to Cosenza... I am sup-
> plied to immense overflowing with letters of all kinds – to
> half the grandees & merchants & bankers of Sicily & Naples
> & what not; so I shall not be much alone... I believe an artist
> friend will come over & join me in Sicily – but there are
> <u>numbers</u> of English there known to me.[1]

Palermo it would be, he reported from Naples a week later,
although the weather had yet to show much improvement:

> It rains here a good deal, & I cannot say is very spring-like...
> Vesuvius is very much changed in form since I was here – a
> new cone is forming, & by no means improves its appear-
> ance. Whether from being stronger & less nervous & irrita-
> ble than formerly I do not know, but I do not suffer so much
> as I used to from the noise of this place, which is neverthe-
> less abominable... the hollow space – being the walls as it
> were of a deep crater, at the bottom (marked ....) of
> which was a little cone rising round the abyss – is all filled
> up, & not only filled, but the cone is rising above it.
> Formerly it was like A – now like B.

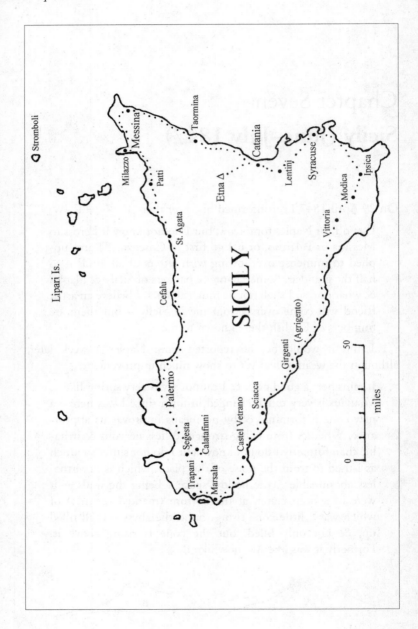

Stromboli

Lipari Is.

Milazzo
Messina
Patti
Taormina
Catania
Etna △
Lentini
Syracuse
Ipsica
Modica
Vittoria
St. Agata
Cefalu

SICILY

Girgenti
(Agrigento)
Sciacca
Palermo
Segesta
Calatafimni
Castel Vetrano
Trapani
Marsala

0   50
miles

5th May. I shall really try to get away tomorrow if possible – if only to escape the <u>cold</u>; would you believe it – I go out in a thick P. jacket, & sleep with my thick plaid over the blankets! One consolation is that I have not seen a single flea yet in Naples.

Another postscript appended two days later finally announced his arrival on the island:

I managed with great running about to get all I wanted, & to obtain numerous letters by 12 on Thursday [the 6th] – at which time, having had my passport done, I went on board the Palermo steamer, & sailing at 2.30 arrived here by 11 a.m. this morning. It was what was called a beautiful passage, but as usual I was ill all night; however, that soon goes when one is on shore, though I always feel dizzy for a day or two… I am in hopes that Mr. Proby, a friend of my friend Mr. Batterby, will go this first tour with me.

In a final postscript he added: '10th. Mr. Proby & I set off tomorrow the 11th.'[2] This was actually the Hon. John Proby, he was the eldest son of the future Earl of Carysfort, although the fact was divulged to Lear only after they had completed their circuit of the island. He was now 24, having come down from Oxford three years earlier after failing to gain an expected First in mathematics. A second disappointment had followed when his father had refused to back his candidature for the family's parliamentary seat in Ireland; he had then taken himself off to Rome to study as an artist. Their mutual friend Batterby, a fellow undergraduate at Balliol College, had written of him on a climbing expedition in the Lake District that 'Proby was the youngest of the party, the swiftest of foot and the most capable of enduring fatigue,'[3] and he thus seemed an eminently suitable companion on the arduous going that lay ahead. Unfortunately, however, he had fallen victim to 'Roman fever' (doubtless malaria) shortly after his arrival the previous autumn and he was never fully to recover from its effects, although Lear's first report of him was that he made 'an excellent fellow traveller'. (The cartoons that illustrate this chapter lay concealed in a pocket of Proby's sketchbook until they were discovered by his great-nephew in 1933, while the text is drawn almost exclusively from Lear's letters to Ann; he did not begin the projected journal until entering Calabria in late July.)

Lear informed his sister in the same letter of 23 May that:

> On the 11th we set off in a carriage, & got to Calatafinni by sunset – 42 miles. The weather was exceedingly hot, indeed much more so than it has been since, & the first day of the disagreeables of Sicily seemed rather unbearable. I do not suppose it is possible to give any idea of the filth & wretchedness of these people. However, as I wished to make drawings of the temple of Segesta, there was no help for it.
>
> Calatafinni is a large town, but we could get nothing eatable but broad beans, which we boiled and ate for 6 days. The bread was full of aniseed – the wine too nasty; the bare walls of our dirty room, with its uneven floor on which no chair could stand, were specimens of Sicilian comfort. Yet as we were out all day, we did not much care about it.
>
> I thought the temple of Segesta more magnificent than when I saw it in 1842; it stands completely alone – on the brink of a tremendous precipice, &, except the remains of an amphitheatre, is the only record of a once great city. The vegetation near is of the most beautiful character. The ground of the hillside is literally & actually a great flower bed & gives you the idea of a Turkey carpet; sweet peas, myrtle, convolvulus, pinks, cistus, & all our garden flowers grow wild as weeds, & the Indian fig, the aloe & acanthus make such hedgerows as cannot be looked at without wonder.

Trapani
May .6. 847

&l are pursued thro' the streets by an innumerable multitude of rabid Mendicants.

This splendid isolation still holds today, diminished only by the faint hum of the traffic on the distant autostrada.

> We passed 3 days most pleasantly at Calatafinni, & left it on Saturday the 15th on mules for Trapani, a city I had never seen; we did not find much to delight us there, nor, excepting the immense number of beggars does it contain anything striking.
>
> However, we went up Mt. Eryx, where Aeneas's father was buried, & did all that was proper. The Sunday 16th we passed at Trapani – we mean to rest always on the Sunday & we read the church prayers & a sermon in the morning; my companion is a very good young man, & I am wonderfully fortunate in having such a one, as he draws constantly, & is of a perfectly good temper.
>
> On the 17th we went on to Marsala, where you know all the wine of that name is made. I had letters [of introduction] to one of the first English factories, & was even lodged & fared most sumptuously, indeed rather injudiciously.[4]

He was less euphoric in a later letter to Fortescue, describing an incident omitted from the letter to his sister: 'The Marsala trip does not pay – & the only break to the utter monotony of life & scenery occurred by a little dog biting the calf of my leg very unpleasantly as I walked unsuspectingly in a vineyard.'[5]

The letter to Ann continued:

> On Wed. the 19th we came on mules to Mazzara Campobello (where there are vast quarries from which the great city of Selinuntium was built) & Castel Vetrano, a most beastly place, from which on the 20th we were but too happy to be off & get to Sciacca – 26 miles – where we passed the afternoon & night.
>
> A long mule day of 44 miles brought us to Girgenti [Agrigento] on the evening of the 21st, & here we are now & have been ever since, working very hard & as comfortable as possible. We have a suite of 3 little rooms, but are very seldom in them, for we are down at the temples before the sun rises & have our dinner sent down to us – sleeping in a hut there afterwards, & returning to our inn by moonrise. Our

health is perfectly good, & we enjoy ourselves immensely. Nothing on earth can be so beautiful as Girgenti with its 6 temples – I speak of the old town – & the flowers & birds are beyond imagination lovely. I must, however, need say that the gnats, fleas, flies, wasps, etc., etc. require much philosophy to bear.

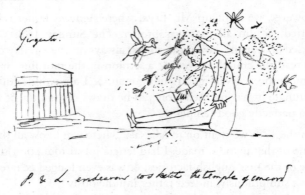

P. & L. endeavour to sketch the temple of concord

It is, however, a great comfort to be able to live so much away from this dirty city. We dine at 12, & our supper consists of 3 ices. Our rooms cost a dollar a day – ditto our dinner; our man & his son to carry our things up & down, prepare dinner, etc. – half a dollar; our breakfast 2 Carlino & our supper 4 – just 3 dollars divided between us.

On Sundays we dress in our 'best clothes', & wash ourselves – which we can't do thoroughly on the weekdays. The coolest day has been like those we had at Eastbourne last year, when you used to sit & fan yourself so; but the moonlight is pleasant enough.

On Friday June 4th we shall leave Girgenti with great regret, & shall proceed to Siracusa – by Modica & Noto (look at your map) – a 4 or 5 days' journey; thence by Sentini to Catania, returning to Palermo about the end of June... I wonder where you will pass the summer – & what sort of summer you will have. They say it will be fine here till Oct. As yet there is no fruit – & in spite of the wonderful fertility & abundance of this island the indolent people make nothing of it, for it is all sent away. It is the greatest mystery to go day after day through vallies of corn, oranges, lemons, olives, pomegranates, grapes – in fact, all sorts of things – & yet even at the large towns you are too fortunate if you can get one or two dirty little rolls & some aniseed! The aloes are beginning to bloom & look very astonishing on all sides.

There is an English consul here, with a very amiable family; but they (the young people) have never been in England, so it is difficult to talk on many subjects. All ladies & rich people here travel in Lettigas – I think an hour of it would kill you, for the chair is slung between two mules & often is quite over a precipice as they walk down or up the mountain paths. The mules who bear them carry large bells heard a long way off to prevent accidents, but I never heard of any occurring. We, however, prefer riding to these hot, close conveyances. When we move from place to place we take food with us, for 'an inn' means merely a room to cook & sleep in this very nasty country.[6]

For once they were able to keep to their timetable, as Lear next reported to Ann on 17 June:

We left Girgenti on the 4th of this month, & we were sorry to do so, having enjoyed our fortnight there very much; & we shall often think of it with pleasure. Our last evening, when we had just got a provision of dollars for the journey, was a disagreeable one, as a waiter at the inn broke open one of our bags, & purloined two piastres. Unluckily [for him] he could not shut the bag again, so we were quite sure of him & had him sent to prison.

It was the felon's bad luck too that the Mafia was not yet in place to secure his release.

The first two days on the road were unremarkable except for some hedges of cactus, which

were really quite wonderful – being large trees from 20 to 30 feet high. It is necessary to be very careful in passing them, as the falling of the thorns, which are all over the leaves, is dangerous.

At Vittoria we found so filthy an osteria or locanda that at any price we thought it better to go on to Ragusa – 12 miles further – on the way to Modica, which was our destination – in order to see a remarkable valley of ancient dwellings called Ipsica. On our way over the mountains from Vittoria – a terribly bad & steep road – a violent storm overtook us, & though the lightning [at] first showed us the way, it was soon as black as night. The only way is to sit quite still on the mule – which goes on as well by night as by day – so that no accidents occurred but our getting to Ragusa wet through & sorry to find none but a bad inn, in which we stayed as short a time as possible.

After a rather better night's sleep at Modica,

we set off very early for Ipsica, an excursion of 7 or 8 miles to a most curious rocky valley, cut into habitations or caves many thousand years ago. We passed the whole of the day there making drawings, & lunched in one of the caves – inhabited by some poor people who gave us some excellent honey.[7]

In his letter to Fortescue Lear allowed himself a somewhat freer rein (and a characteristic play on words) in describing these cave-dwellers or troglodytes:

At the caves of Ipsica we became acquainted with a family of original Froglodytes: they are very good creatures, mostly sitting on their hams, & feeding on lettuces & honey. I proposed

Ipsica. June 3. 1847

? ad. visit the one remaining family of Froglodytes now existing, and are introduced by the Paternal Frog to his family.

bringing away an infant Frog, but Proby objected.[8]

He doubtless objected too to any suggestion of a cave for the night and they returned to Modica, 'a picturesque town', which occupied them in sketching for another day.

On 8 June, as he told Ann, they 'set off in a carriage by Noto to Syracuse':

> At Noto, the chief town of the province, we found barely anything to eat – so extraordinary is the system of things regarding inns in this country; you pass through every sort of luxuriant vegetation for days & days, & yet you can absolutely get <u>nothing</u> – <u>nothing</u> in any of the towns you come to. A stale lettuce, bad bread, & doubtful eggs is all you are sure of to prevent starvation.

Syracuse, by contrast, offered an 'excellent hotel', and they passed a 'very happy' week there (although Lear later referred to his disappointment at Fortescue's failure to make his expected appearance).

> There is nothing in the world like a Syracuse garden. A hasty glance over the flat country would lead you to suppose it contained nothing, but the vast quarries whence this enormous city was dug are now used as gardens, & being sheltered are really quite like Paradise. Every kind of tree & flower grows luxuriantly in them, & they are as full as possible of nightingales. Every day we had our dinner brought to one [of] these; that containing the Ear of Dionysius is as beautiful as [it is] curious.

The quarries of Syracuse, first made famous by Thucydides in his harrowing description of the incarceration in them of the Athenian prisoners from the ill-starred Sicilian Expedition of 415 BC, were chosen by Lear as the subject of one of his largest and best-known oils. Recently cleaned and restored, it stole the show at the 2004 exhibition of Pre-Raphaelite art at Tate Britain.

> From Syracuse on the 14th we came, by the loveliest scenery imaginable, to Sortino, & by evening to Lentini – whence Mt. Etna appears very gigantic. On the 15th we rode over the hot bare plain of Catania, & were in this very decent inn by noon. Our time here has passed in sketching a little on the

lava which you know destroyed the Catania of 1666, & whence there are fine views of the city & Mt. Etna. On Saturday, resolving to go up to the top of the mountain, we set off early & went first to the Val di Bove, a most awful chasm of valley below the crater – exceeding in grandeur & terror anything of the kind I ever saw; thence we returned to Nicolosi, & passed our Sunday there – going up in the evening through what is called the woody region of Etna to a little hut in the forest, where, well wrapped up in additional clothes, we supped & slept comfortably enough.

At midnight we started on mules & with a light, & after two hours climbing reached the snow, beyond which it is necessary to go on foot. Here the trouble begins: fancy two hours of climbing up & slipping down, over the steepest hill of frozen snow. I never was so disgusted. Sometimes I rolled back as far as 20 minutes had taken me up. It was impossible to keep one's footing, even with a spiked stick. By the aid of the guide, however, we reached the top of this horrible height, & rested in another hut called Casa Inglese. Then we crossed a plain of snow which surrounds the cone & began to climb that, an operation as difficult as the last, as it is nearly perpendicular & made up of fine ash & sulphur, into which you plunge up to your knees at each step.

This, however, is not the obstacle that prevents your progress, but rather the extreme rarity of the air which takes different effects on different persons. Some it stupifies, others it causes to vomit. Had it made me very ill, I should have turned back, but it only caused me to feel as if I were drowning, & made me lose my breath almost & my voice altogether. A sort of convulsive catching [of the breath] was very disagreeable, & at times was so violent that for a moment or two I lost the use of my limbs & fell down. Being on the ground, however, restored one's breathing, & so we got on by very slow degrees – climbing & falling alternately. The fatigue is certainly immense, but one is amply repaid by the extraordinary scene above – where you look on the whole island of Sicily just like a great pink map in the sky, with the sea around it so blue & the dark purple triangular shade of the mountains over that part furthest from the sun, which rose just before we got to the mouth of the crater.

Given the congenital weakness of Lear's lungs, this feat might be thought worthy of an honourable mention in any anthology of mountaineering.

We did not remain long there, as you may suppose on my telling you that the sulphur we sat on burned our clothes very much, & was horribly hot – yet one was too glad to bury one's hands in it, one's body & head being wrapped up in cloaks & plaids through all which one shivered in the icy wind, which blew like knives from the north (Etna, you know, is nearly as high as Mt. Blanc). We came down ridiculously fast: you stick your heels in the ashy cone, slide down almost without stopping to the bottom, & with a spiked stick you shoot down the ice hill we had taken so long to surmount in 10 minutes. We reposed & fed at Nicolosi, having taken a stock of bottled porter, etc. with us, & by evening were once more at Catania.

Today, I feel greatly better for my excursion, & tomorrow we start for Taormina – & so by Messina & the north coast to Palermo, where I hope to be very early in July. My companion is a most excellent creature, & I hope he will not leave me at Palermo. If he does, I shall remain some longer perhaps in Sicily…[9]

They completed the circuit more or less to schedule, arriving back at Palermo on 10 July, from where Lear wrote the following day describing this final stage to his sister:

On the 23rd we went in a carriage along the coast to Giardini & Taormina, & there finding a very homely but comfortable little private lodging, we stayed till the 29th, when we came down again to Giardini. Taormina is perhaps one of the most wonderful places in the world. It takes about two hours to get up to it, by a zigzag road without any parapet – sometimes hanging sheer over the sea. The views on all sides are most astonishing, particularly the ruins of the theatre, which overlook Mt. Etna & are very perfect – Taurominium having been a celebrated Greek city. We enjoyed ourselves very much at Taormina indeed.

On the 30th we hired some mules & set off by the coast road, stopping at Via Paola for two or three hours at noon & reaching Messina – where there is an excellent hotel – by dusk. Messina is a most lovely place, & having been quite shaken down by the earthquake of 1780 looks all new. The view of the Straits over to the Calabrian mountains is very beautiful. We were, however, too anxious to reach Palermo before this day – the first of the immense festa of Santa Rosalia – to allow us to linger long at Messina, as we knew that it would be very difficult to get rooms if we did not arrive here early. So we set off on July 3rd to return by the north coast, & as far as possible in a carriage.

When we had passed the high hills behind Messina we soon lost sight of Calabria, & saw all the Lipari isles – ugly things – all in a row like tea-cups turned topsy-turvy. Milazzo, where there is a good castle, was the first place we visited & stopped at to dine – nor could we get further than Barcelona for our night's rest. On the 4th – Sunday – we were obliged to take on the carriage to Patti, where we rested for the rest of the day, having seen the ruins of Tyndarus by the way.

Here – at Patti – where the carriage road ceases – the miseries begin, concerning which in answer to your numerous questions I will try to write somewhat of explanation; at present I will go on with my tale. We engaged some mules & a man, whom I could not in the <u>least </u>understand, to go as far as Cefalu, but – <u>most fortunately</u> for us – one of the best guides in Sicily was returning to Palermo with 5 mules – so we forsook our first bargain & took to him, much to our future comfort. Indeed, what we could have done without him I know not.

On the 5th, then, we started; I had a nice little grey mule, the best I ever rode on; Proby, [a] stupid horse; Guiseppe Campi with a baggage beast & two more rode in front. The heat was great. You have to toil only by a narrow path up

cape after cape & round the points, then descending to the
shingly beach, & ever more seeing the point you are going to
sleep at in the distance; nay, what do I say? We saw [on the
5th] the point of Cefalu where we were to sleep on the
Wednesday night – the 7th. The bright sky & clear air makes
all this look lovely, but after 7 or 8 o'clock the heat is frightful & the journeying tedious.

At a most wretched little town, Brolo (which was pretty, however), we stopped at noon. The people of the Locanda would
absolutely do nothing whatever – but Guiseppe was an angel
of comfort, & he got us a capital dish of anchovies – fresh – &
an omelette, so – as we had brought wine from Messina – we
managed very well. A long afternoon of sea beach mule work
brought us to St. Agata, a village by the sea side – our sleeping
place. This was as hopeless a spot as I ever saw – not even a
glass of water could be had. A great fat pig, 7 cats & 4 dogs
were all in the bedroom, & to make things worse, the people
were utterly sulky. For 2 days I had a swelled face, & Proby had
a bad headache – so we were not very lively – but the imperturbable Joseph, after putting up his 5 mules & bringing us
our luggage, absolutely turned us out an astonishing dish of
capital macaroni & an omelette – besides 4 figs. However, it
seems too dreadful to see the sea & get no fish – to see corn,
wine & oil, & yet starve; had we come with the Patti peasant,
I believe we should have expired of disgust & hunger.

Another 'hard day's work' ensued, although it was softened by the
continuous scent of myrtle and oleander in full bloom.

At noon we came to St. Stefano, a place with more preten-
sions but filthier than the last – I took 28 fleas out of one
sock – within a minute or two of my arrival. Cefalu was in
sight, but [with] 24 miles of bad road it was too late to
attempt – so we resigned ourselves for the night, during
which I amused myself by flea-catching. Wed. the 7th, a
most broiling path – high up on the hills, or low down on
the sea sand – brought us to that magnificent place, Cefalu
– where I was with L. Acland in 1842! Here there is a decent

Locanda, & very nice obliging people. We had such fish dinners!! & such figs! Sea-eggs – cuttle-fish – & all kinds of
marine curiosities. Cefalu cathedral was built by King Roger
2nd on his escape from ship-wreck, & it is a Norman cathedral of great beauty; I hardly know any place so grand.

They finally reached Palermo on the 10th and found

the bay as gay as gay can be, for the French Mediterranean
fleet is here with one of the Princes – & the King & Queen
of Naples are here – & the city is crammed full full full full!!
By the ill luck of 2 Englishmen who had ordered rooms here
but had missed the steamer, we profited – & though the
price was exorbitant, yet we took them, as the annoyance of
no lodging is horrible in such a time of tumult.

The Marina of Palermo you have heard me speak of; it is at
present all over temporary Gothic edifices – all for fireworks
– & at sunset last night was a wondrous scene of gaiety; at 10
immense music began to perform, & continued to do so till
one or two in the morning. All this brilliant week is no particular delight to me who has lived so long in the south, but
my companion is naturally much interested in the sights. As
for the procession of Sta. Rosalia in her carriage, that of
course I must see, & the fireworks – but otherwise, I shall try
to be as quiet as I can, being extremely well & not wishing
to heat myself. My swelled face went off decorously, & sea-
bathing every night does me great good.

This was just as well, since there was no prospect of any steamer sailing until the festa was over. Whether Proby would accompany him to
Calabria was also left hanging in the air, as Lear was still hoping that
Fortescue would appear in time to take his place. In the meantime he
set himself to answer some of his sister's many questions:

The Sicilians do not like work; the poorer cultivate as much
& no more garden stuff as they can eat themselves, for they
live on it. If they have more land, they either sell the produce
to regular customers – the clergy, or upper people – or it is
sent away to the larger cities, where you can certainly always
have plenty. This partly explains the difficulty of getting

fresh fruit & vegetables. Everything is gathered very early & towards noon is eaten, or spoils by the heat – for these nasty people take no pains to preserve anything. Lettuces <u>might</u> be kept in water – but water is scarce, so even a salad is unobtainable if you don't seize it at sunrise.

Milk, do you want? The goats are driven in from the country at <u>sunrise</u>, are milked in the street, & off they go again; if then you do not run about with a milk jug, no hope of milk – for 2 hours turns it sour. Oil, vinegar, salt, pepper – matters collected, or grown by richer people – are either consumed in small quantities by each household or exported altogether. Fish? If much is taken at <u>sunrise</u>, the happy catchers eat it, & there is none for the passer-by at noon; if they catch less – so much the less chance for you. Eggs? You cannot make a hen lay when you please, & the morning produce of the hen roost is all gone by noon. Meat? This is rarely killed & as it were by <u>subscription</u>, everybody taking a part & cooking it directly or it would be bad very soon.

Wine? Private houses possess good wine – but the Locandari have it not. From the scarcity of passengers, & the inveterate habit of bringing one's [own] food, it is not worth their while to keep any food in the house – so that innkeeping in Sicily chiefly consists in showing the guest into a beastly room, & shrugging the shoulders at him if he asks for anything to eat. Fowls they eat themselves, but will not procure for you. The shops are tolerable in large cities, but of course bad in the towns. Catania is a magnificent place; Messina & Palermo & Syracuse the next, & these contain good hotels; all the rest are good for nothing – but Taormina & Giardini.

As for the people, all the grandees live in the great cities, or in villas on their own property. Much of the population consists of clergy & monks & nuns. A vast proportion are beggars, & more horrible objects no one could imagine. The day we stopped at Via Paola, we threw some bread out of the window to one, & directly after there were about 20, lame, blind, monsters, idiots, & all more loathsome than the most vivid idea

can suppose Lazarus to have been. At Catania, where Proby &
I went every night to make our supper or ices at the principle
shop, surrounded by the great residents either on chairs or in
carriages, there was an outer circle of beggars, who used to
rush at us on our retreat; one or two blind we gave to, but
some we were obliged to beat & kick off. Indeed, it is <u>impos-
sible</u> to give in the towns: all along the roads we did so.[10]

Lear seems here to be saying that, if Ann ever did get to Rome, she
should certainly give up any idea of going on to Sicily.

After a week of suspense, he seems to have received word that
Fortescue was expected at Naples, for in his next letter to Ann he
reported that, instead of crossing over into Calabria from Messina, as
originally planned, 'Proby & I left Palermo by a bad steamer, full –
noisy – & nasty; but we had a most beautiful passage over a sea of
glass, & arrived at Naples on the 20th.'[11] He was once more to be disappointed, however, as he later complained:

We returned to Naples – & there, as at Palermo, was [Sir
Francis] Scott &, to my disgust, no Fortescue. I fear when Scott
sent up your card, & then entered too soon himself – I fear my
visage fell very rudely. But I wish much now I had seen more
of Sir F. Scott, as he improves immensely on knowing him.[12]

Proby too seems to have borne some of his frustration. Lear told his
sister that:

I am sorry my companion, as his health improves, <u>does not</u>
in temper; he is sadly imperious & contradictory at times,
which is rather trying as his visit to Calabria is entirely
dependent on my letters of introduction. However, there is
some allowance to be made, as I find he is heir to a rank
which I had no knowledge of as being about to be his, or I
should not have travelled with him.[13]

Happily for them both, however, this brush was soon forgotten. At
the end of their time in Calabria Lear was able to report that:

Proby makes a perfectly excellent companion – & we now go
on with perfect comfort & smoothness; indeed, I now like him
so much, that I do not at all like to think of his leaving me.[14]

Chapter Eight
Southern Calabria (July-August 1847)

Lear landed again at Messina with Proby on 25 July, after another not wholly agreeable voyage, as he told Ann in his last letter before embarking on his *Journal of a Landscape Painter in Southern Calabria*:

> The sea <u>was very rough</u>, though the sky was bright blue. Almost everyone was horribly ill – even Proby, a good sailor; but, to my extreme wonder, I was not even <u>squeamish</u>!!! I ate a large dinner, & slept on deck soundly all night! Is that not curious?!'[1]

To Fortescue, however, he made lighter of it: 'I have crossed the sea from Naples to Sicily so often this year that I know nearly all porpoises by their faces, & many of the Merluzzi [mermaids].'[2]

The *Journal* opens:

> In the afternoon, having hired a boat to cross the straits, Proby and I were ready to start from Messina. Leaving a portion of our luggage there we took enough for a month or six weeks' journey through the nearest province [of the Kingdom of Naples], or Calabria Ulteriore Prima; and, well supplied with letters to those persons in its chief city who would send us on our way through the interior, we set sail for Reggio.

They formed a favourable first impression of the town, with 'its endless cactus and aloe lanes, fig gardens, and orange groves. Reggio is indeed one vast garden, and doubtless one of the loveliest spots to be seen on earth.' Nor did 'those persons' disappoint. The Direttore 'readily promised letters to Bova and other out of the ways places in the toe of Italy'; the Consigliere da Nave, 'a great ally… prepared fifteen notes

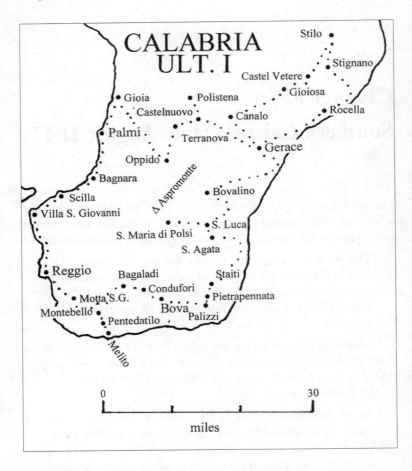

to the principal proprietors in towns we should pass through'; and the Musitano family, in addition to providing several letters, 'took no little pains to procure us such a guide and mule as we wanted – not always an easy task'. By the following afternoon, however, they

> had engaged a muleteer for an indefinite time, the expense for both guide and quadruped being six carlini daily; and if we sent him back from any point of our journey it was agreed that his charges should be defrayed until he reached Reggio.

Our man, a grave, tall fellow of more than fifty years of age, and with a good expression of countenance, was called Ciccio, and we explained to him that our plan was to do always just as we pleased – going straight ahead or stopping to sketch, without reference to any law but our own pleasure; to all of which he replied by a short sentence ending with 'Dogo; dighi, dóghi, dághi, dà' – a collection of sounds of frequent recurrence in Calabrese lingo, and the only definite portion of that speech that we could perfectly master. What the 'Dogo' was we never knew, though it was an object of our keenest search throughout the tour to ascertain if it were animal, mineral or vegetable. Afterwards, by constant habit, we arranged a sort of conversational communication with friend Ciccio, but we never got on well unless we said 'Dogo si' or 'Dogo no' several times as an ad libitum appogiatura, winding up with 'Dighi, dóghi, dághi, dà,' which seemed to set all right.

Ciccio tied four packets (one of vestments, &c., another of drawing materials for each man), plaids, umbrellas, &c., on a quiet-looking steed, touching whose qualities its owner was wholly silent, thereby giving me, who go by contraries in these lands, great hope that it might be worth a good deal, for had it been a total failure one might have looked for a long tirade of praises. And so, all being adjusted – off we set.

The road led over the torrent-bed and by the Villa Musitano, through suburban villages for two or three miles, and for a considerable distance we passed numerous odiferous silk factories and many detached cheerful-looking houses, with lofty pergolate or vine trellises spanning and shading the whole public road from side to side. Beyond, the broad dusty highway was uninteresting in its foregrounds, but the blue straits of Messina was ever on our right, with Etna beyond, while on the left a wall of hills, with Castel San Nocito and San Vito perched upon their summits, sufficed for men who were all alive for impressions of Calabrese novelty. Always in sight also was the town of Motta San Giovanni, our night's resting-place, but so high up as to promise a stout pull to reach it...

High winds prevented our making any drawing, and indeed it was nearly Ave Maria when we had risen above the weary sandy gorges immediately below the town, which stands at a great elevation and overlooks earth and sea extensively. With little difficulty we found the house of Don Francesco Maropoti, who received us with hospitality and without show of ceremony, only apologising that, owing to his being alone in this his country residence, our reception could not be in point of fare and lodging all he could wish. Indeed, this worthy person's establishment was not of the most recherché kind, but I had warned my companion (hitherto untravelled in these regions) that he would probably meet with much simplicity, much cordiality, and heaps more of dirt throughout Calabria.

There is always in these provincial towns a knot of neighbours who meet in the house of the great man of each little place to discuss the occurrences of the day for an hour or two before supper; already a long perspective of such hours oppressed me, loaded with questions about Inghilterra and our own plans and circumstances. 'What ever is there to see in Bagaládi?' said our host's coterie with one voice when they heard that we wanted to go there; and one elder was fiercely incredulous, proposing that if, as we said, we were in search of the beautiful or remarkable, we should set out directly for Montebello or Melito, or any place but Bagaládi. He also explained the position and attributes of England to the rest of the society, assuring them that we had no fruit of any sort, and that all our bread came from Egypt and India; and as for our race, with a broad contempt for minute distinctions he said we were 'tutti Francesi', an assertion we faintly objected to, but were overruled... so we soon retired and, on perceiving very clean beds, were not slow in congratulating ourselves on the prosperous commencement of our Calabrian tour.

At six the next morning their pencils and sketchbooks were at the ready,

but a drizzling rain, augmenting rapidly, forbade delay; so we followed Díghi Dóghi Dà along lanes and paths, over the slope of bare hills, and up a long ravine, till the weather cleared and we arrived at an elevated plateau, whence the whole 'Toe of Italy' is finely discernible, a sea of undulating lines of varied forms down to the Mediterranean; a few towns glittered here and there, and towering over the most southern extremity of land, a high cluster of rocks, the wild crags of Pentedátilo, particularly arrested our attention. Before us, eastward, is the lofty chain of mountains, on the last or southernmost peak of which Bova, whither we are bound, is visible; but when we asked whether we should reach that town today, the silent Ciccio turned up his chin and shook his head with an air of decided negative which rendered language wholly unnecessary.

The sun came out as we descended a steep mountain path towards a white fiumara or dry torrent-course, along which we toiled and broiled patiently for an hour or two. Lonely places of devastation are these fiumaras; blinding in their white or sandy brilliancy, barring all view from without their high cliff-sides, and recalling by the bare tract of ground right and left of their course how dismal and terrible the rage of their wintry watery occupant has once been throughout its destroying career. Bagaládi was yet far distant, and we glad to meet in a garden of pear-trees some chance labourers, who gave us as much fruit as we wished. Bitterly they complained of their abodes – 'We do not know what we are to reap; sow we never so much, the torrent swells and carries away all our work.' Even with the bright blue sky above, I confess to a heart-heavy feeling among these stern scenes, where nature appears independent of man, and where any attempt on his part to set up his staff permanently seems but allowed for a season, that his defeat may be the more completely observable after years of laborious cultivation.

It was 2 pm before they eventually arrived, to find their hosts already in bed for the afternoon;

but, notwithstanding our unseasonable arrival, Don Peppino Panutti (a good hearty fellow, head of the district police) and a very pretty little woman, his wife, received us in the most friendly manner imaginable and soon refreshed us with a substantial meal of macaroni, &c., good wine and sparkling snow. Much did these good people press us to stay all night. Condufori, the next village, was yet several hours distant; nor could we be sure of meeting with so clean a dwelling and such agreeable hosts. So we agreed to remain, and make the cloud-capped Bova our next day's journey; besides, we had footed it for than seven hours under a hot sun and had need of rest, which we were glad to obtain after dinner.

The contrast between the 'very pretty little woman' and their previous hostess had an explanation:

we found she was a Livorneses by birth, and moreover had seen Malta, Constantinople and various other parts of the world, having gone for awhile to join her father in some remote place, whither he had fled from Livorno on account of what Donna Giacinta Panutti quietly called 'A little accident; that is to say, he killed someone.'

Their reception at their next stop, Condufori, served only to confirm her exceptional qualities:

questioned on the characteristics of its inhabitants, Ciccio would only volunteer 'They are Turks', adding that 'we had done well to sleep last night at Bagaládi – díghi, dóghi, dà.'

And so it proved: the Don was away and his elderly sister would have nothing to say to us. 'I am a woman, I am a woman,' she constantly declared – a fact we had never ventured to doubt, in spite of her immoderate size and ugliness – 'I am a woman, and know nothing.' No persuasions could soften her, so we were actually forced to turn away in hunger and disgust. As for Ciccio, he merely took his short pipe from his lips and said 'They are Turks – dóghi, dà.'

They had little luck either at the sole inn, which was little more than a

wretched hut... more than half choked up by the bed of a sick man, with barrels, many calf-skins filled with wine and a projecting stone fireplace. Moreover, it was as dark as Erebus; so in the palpable obscure I sat down on a large live pig, who slid away, to my disgust, from under me and made a portentous squeaking, to the disquiet of a horde of fowls perched on every available spot above and below.

The little light the place rejoiced in was disturbed by a crowd of thirty or forty 'Turks', who glared at us with the utmost curiosity and talked in their vernacular tongue without ceasing. We had also a glimpse now and then of our Hebe handmaid, the assistant or 'waitress' in the establishment, a woman with one eye whose countenance struck both of us a model of a Medusa; nor was her mistress (the hostess) much better... Besides, Bova was a weary way off, and Díghi Dóghi Dà made signs of impatience, so he paid for our lunch and off we went once more into the blazing fiumara.

We had not gone far before a chuckling sound was heard to proceed from the hitherto imperturbable Ciccio, who presently went into convulsions of suppressed laughter which continued to agitate him for more than an hour, only broken by the words 'I am a woman, I know nothing – díghi, dà...'

The climb to Bova was still more arduous, but not without its rewards: 'The immense perspective of diminishing lines and torrents, finished by the complete and simple outline of Etna beyond the sea, is certainly one of the very finest scenes to be found even in beautiful Italy.' On their arrival Don Antonio Marzano

received us with the greatest hospitality... Like most of the landowners hereabouts, he was educated at Naples. Albeit a scholar as regards Latin and Greek authors, his knowledge of English geography and personages is limited, and he refers in rather a misty manner to our 'glorious compatriot, the great Fox,' who, he says, once came to Bova to study geology, 'but whether it was before or after he governed England with Lord Pitt' – this he did [not] clearly know. According to our friend, Bova (with the four villages whose inhabitants speak a corrupt Greek and are called Turks by their neighbours) is a real old Grecian settlement, or rather, the representative of one formerly existing at Amendolia and dating from the time of Locris and other colonies. The Bovani are particularly anxious to impress upon the minds of strangers that they have no connection with the modern migrants from Albania, &c. [claiming to be, among other things, a source of wondrously good honey and the birthplace of Praxiteles].

Their departure, after three days shared between resting and sketching, left them with an equally vivid impression:

Descending the narrow street of steep stairs – for whosoever leaves Bova must needs so descend, unless he be a bird – we passed the public prison, and lo! glaring through the bars was the evil countenance of the woman whom, in the tavern-hut of Condufori, we had remarked as a species of Medusa; she had been sent hither last night for having murdered one of her fellow Turks.

By mid-day they had reached Palizzi, than which

no wilder nor more extraordinary place can well greet the artist eye. Leaving Proby to finish a drawing, I went forward to seek some shelter against the heat and, reaching the castle, soon found myself in the midst of its ruined area where, though full of incidental picturesqueness – namely, a cottage, a pergola, seven large pigs, a blind man and a baby – I could get no information as to the whereabouts of the taverna; until, alarmed by the lively remonstrances of the pigs, there appeared a beautifully fair girl who directed me down to the middle of the town. The light hair and Grecian traits, like those of the women of Gaeta, seemed to recall the daughters of Magna Graecia.

The streets of Palizzi, through which no Englishman perhaps had as yet descended, were swarming with perfectly naked, berry-brown children, and before I reached the taverna I could hardly make my way through the gathering crowd of astonished mahogany Cupids. The taverna was but a single dark room, its walls hung with portraits of little saints and its furniture a very filthy bed with a crimson gold-fringed canopy containing an unclothed opthalmic baby, an old cat and a pointer dog, all the rest of the chamber being loaded with rolls of linen, guns, gourds, pears, hats, glass tumblers, puppies, jugs, sieves, &c.; still, it was a better resting-place than the hut at Condufori, inasmuch as it was free from many intruders.

Until Proby came and joined me in despatching a feeble dinner of eggs, figs and cucumber, wine and snow, I sat exhibited and displayed for the benefit of the landlord, his wife and family, who regarded me with unmingled amazement, saying perpetually, 'Oh, where <u>do</u> you come from? Oh, what <u>are</u> you going to do? Oh, what <u>can</u> you be?' And indeed, the passage of a stranger through these outlandish places is so unusual an occurrence that on no principle but one can the aborigines account for your appearance. 'Have you no rocks, no towns, no trees in your country? Are you not rich? Then what can you wish <u>here</u>? – <u>here</u>, in this place of poverty and isolation? What <u>are</u> you doing? Where <u>are</u> you going?' You might talk for ever, but you could not convince them you are not a political agent sent to spy out the nakedness of the land, and masking the intentions of your government under the thin veil of portraying scenes, in which they see no novelty and take no delight.

The attentions of the naked children, together with the 'frying heat', the 'alarming prickles' of the ubiquitous cactus and the 'poisonous stench' of soaking hemp curtailed their attempts to sketch, and by 3 pm they had set out for Staiti via the celebrated eyrie of Pietrapennata (literally, 'winged rock'):

> As we slowly toiled up to this most strange place, wholly Calabrese in aspect with its houses jammed and crushed amid extraordinary crevices, its churches growing out of solitary rocks and (what forms the chief character of these towns) all its dwellings standing singly, the bagpipers were playing and all the peasant population thronging upwards to their evening rest.

They found their host for the night, Don Domenico Musitani,

sitting in the Piazza – an obese and taciturn man, who read
the introductory letter and forthwith took us to his house;
which, among many unpleasing recollections, will certainly
ever rank as one of the most disagreeable. Life in these
regions of natural magnificence is full of vivid contrasts. The
golden abstract visions of the hanging woods and crags of
Pietrapennata were suddenly opposed to the reality of Don
D. Musitani's rooms, which were so full of silkworms as to
be beyond measure disgusting. To the cultivation of this
domestic creature all Staiti is devoted; yellow cocoons in
immense heaps are piled up in every possible place, and the
atmosphere may be conceived rather than described, for
there is no more sickening odour than that of many thousand caterpillars confined in the closest of chambers.

In their bedroom they also had to compete for space with numerous dogs, hens and pigeons, and at dinner too they were joined by a
motley of other guests. These included the town's resident judge, 'a
well-bred man', who, 'when speaking of his "life of exile" here, said,
in the saddest of tones, "O Lord, Signori! Compare Napoli and Staiti!
Compare Paradise and Hell!"'. That might have struck Lear as an
invidious comparison indeed. It was the silkworms, however, that
continued to dominate their thoughts, so

that we felt more than half sure, on contemplating three or
four suspicious-looking dishes, that those interesting lepi-
doptera formed a great part of the groundwork of our banquet
– silkworms plain boiled, stewed chrysalis, and moth tarts.

These fears were compounded by the sight of their 'fat hostess
amusing herself by catching unwary dragonflies and holding them in
the candle'.

Having devoted the next day to sketching the 'most strange' features
of Pietrapennata, they returned for a second evening of 'supper and
silkworms, screaming children and howling dogs; the fat lady shouted
and scolded, and anathematised the daddy-longlegs who flew into the
candles'. Lear began to speculate on what lay ahead of them at Santa
Maria di Polsi, their next stop. 'On the map it is most inviting,' he
observed ironically, 'and deep among the horrors of Aspromonte.'

After an early start to catch the 'many charming views' around the village of Bruzzano, they stopped to indulge themselves in 'the best Calabrian wine we had yet tasted', until the usually taciturn Ciccio intervened to inform them that there was no more time to be lost if they were to make Santa Maria by the following evening.

They were faced with a choice of route: either via Feruzzano, which looked uninteresting and where they did not have any introductions; or via Santa Agata, which lay considerably further on but where they had an introduction to the Barone Franco. They

> finally decided on this difficult question by that intellectual process of reasoning generally known as 'tossing up'. Heads? Tails? Heads – Sta. Agata.

> Down, therefore, we went into a new scene – ridges and lines beyond lines of chalky-bright heights, town-crowned heights and glaringly white fiumaras, a great tract from hill to sea of glitter and arid glare.

The journey was made even more torturous by the blasting heat of a sudden *sirocco* wind:

> It was as much as either of us could do, aided by some water-melons, to reach that longed-for spot, the convent of Bianco, beyond which we looked earnestly to ever-rising grounds with fresh woods and bluer mountains beyond, speaking of air and endurable existence once more.

> At last, behold us at the monastery door. O fallacious hopes! All the monks were fast asleep, so we could only penetrate into a courtyard where, indeed, was a well of clear water, and an iron bucket chained thereto... so off we set again. 'Coraggio, díghi, dóghi, dà,' said Ciccio, and we climbed on.

Again they were to be disappointed, for the next village proved not to be Santa Agata, as they had imagined. Nor were the omens any better when they at last arrived there, for they found the Barone absent, and the rest of the family 'dirty and sad'. At supper, however, their fears for the menu were dispelled by

> an unexpected display of macaroni, eggs, olives, butter, cheese and undeniable wine and snow, on a table covered

with the whitest of linen and sparkling with plate and glass, arrangements at variance with the outward appearance of the mansion.

Lunch at Santa Luca, their next stop, yielded a still more agreeable surprise, in spite of a warning from the Don Giacomo Stranges: '"You must take what you can find," said he; "there is no time to get anything: there are no markets here, signore – we are not in Naples."' In fact they were presented with 'heaps of macaroni, marrows and tomatoes, and a roast hare, and that is not matter for complaint in the heart of Calabria'.

Questioned again on England's produce and answering that it included, if not grapes, then a rich variety of other fruit, they received the reply: '"Oh, but that's not possible," and a polite grin of incredulity'.

> The worthy man pressed us much to stay, to see all the hills. 'Since you are come to this out-of-the-way place, what difference can a week or two make? Stay, and hunt – stay, and make this your home!'

> 'Alas, good Don Giacomo! So we would gladly, but life is short and we are trying hard to see all Calabria in three months.'

It was half past six before they were eventually able to shake him off, and the light soon began to fade as they made their way up another *fiumara*, overhung on either side by enormous oleander trees:

> A circuitous toil to the head of a second large torrent, skirting a ravine filled with magnificent ilex, brought us to the last tremendous ladder-path that led to the 'serra' or highest point of the route, wherefrom we were told we should perceive the monastery. Slowly old Ciccio and his horse followed us, and darker grew the hour. 'We shall arrive late, if we do not die before we get there,' quoth he – 'díghi, dóghi, dà!' But alas! when we did get at the promised height, where a cross is set up and where, at the great festas of the convent, the pilgrims fire off guns on the first and last view of the celebrated Calabrian sanctuary – alas! it was quite dark, and only a twinkling light far and deep down, in the very bowels

of the mountain, showed us our destination. Slow and hazardous was the descent, and it was nine o'clock ere we arrived before the gate of this remote and singular retreat.

Their desperate knocks were answered at last by a 'most affable' Father Superior, who advised them that he had little to offer by way of accommodation. When they indicated that they were happy to accept whatever that little might be,

> wonder and curiosity overwhelmed the ancient man and his brethren, who were few in number and clad in black serge dresses. 'Why had we come to such a solitary place? No foreigner had ever done so before!' The hospitable father asked us a world of questions, and made many comments upon us and upon England in general, for the benefit of his fellow-recluses. 'England,' said he, 'is a very small place, although thickly inhabited. It is altogether about the third part of the size of the city of Rome. The people are a sort of Christians, though not exactly so. Their priests, and even their bishops, marry, which is incomprehensible and most ridiculous. The whole place is divided into two equal parts by an arm of the sea, under which there is a great tunnel, so that it is all like one piece of dry land.' Ah – that celebrated tunnel!

> A supper of hard eggs, salad and fruit followed in the refectory of the convent, and we were attended by two monstrous watch-dogs, named Assassino and Saraceno, throughout the rest of the evening, when the silence of the long hall, broken only by the whispers of the gliding monk, was very striking. Our bedrooms were two cells, very high up in the tower of the convent, with shutters to the unglazed windows as a protection against the cold and the wind, which were by no means pleasant at this great elevation. Very forlorn, indeed, were the sleeping apartments of Sta. Maria di Polsi!

They awoke to light rain, but it presently cleared and they were soon busy again with their sketchbooks:

> Assuredly, Sta. Maria di Polsi is one of the most remarkable scenes I ever beheld. The building is picturesque, but of no great antiquity and with no pretensions to architectural taste;

it stands on a rising ground above the great torrent, which comes down from the very summit of Aspromonte, the highest point of which – Montalto – is the 'roof and crown' of the picture. From the level of the monastery to this height rises a series of screens covered with the grandest foliage, with green glades and massive clumps of chestnut low down – black ilex and brown oak next in succession and, highest of all, pines. The <u>perpendicular</u> character of the scene is singularly striking, the wooded rocks right and left closing it in like the side slips of a theatre; and as no other building is within sight, the romance and loneliness of the spot are complete.

The monastery, they were not surprised to learn, was frequently snowed in for months on end during the winter, but this was regarded as no hardship by an order dedicated to a life of the strictest seclusion. On their departure the Father Superior presented them with a print of the Madonna di Polsi, the original, he claimed,

having been discovered by a devout ox, who inveigled one of the early Norman Conquerors of Sicily all the way from Reggio to this place for the particular purpose of inducing him to build a monastery. The excellent ox, said the monk, led on the prince from hill to hill till he reached the proper spot, when, kneeling down, he with his pious horns poked up the portrait of the Virgin Mary which was miraculously waiting some inches below the ground for its bovine liberator.

They descended again by the same *fiumara* almost down to the coast, before returning inland to the sizeable town of Bovalino, where they had an introduction to the Conte Garrolo, who turned out to be exactly what his name implied. They

fortunately found him just returned from the country; the small rooms of his house betokened the literary man, heaps of books, maps, globes and papers filling up all corners and great wealth of very old-fashioned furniture leaving small space for sitting or standing. The Conte himself was a most good-natured and fussy little man, excessively consequential and self-satisfied but kind withal, and talking and bustling in the most breathless haste, quoting Greek and Latin, hinting at antiquities and all kinds of dim lore and obscure science, rushing about, ordering his two domestics to and fro, explaining, apologising and welcoming, without the least cessation.

He had come from a villa, a villetta, a vigna – an old property of his family – Giovanni Garrolo, Gasparo Garrolo, Luca Garrolo, Stefano Garrolo – he had come just now, this very minute; he had come on a mule, on two mules, with the Contessa, the amiable Contessa, he had come slowly – pian, pian, piano, piano, piano – for the Contessa expected to be confined shortly – perhaps today – he hoped not; he would like us to be acquainted with her; her name was Serafina; she was intellectual and charming; the mules had never stumbled; he had put on the crimson-velvet housings, a gilt coronet embossed, Garrolo, Garrolo, Garrolo, Garrolo, in all four corners; he had read the Contessa an ode to ancient Locris all along the road, it amused her, a Latin ode; the Contessa enjoyed Latin; the Contessa had had six children, all in Paradise, great loss, but all for the best; would we have some snow and wine? Bring some snow, bring some wine. He would read us a page, two pages, three – Locri Opuntii, Locri Epizephyrii, Normans, Saracens – Indian figs and Indian corn – Julius Caesar, and the Druids, Dante, Shakespeare – silkworms and mulberries – rents and taxes, antediluvians, American republics, astronomy and shellfish – like the rushing of a torrent was the volubility of Conte Garrolo, yet one failed to receive any distinct impression from what he said, so unconnected and rapid was the jumbling together of his subjects of eloquence.

As the evening drew on, they fell to wondering

if the Contessa would talk a tenth part as much, or as loudly. Supper was ready sooner than in most of these houses, and when it was served, in came the Contessa, who was presented to us by her husband with a crash of compliments and apologies for her appearance, which put our good breeding to the severest test; in all my life I never so heartily longed to burst into merriment, for the poor lady, either from ill-health or long habitual deference to her loquacious spouse, said nothing in the world but '[Sig]Nirr si' or 'Nirr no', which smallest efforts of intellectual discourse she continued to insert between the Count's sentences in the meekest way, like Pity between the drummings of Despair in Collins' Ode to the Passions.

'Excuse her, excuse her,' thundered the voluble Count, 'excuse her – supper, supper, to supper – the table is ready, is ready.'

'Nirr si.'

'Quickly, quickly, quickly, quickly.'

'Nirr si, nirr no.'

'Sit you down, sit you down (her sister died four months ago).'

'Nirr si.'

'Eat! Eat!'

'Nirr no.'

'Macaroni? Chicken? (her mother's dead, she cries too much) Anchovies? Soup? Eggs?'

'Nirr no.'

'Signori strangers, have some wine. Contessa, be merry.'

'Nirr si.'

It was a most trying and never-ending monologue, barring the choral nirr si and no, and how it was we did not go off improperly into shrieks of laughter I cannot tell, unless that day's fatigue had made our spirits tractable. Instantly after supper the Contessa vanished, and the Count bustled about like an armadillo in a cage, showing us our room and bringing in a vast silver basin and jug, towels, &c., with the most surprising alacrity, and although the ludicrous greatly predominated in these scenes, yet so much prompt and kind attention shown to the wants of two entire strangers by these worthy people was most pleasing. For all that, how did we laugh when we talked over the ways of this amazing Count Garrolo!

August 10th. The bustling Count whisked us all over the town, into the church, the castle, the lanes – showed us the views, the walls, the towns, the villages, manuscripts, stables, the two mules and the purple velvet saddle and crimson housings with coronets and Garrolo, Garrolo, Garrolo, Garrolo – tutto-tutto-tutto – put us in charge of a peasant to show us a short cut to Ardore – shook hands fifteen times with each of us and then rushed away with frantic speed to write down some poetical thoughts; to give orders to the staff (those two servants, how they must have worked!); to sell a horse; to buy some grain; to pick some flowers; to console the Contessa.

'Addio! Addio!'

Addio, Count Garrolo! A merry obliging little man you are as ever lived, and the funniest of created counts all over the world.

It was noon before they felt sufficiently out of earshot of the garrulous Conte to pause for a watermelon, and shortly afterwards came to the Torre di Gerace, a single tower of the Middle Ages, standing on the edge of the seashore at the spot which antiquaries recognise as the indubitable site of ancient Locris. Foundations of antique buildings exist for a great extent in all the vineyards around, and innumerable coins are dug up by the labourers.

After another four hours heading inland again they reached Gerace itself,

a large cathedral town full of beautifully-placed buildings situated on a very narrow edge of rock, every part of which seems to have been dangerously afflicted by earthquakes – splits, and cracks, and chasms – horrible with abundant crookedness of steeples and a general appearance of instability in walls and houses. Towards the north-west, the sharp crest of rock ends abruptly in a precipice, which on three sides is perfectly perpendicular. Here are the dark and crumbling ruins of a massive Norman castle, from which by a scrambling path you may reach the valley below; but all other parts of the town are accessible only by two winding roads at the eastern and less precipitous approach… In fact, Gerace is by far the grandest and proudest object in general position, and as a city, which we have yet seen in Calabria.

Their host for the next three days, Don Pasquale Scaglione, 'a prepossessing and gentlemanlike person, welcomed us warmly,' treating them to 'an admirable dinner of soup, fish, boiled and fried meat, and potatoes, all plain and excellent', washed down with 'sundry glasses of an old wine much esteemed by the Calabrese and called Greco'. There was a price attached, however: after showing them his extensive collection of ancient Greek and Roman coins,

> our good host victimised us fearfully by reading aloud chapter after chapter of a work which he is writing on Locris – an 'opus magnum' which, however learned, was vastly dull. All hints about repose were vain; so when Proby fell fast asleep, and I was nearly following his example, I was about to beg we might retire when the author himself yawned, and paused, and fell into the arms of the drowsy god…[3]

Chapter Nine
Southern Calabria (August 1847)

Lear and Proby received an altogether different welcome when they arrived that evening at Rocella, their next port of call along the coast,

once a stronghold of the Caraffa family, now a collection of scattered houses below and a knot of others on the double fortress rock... all, as we could see by their ragged walls against the sky, in utter ruin.

Ciccio shouted aloud, but no signs of life were given in the total darkness. We tried this turning – it was blocked up by a dead wall; that way you stumbled among sleeping horses; the next path led you to the precipice. We despaired, and remained calling forth 'ai! ai! Don Guiseppe Nanni! Oo! ooo! ai! ai!' till we were hoarse, but there was no other way of attracting attention. At last (as if there had been no steps taken at all to arouse the neighbourhood) a man came, as it were casually, forth from the dark ruins, holding a feeble light and saying mildly, 'What do you want?' 'We seek Don Guiseppe Nanni's house,' said we. 'This is it,' said he. So we walked, with no small pleasure, into the very place under whose windows we had been screaming for the last hour past.

Subjected once again to the usual inquisition, Lear confessed to

having been more than once fast asleep, and, waking up abruptly, answered at random, in the vaguest manner, to the applied catechetical torture. I will not say what I did not aver to be the natural growth of England – camels, cochineal, sea-horses, or gold-dust; and as for the celebrated tunnel, I fear I invested it drowsily with all kinds of fabulous qualities.

Supper was at last announced, and an addition to our party was made in the handsome wife of Don Ferdinando and other females of the family, though I do not think they shared greatly in the conversation. Vegetables and fruit alone embellished the table. The world of Rocella particularly piques itself on the production and culture of fruit; and our assertion that we had fruit in England was received with thinly-hidden incredulity.

'You confess you have no wine – no oranges – no olives – no figs; how, then, can you have apples, pears, or plums? It is a known fact that no fruit does or can grow in England, only potatoes, and nothing else whatsoever – this is well known. Why, then, do you tell us that which is not true?'

It was plain we were looked upon as vagabond impostors.

'But indeed we do have fruit,' said we, humbly; 'and what is more, we have some fruits which you have not got at all.'

Suppressed laughter and supercilious sneers, when this assertion was uttered, nettled our patriotic feelings.

'Oh, what fruit can you possibly have that we have not? Oh, how you are laughing at us! Name your fruits, then – these fabulous fruits!'

'We have currants, gooseberries and greengages.'

'And what are gooseberries and greengages?' said the whole party, in a rage. 'There are no such things – these are fantasies!'

So we ate our supper in quiet, convinced almost that we had been telling lies; that gooseberries were unreal and fictitious; greengages a dream.

They escaped at first light for a morning's sketching, but another trial awaited them on their return for lunch:

They had procured dishes of the largest pears and apples to be found in Rocella by way of desert [sic], and they watched our faces for signs of mortification thereat, evidently attributing our non-amazement to our firm resolve not to tell the truth and betray our country's horticultural failings.

24 hours later, at the table of Don Cicillo Caristò in Stignano, their composure was equally tested by

> a most confused assemblage of large dogs under the table who fought for casual crumbs and bones, and when they did not accidentally bite one's extremities, rushed, wildly barking, all about the little room. But the most remarkable accident during our stay was caused by a small juvenile Caristò who, during the mid-day meal, climbed abruptly on to the table and, before he could be rescued, performed a series of struggles among the dishes, which ended by the little pickle's losing his balance and collapsing suddenly in a sitting posture into the very middle of the macaroni dish, from which Proby and I rejoiced to think that we had been previously helped.

On their arrival at Stilo in the evening, it was all change again in the hands of Don Ettore Marzano, 'a thoroughly hearty, as well as polite, young man,' whose 'large house was well kept and comfortable (speaking of things as they are in Italy), though without attempt at splendour', and who forbore from interrogating them for their supper. Another novelty was

> a domestic [who] stood at meal-time close to the table and in order to dissipate the flies, which at this season are legion, flapped a long flapper of feathers, Laputa-wise, close to our faces. No sooner did we begin to speak than whizz – flick – down came the flapper so as to render conversation a rather difficult effort.

Lear was similarly impressed by the courtesy shown them by the town's population at large during their two days there:

> No one met or overtook me on the way to Bigonzi without a word or two of salutation; there were few who did not offer me pears, and parties of women laden with baskets of figs would stop and select the best for us. Nor did anybody ask a question beyond 'What do you think of our mountains?' or 'How do you like our village?' In the town of Stilo we were

sometimes followed by not less than fifty or a hundred people, but ever with the utmost good feeling and propriety.

Taking to the hills again, they arrived at Motta Placánica,

one of the most truly characteristic of Calabrian towns. Like
others of these strange settlements, this place has no depth
but is, as it were, surface only, the houses being built one
above another, on ledges and in crevices, over the face of a
large rock rising into a peak, its highest pinnacle being graced
by a modern palazzo. The strange effect which these towns
have, even upon those long used to the irregularities of South
Italian village architecture, is not to be imagined; Motta
Placánica seems constructed to be a wonder to passers-by.

More surprises awaited them at Castel Vetere, which they found,

though mean in appearance from below, full of houses of a
large size and indicating wealth and prosperity. To that of
Don Ilario Asciutti we went, narrowly escaping the midday
autumn thunder-storm, and found a large mansion, with a
hall and staircase, ante-room and drawing-room very surprising as to dimensions and furniture; the walls were
papered and hung with mirrors, prints, &c.; chiffoniers,
tables and a bookcase adorned the sides of the rooms, and
there were footstools, with other unwonted objects of Trans-
Calabrian luxury. The famiglia Asciutti were polite and most
friendly; there were two smart sons, just come from college
in Naples; a serene and silent father; and last, not least, an
energetic and astute grandsire, before whose presence all the
rest were as nothing.

Grandad Asciutti was as voluble as Conte Garrolo, but with
more connected ideas and sentences, and with an overpow-
ering voice; an expression of 'L'état, c'est moi' in all he said
and did. The old gentleman surprised us not a little by his
information on the subjects on which he held forth – the
game laws of England, and Magna Carta, the Reformation,
the Revolution of 1688, Ireland, and the Reform Bill. He
was becoming diffuse on European politics, having already
discussed America and the Canadas, and glanced slightly at

slavery, the East and West Indies and the sugar trade, when, to our great satisfaction, all this learning, so wonderful in the heart of Magna Graecia, was put to a stop by the announcement of dinner. This, however, provided only the briefest of respites from the didacticism of the erudite grandfather, who harangued loftily from his place at the end of the table. It was Wednesday and there was no meat, as is usual on that day in South Italian families.

'It would be better,' said the authoritative elder, 'if there were no such thing as meat – nobody ought to eat any meat. The Creator never intended meat, that is the flesh of quadrupeds, to be eaten. No good Christians ought to eat flesh – and why? The quadruped works for man while alive, and it is a shame to devour him when dead. The sheep gives wool, the ox ploughs, the cow gives milk, the goat cheese.'

'What do the hares do for us?' whispered one of the grandsons.

'Hold your tongue!' shouted the orator. 'But fish,' continued he, 'what do they do for us? Does a mullet plough? Can a prawn give milk? Has a tunny any wool? No. Fish and birds also were therefore created to be eaten.'

A wearisome old man was Grandad Asciutti! But the alarming point of his character was yet to be made known to us. No sooner, dinner being over, did we make known our intention of proceeding to sleep at Gioiosa on account of our limited time, than we repented having visited Castel Vetere at all. 'Oh, heaven! Oh, rage! Oh, what do I hear? Oh, who am I? Oh, who are you?' screamed Grandad, in a paroxysm of rage. 'What have I done that you will not stay? How can I bear such an insult? Since Calabria was Calabria, no such affront has ever been offered to a Calabrian! Go – why should you go?' In vain we tried to assuage the grandsire's fury. We had stayed three days in Gerace, three in Reggio, two in Bova and in Stilo, and not one in Castel Vetere! The silent father looked mournful, the grandsons implored; but the wrathful old gentleman, having considerably endangered the furniture by kicks and thumps, finally rushed downstairs in a frenzy, greatly to our discomfiture.

The rest of the family were distressed seriously at this incident, and on my sending a message to beg that he would show us a new palazzo he was constructing (himself the architect) for the increased accommodation of the family Asciutti, he relented so far as to return, and after listening favourably to our encomiastic remarks, bade us a final farewell with a less perturbed countenance and spirit.

In the event, their reception at Gioiosa proved hardly less of a trial. They were informed that their intended host, the Baron Rivettini, was elsewhere, and it was only with great difficulty that they were able to persuade a servant to lead them to him.

In a spacious salone on the first floor sat a party playing at cards, and one of them, a minute gentleman with a form more resembling that of a sphere than any person I ever remembered to have seen, was pointed out to me as the Baron by the shrinking domestic who had thus far piloted me. But excepting by a single glance at me, the assembled company did not appear aware of my entrance, nor, when I addressed the Baron by his name, did he break off the thread of his employment, otherwise than by saying, 'One, two three – yes, sir – four, five – your servant, sir – make fifteen.'

'Has your Excellency received an introductory letter from the Cavalier da Nava?' said I.

'Five, six – yes, sir – make eleven.'

This, thought I, is highly mysterious.

'Can I and my travelling companion lodge in your house, Signor Baron, until tomorrow?'

'Three and six make nine,' pursued the Baron, with renewed attention to the game. 'Ma perchè, signore?'

'Perchè, there is no inn in this town, and, perchè, I have brought you a letter of introduction,' rejoined I.

'Ah, si si si, signore, pray favour me by remaining at my

house – two and seven make nine – eight and eleven make nineteen.'

And again the party went on with the game...

When I returned to the Palazzo Rivettini, all the scene was changed. Coffee was brought to us and a large room was assigned for our use, while all the natural impulse of Calabrese hospitality seemed, for the time at least, to over-power the mysterious spell which, from some unknown cause, appeared to oppress those inhabitants of Gioiosa with whom we were brought in contact. But the magic atmos-phere of doubt and astonishment returned in full force as other persons of the town came in to the evening conver-sazione. Few words were said but those of half-suppressed curiosity as to where we came from; and the globose little Baron himself gradually confined his observations to the sin-gle interrogative 'Perchè' which he used in a breathless man-ner, on the slightest possible provocation. Supper followed, every part of the entertainment arrayed with the greatest attention to plenty and comfort; but the whole circle seemed ill at ease, and regarded our looks and movements with unabated watchfulness, as if we might explode, or escape through the ceiling at any unexpected moment; so that both hosts and guests seemed but too well pleased when we returned to our room, and the incessant 'Perchè? perchè? per-chè?' was, for this evening at least, silenced.

By all this mystery – so very unusual to the straightforward and cordial manners of these mountaineers – there was left on my mind a distinct impression of some supposed or antic-ipated evil.

Hoping to make an early escape, they rose before sunrise – only to be confronted by their host, who was waiting outside the door and who then subjected their passports to a minute examination:

Every particular relating to our eyes, noses and chins was written down; nor was it until after endless interrogatories and more perchès than are imaginable that we were released. Even then at breakfast our usual practice of taking a small piece of bread with our coffee renewed the universal surprise and distrust of our hosts.

'Bread!' said the Baron, 'perchè bread? Oh, heaven!'

'I never take sugar,' said Proby, as some was offered to him.

'Sant' Antonio, you don't take sugar? Perchè? O Dio! Perchè do you never take sugar?'

'We want to make a drawing of your pretty little town,' said I; and, in spite of a perfect hurricane of 'perchès', out we rushed, followed by the globular Baron in the most lively state of alarm, down the streets, across the river on stepping-stones, and up the opposite bank, from the steep cliffs of which, overhung with oak foliage, there is a beautiful view of Gioiosa on its rock.

'For Heaven's sake! Oh, Saint Peter! Whatever do you want to do?'

'I am going to draw for half-an-hour,' said I.

'Ma – perchè?'

And down I sat, working hard for nearly an hour, during all which time the perplexed Baron walked round and round me, occasionally uttering a melancholy 'O signore, ma perchè?'

'Signore Baron,' said I, when I had done my sketch, 'we have no towns in our country so beautifully situated as Gioiosa!'

'Ma perchè?' quoth he.

I walked a little way and paused to observe the bee-eaters, which were flitting through the air above me and under the spreading oak branches.

'For the love of Heaven, what are you looking at? Whatever have you seen?' said the Baron.

'I am looking at those beautiful blue birds.'

'Perchè? perchè? perchè?'

It was evident that do or say what I would, some mystery was connected with each action and word; so that, in spite of the whimsical absurdity of these eternal wherefores and whys, it was painful to see that, although our good little host strove to give scope to his hospitable nature, our stay caused more anxiety than pleasure.

Their purchase of some sugarplums, for which Gioiosa was famous, provoked still more questions, and even after they had finally taken their leave they were arrested by the sight of their host

thrusting his head from a window and calling out, 'Stop! Why are you going? Why don't you stay for dinner? Why birds? Why drawings? Why sugarplums? Why, why, why why?' till the last 'perchè' was lost in distance as we passed once more round the rock and crossed the river Romano.

Long did we indulge in merriment at the perturbation our visit had occasioned our host, whom we shall long remember as 'Baron Wherefore'. Nevertheless, a certainty impresses me that so much timidity is occasioned by some hidden event or expectation.

As they pushed on up to Cánalo, their ascent grew progressively steeper and more arduous until it became

a wilderness of terror, such as it is not easy to describe or imagine. The village itself is crushed and squeezed into a nest of crags immediately below the vast precipices which close round the Passo del Marcante, and when on one side you gaze at this barrier of stone and then, turning round, perceive the distant sea and undulating lines of hill, no contrast can be more striking... I have never seen such wondrous bits of rock scenery.

They were equally appreciative of the contrast between their next host, an elderly man, and his recent predecessors:

Good old Don Giovanni Rosa amused and delighted us by his lively simplicity and good breeding. He had only once in his long life (he was eighty-two) been as far as Gerace, but never beyond. 'Why should I go?' said he; 'if, when I die, as I shall ere long, I find Paradise like Cánalo, I shall be well pleased. To me my Cánalo has always seemed like Paradise – I am in want of nothing.'

Considering that the good old man's Paradise is cut off by heavy snow four months in the year from any external communication with the country round, and that it is altogether (however attractive to artists) about as little convenient a place as may well be imagined, the contented mind of Don Giovanni Rosa was equally novel and estimable.

The only member of our host's family now living is a grandson, who was one of our party, a silent youth who seemed never to do or say anything at any time. Our meals were remarkable, inasmuch as Paradiso cookery appeared to delight in singular experiments and materials. At one time a dish was exhibited full of roasted squirrels, adorned by funghi of wonderful shapes and colours; at another, there were relays of most surprising birds, among which my former ornithological studies caused me to recognise a few corvine mandibles, whose appearance was not altogether in strict accordance with the culinary arrangements of polite society.

Lear and Proby spent the next two days busily capturing 'the wondrous scenery', distracted only by

a poor harmless idiot following us wherever we went, sitting below the rock or path we took for our station and saying, without intermission, 'Oh, little Englishmen, give me a farthing – wh——-ew!', the which sentence and whistle accompaniment he repeated all day long.

After taking a fond farewell of their 'agreeable, kind and untiringly merry' host, they returned by a more southerly route to Gerace and the Palazzo Scaglione, where

all the family were delighted to welcome us back, including little Cicillo and his sister, to whom the sugarplums were a source of high edification; and it was great sport for us to tell them of all our adventures since we had left them, save that we did not dilate on the facetiae of the Baron Rivettini.

All Gerace was in a fever of preparation for a great Festa, to take place on the following day; and in the evening Proby and I, with Padre Abbenate and Don Gaetano Scaglione, inspected the site of the entertainment, which was arranged at the west end of the rock, on the platform by the ruined castle. Here were bagpipers and booths, and dancing and illuminations, all like the days and doings of Tagliocozzo in the fête of 1843, but on a smaller and more rustic scale. The Sottintendente, Don Antonio Buonafede, was presiding at the preliminary festivities. There was also, as in the Abruzzo, a temporary chapel erected in the open air, highly ornamented and decked with figures of saints, &c.; but the usual accompaniments of dancing were expected to be rather a failure, as the Bishop of Gerace had published an edict prohibiting the practice of that festive amusement by any of the fairer sex whatever.

It had its desired effect: while all the men from miles around disported themselves,

> black-hooded women, ranged in tiers on the rock-terraces, sat like dark statues against the amber western sky; the gloomy and massive Norman ruins frowned over the misty gulf beneath with gloomier grandeur; the full moon rose high and formed a picturesque contrast with the festa lights, which sparkled on the dark background of the pure heaven; and all combined to create one of those scenes which must ever live in the memory, and can only be formed in imagination, because neither painting nor description can do them justice.

From Gerace the travellers headed into the hinterland again to cross the 3,000-foot Passo di Mercante, then descended more gently to Castelnuovo (now called Cittanova), so named because it replaced the town obliterated by the devastating earthquake of 1783. Their host, Don Vincenzo Tito,

> seemed to hesitate as to his reception of us; but after a long scrutiny, and many interrogations, he apparently decided in our favour and, showing us some good rooms, ordered a dinner for us anew, his own being finished. But the manner of our host was abrupt, restless and uneasy; and his frequent questions as to whether we had heard anything from Reggio, &c., &c., gave me a stronger suspicion than ever that some

political movement was about to take place. Although long accustomed to hear that some change of affairs was anticipated in the kingdom of Naples, and equally in the habit of studiously remaining as far as I could in ignorance of all political acts or expressions, I half concluded that now, as often before, the suspicious reserve of Don Vincenzo, and possibly that of Baron Rivettini also, proceeded from some false rumour afloat. Nevertheless, I confess that more than one trifling occurrence in the last two days had increased my feeling that 'something is about to happen'.

The products of their afternoon's sketching served only to increase their host's wariness of them, and they made another dawn start for a brief excursion to Polístena, 'a large town where riven rocks, a broken bridge, shattered walls and desolate streets bore witness to the fatal catastrophe of 1783':

> We easily found the home of Morani's family – 'that famous painter', as the town's-people called him, and entering it were welcomed by his mother and sisters, who seemed pleased that any stranger should inquire after his dwelling. 'These,' said two very nice girls, throwing open the door of a small room, 'are all the works we possess done by our brother' – little supposing that to an Englishman one of the portraits possessed the highest possible interest. It was a small drawing made from Sir Walter Scott during his visit to Naples; and though neither remarkable for beauty of execution nor pleasing as a likeness, it was highly interesting as the last record of that great man taken from life. 'They say this was a famous author,' said our two hostesses…

On their return to Castelnuovo Don Tito treated them to another

> hospitable meal; but on my asking for a letter of introduction to Palmi, he drew back and abruptly declined. 'There is a locanda there,' said he, which refusal, so different to the way in which the Abruzzesi used to say 'Go to our cousin this, or uncle that, but not to a locanda,' or 'What a disgrace to go to a locanda! Are there then none of our relations in that town?' rather revived my suspicions.

It was thus in a state of growing unease that Lear and Proby set out again on 'a delightful road through never-ending olives, with wondrous glimpses of a perfect sea of foliage down to the Gulf of Gioia'. This was their first sight of Calabria's west coast since they had left Reggio. After passing through Terranova (now Taurianova), 'once the largest town of this district but utterly destroyed by the fearful event of 1783,' they arrived at Oppido, by the light of a full moon, 'well tired', only to find that their prospective host was

> away and all his palazzo shut up for repairs! Our only hope and help, therefore, was in a most wretched locanda – a very horrid den: at its door we sat, and prolonged our supper of eggs till late; but the numbers of formidable vermin were so great and distressing in the sleeping apartments that we could not contemplate the animated beds without a shudder; whereon we sat and waited till daybreak, as best we might.

On Ciccio's advice they turned west again and made for the coast through humid, mosquito-laden fields of water melon in order to pick up the main carriage road between Naples and Reggio at 'pestiferous Gioia, a mere village, consisting of some large warehouses and a huge osteria which stands close to the sea-shore'.

> In this public resort, a tenement containing two huge rooms mostly filled with the oily, but by no means odiferous, produce of the neighbourhood, we sought food and rest, though our prospect of the latter was small; for the wary Ciccio said, ever and anon, 'If you sleep, you are dead, díghi, dóghi, dà!', and if we ever closed our eyes for a moment, all the people of the osteria shrieked out with one voice, 'Oh, holy heaven, wake up! Wake up!' Gioia is indeed one of the most mournful of places; for, although the trade carried on from it in oil is very considerable and numerous workmen are transporting barrels, &c., on every side, these are all people of the adjacent city of Palmi, who come hither at morn and return home at night. There is no drinkable water in the place, and the few poor wretches who are left in charge of the warehouses are melancholy and horrible objects – malaria-fever being written on every line of their face and form.

The sun was now at its zenith, yet, perhaps not surprisingly, they

> preferred to set off as early as we could along the burning high-road towards Palmi. How undeniable is the simplicity of those who think they have 'done' Calabria by travelling in a carriage from Naples to Reggio! All the beautiful incidents of pastoral or mountain life, all the romance of a wandering artist's existence is carefully banished from your high-road tourist's journey, and the best he can boast of is an extended view from some elevated point of road. We looked back with fond regret to the mountains of Aspromonte, or to the shady paths in the groves of the upper plain of Gioia, and voted all highways eminent nuisances and vulgarities.

Palmi, an already well-established seaside resort,

> is placed on the high cliffs of its western coast immediately opposite the Lipari Isles which, in shape somewhat like a row of inverted cups and saucers, here adorn the horizon... We went to a locanda which had been named to us by someone on the road, but in going thither old Ciccio twice shook his head and said 'Non credo – díghi, dóghi, dà,' wherefrom we did not augur any great success in our search.

> When we arrived at the bottom of the scala or staircase, all the upper part of it was filled up by the most Brobdingnagian of living landladies; moreover, this enormous woman was peculiarly hideous, and clad in the slightest and most extraordinary of simple costumes.

Her state of undress might have been excused by the heat, but Lear also observed that she was far from sober, being 'as unsteady on her feet as clamorous with her tongue'.

> 'Let us try some other locanda,' said we to each other, and were turning away when the monster landlady shouted out, 'Oh, my sons, come in, come in'; but seeing that her invitation made no impression, 'Go to the black devil!' quoth she, accompanying her words with a yell and an abrupt ejection of a large broom from her right hand down the staircase, so that we fairly fled without further discussion and followed

the silent but grinning Ciccio to another locanda.

Happily this proved more acceptable. When it came to settling up in the morning, however, the bill was found to be 'by no means so unexceptionable as the dinner and style of the accommodation'. By dint of some heated haggling they succeeded in reducing it to a seventh of the original sum, although even that Lear considered exorbitant.

Sending Ciccio with the horse and baggage by the road, we descended to the Scala and embarked in a boat for Bagnara, which, placed on a peninsular rock, projects grandly into the water beyond the bay of Palmi. The cliffs are infinitely majestic between the two towns – descending in sheer and perpendicular crags to the sea, and were it not for the absence of buildings the coast would have often reminded me of that of Amalfi, or Positano; as far as the motion of a boat in a very rough swell would allow me to observe them, I enjoyed these scenes extremely, but I was glad to approach the shore once more…

Bagnara rises from the water's edge in an amphitheatre of buildings, crowned by a high rock which is joined to the mountain above by a castle and aqueduct, and is assuredly one of the most imposing and stately towns in appearance which we have yet seen. The arches of the aqueduct span a chasm in the rock-peninsular on which it stands, and while a castle adorns the seaward portion, the land-cliffs are studded with a glittering row of buildings, many of which nestle down to the very shore below the torn and cracked ravines into which the precipices are shivered. A smooth half-moon of sand extends to the foot of the rocks, and gives a calm and pleasant air to the whole picture.

We wound up the path which leads to the upper town, and passing through the arches of the viaduct (for it serves for a road as well as to transport water) were even more delighted by the sight of the southern side than we had been with the northern. Bagnara from this point of view is wonderfully striking, and few coast scenes of Western Calabria can rival it.

It grew late ere we finished sketching, and a courteous priest directed us to a good inn, where we found Ciccio arrived before us.

August 27th. We had no squabble with the host of our very comfortable and quiet locanda here; few people ever stop at Bagnara, so the world is less acquainted with the modes of high-road depredation. There is a good carriage route all along the coast, which decided us on sending Díghi-dóghi-dà to Scilla, and we loitered forward, making drawings as we proceeded, until we reached that town about noon and found (so much for 'roughing it' on this side of Calabria) another very clean inn by the sea-side, just beyond a most picturesque rock and castle.

Scilla is one of the most striking bits of coast scenery, its white buildings and massive castled crag standing out in noble relief against the dark blue waves – while the Lipari Isles and Stromboli, with the Faro of Messina, form a beautiful background. But beyond the general appearance of the place, which from all points of view is very imposing, there is but little to note down...

In spite of the favourable appearance of our locanda, we could get nothing to eat but a very antique fowl, which baffled knives and forks, and we anticipated from such bad fare, and from the landlord's continual compliments, that the charges would be proportionally heavy.

Once again Lear's forebodings were proved right. After paying the inflated bill they made another attempt at sketching, attracting the attentions of a considerable crowd of onlookers:

'These men,' said an old man as we were thus busily employed, 'are all persons sent by their government to gather intelligence on our Kingdom' – a conceit universally ridiculed by Englishmen, but not quite so absurd as it may seem, if we reflect that the conquest of many countries by others has been preceded by individual observation and research.

Hurried on their way from the locanda by an 'outcry of feminine shrieks and masculine curses, which followed us long after we left the

place,' they made hotfoot for Villa San Giovanni, where they grate-
fully took their time over an excellent lunch. Setting out again at four,
they reached Reggio, their starting point, just before dusk:

> ... with its lamps here and there, its broad streets and its
> numerous inhabitants, [Reggio] seemed to us a sort of Paris
> in bustle and splendour after such places as Cánalo and
> Gerace.

> We again settled ourselves in the Locanda Giordano, and
> closed our day by a call on Consigliere da Nava to thank him
> for the letters by which he had so ably and good-naturedly
> assisted us throughout our journey. Had we not indeed been
> furnished with these introductions, much of the interest, and
> nearly all the comfort, of our tour would have been denied
> us, and the recollections of Southern Calabria would have
> been far other than those we now enjoyed.[1]

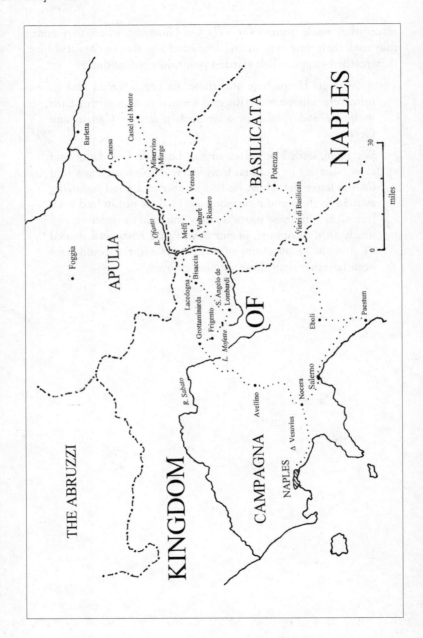

Chapter Ten
Basilicata (September-October 1847)

On 29 August the *Journal* resumes:

> A day of arrangements for past and future. Ciccio received his thirty-one dollars and a half, with four more for good service; whereon the angel guide burst into tears, and said he should have thought it quite enough to have worked for such nice people as we two for his stipulated pay only; he moreover declared that we appeared to him in the light of sons and nephews, and that he would live or die for us, as, how and when we pleased. Díghi-dóghi-dà was indeed a most meritorious fellow.[1]

This was not a final parting, however, for Lear retained Ciccio to accompany him to the spectacular mountain village of Pentedatilo, of which they had caught only a glimpse, before rejoining Proby to embark on a tour of the eastern half of Calabria. In a letter to Ann outlining their projected itinerary, he had warm words too for the latter , 'who I find one of the best creatures possible, & I dare say it was my own ill temper that made him seem hasty. We get on perfectly well together now, & I shall be very sorry to part with him.'[2]

After leaving Proby in Messina, Lear and Ciccio set out three days later armed with an introduction to the Don of Melito, which Lear had counted on using as his base. However,

> albeit Don Pietro [Tropaea] gave me a most friendly welcome, it is not to be disguised that his casino was of the dirtiest; and when I contemplated the ten dogs and a very unpleasant huge tame sheep which animated his rooms, I congratulated myself that I was not to abide long with them.

Moreover, it appeared to me that some evil, general or particular, was brooding over the household, which consisted of a wife, haggard and dirty in appearance and agitated in a very painful degree; an only son, wild and terrified in every look; and a brother and nephew from Montebello, strange, gloomy and mysterious in aspect and manner. The host also apologised for being ill at ease and unwell. The singular uneasiness of the whole party increased presently at the sound of two or three guns being fired, and Donna Lucia Tropaea, bursting into tears, left the room with all the family but Don Pietro, who became more and more incoherent and flurried, imparting the most astounding revelations relative to his lady and her situation, which he declared made all the family and himself most afflicted and nervous.

These excuses for so remarkable a derangement as I observed in the manner of all the individuals of the family did not deceive me, and I once more suspected, more strongly than ever, that 'something was to be foreseen'. The feeling was confirmed at supper-time, when the assembled circle seemed to have agreed among themselves that it was impossible to conceal their alarm, and a rapid succession of questions was put to me as to what I knew of political changes about to take place immediately.

'Had I heard nothing? Nothing? Not even at Reggio?'

'Indeed I had not.'

'Bosh! It was folly to pretend ignorance: I must be aware that the country was on the very eve of a general revolution!'

It was useless to protest, and I perceived that a sullen ill-will was the only feeling prevalent towards me from persons who seemed positive that I would give no information on a subject they persisted in declaring I fully understood. So I remained silent, when another brother from Montebello was suddenly announced, and after a few whispers a scene of alarm and horror ensued.

'The revolution has already begun!' shrieked aloud Don Pietro; sobs and groans and clamour followed, and the moaning hostess, after weeping frantically, fell into a violent fit and was carried out, the party breaking up in the most admired disorder, after a display, at least so it appeared to me, of feelings in which fear and dismay greatly predominated over hope or boldness.

As for me, revolution or no revolution, here I am in the toe of Italy all alone, and I must find my way out of it as best I may; so, wrapping myself in my plaid and extinguishing the light, I lay down in the front room on the bed allotted me, whose exterior was not indicative of cleanliness or rest.

Lear's instinctive distaste for sound and fury of any description disqualified him as an ally to the rebel cause. As he complained in a letter to Fortescue, 'What is the use of all these revolutions which lead to nothing? As the displeased turnspit said to an angry cookmaid.'

Hardly was I forgetting the supper scene in sleep, when a singular noise awoke me. After all, thought I, I am to encounter some real Calabrian romance, and as I sat up and listened the mysterious noise was again repeated. It proceeded from under my bed, and resembled a hideous gurgling sob four or five times reiterated. Feeling certain that I was not alone, I softly put out my hand for that never-to-be-omitted night companion in travelling – a phosphorus box – when before I could reach it my bed was lifted up by some incomprehensible agency below, and puffing and sobs, mingled with a tiny tinkling sound, accompanied this Calabrian mystery. There was no time to be lost, and having persevered in obtaining a light in spite of this disagreeable interruption, I jumped off the bed, and with a stick thrust hastily and hardly below the bed to put the intruder, ghostly or bodily, on to fair fighting ground – Baa-aa-a!'

Shade of [the Gothic-horror novelist] Mrs. Radcliffe! It was the large dirty tame sheep! So I forthwith opened a door into the next room, and bolted out the domestic tormentor.

For once, none of the host family was up to see them off in the morning, but when Ciccio was questioned on the significance of this he replied only with 'a clucking sort of glottal ejaculation; nevertheless, he seemed anxious and gloomy'.

The route to Pentedatilo lay along the bed of a steep-sided ravine and it was not until they worked their way up onto higher ground, almost directly beneath the village, that they caught their next sight of it:

> The appearance of Pentedatilo is perfectly magical, and repays whatever trouble the effort to reach it may so far have cost. Wild spires of stone shoot up into the air, barren and clearly defined, in the form (as its name implies) of a gigantic hand against the sky, and in the crevices and holes of this fearfully savage pyramid the houses of Pentedatilo are wedged, while darkness and terror brood over all the abyss around this, the strangest of human abodes. Again, a descent to the river and all traces of the place are gone, and it is not till after repassing the stream and performing a weary climb to the farther side that the stupendous and amazing precipice is reached; the habitations on its surface now consist of little more than a small village, though the remains of a large castle and extensive ruins of buildings are marks of Pentedatilo having once seen better days.

As soon as Lear got to work with his sketchbook

> the whole population bristled on wall and window, and the few women who passed me on their way to the hanging vineyards which fringe the cliffs low down by the edge of the river screamed aloud on seeing me and rushed back to their rocky fastnesses. As it is hardly possible to make these people understand ordinary Italian, a stranger might, if alone, be awkwardly situated in the event of any misunderstanding. Had the Pentedatilini thought fit to roll stones on the intruder, his fate must have been hard; but they seemed full with fear alone.

Not surprisingly, he chose discretion over valour and moved on higher up the ravine to Montebello, where he had an invitation to lunch with Don Pietro Amazichi. The latter,

> though receiving me with every kindness and hospitality, was as much agitated as my acquaintances at Mélito. It seems evident that coming events are casting rapidly deepening shadows, and in vain again do I try to persuade my hosts that I am not in the secret. 'It is <u>impossible</u>,' they said; 'you only left Reggio yesterday, it is true; but it is certain that the rev-

olution broke out last night, and everyone has known for days past what would happen.'

On which there was another scene. The lady of Montebello, less feeble than she of Mélito, gave way to the deepest affliction; her exclamation of 'My sons! My two sons! I have parted from them for ever in this world!' I shall not easily forget; and the husband strove to comfort her with such deep feeling that I became truly grieved for these poor people, ignorant though I was actually of pending circumstances.

By now thoroughly alarmed on his own account, Lear decided to return post haste in order to find out what was happening for himself. As it turned out, he was to witness the outbreak of the Risorgimento, the civil war that would convulse the whole of Italy for the next 20 years:

At the hour of one in the night we reached Reggio, and here the secret divulged itself at once. How strange was the scene! All the quiet town was brilliantly lighted up, and every house illuminated; no women or children were visible, but troops of men, by twenties and thirties, all armed, and preceded by bands of music and banners inscribed 'Viva Pio IX' or 'Viva la Constituzione', were parading the high street from end to end.

'What's happened, Ciccio?' said I.

'Oh, don't you see?' said the unhappy muleteer, with a suppressed groan. 'Oh, don't you see? It's a revolution! Díghi, dóghi, dà!'

No one took the least notice of us as we passed along, and we soon arrived at Giordano's Hotel. The doors were barred, nor could I readily gain admittance; at length the waiter appeared, but he was uproariously drunk.

'Is Signor Proby arrived by boat from Messina?' said I.

'Oh, what boat! Oh, what Messina! Oh, what beautiful revolution! Ai! ao! Orra birra burra – ba!' was the reply.

'Fetch me the keys of my room,' said I; 'I want to get at my trunk –'

'Oh, what keys! Oh, what room! Oh, what trunk! Ai, ai!'

'But where are the keys?' I repeated.

'There are no more keys,' screamed the excited cameriere; 'there are no more passports, there are no more Kings – no more laws – no more judges – no more anything – nothing except love, liberty, friendship and the constitution – there are the keys – ai! o-o-o-o-o-orra birra bà!!'

Without disputing the existence of love, liberty, friendship or the constitution, it was easy to see that matters were all out of order, so, taking Ciccio with me, I went hastily through the strangely-altered streets to Cavaliere da Nava's house. From him, whom with his family I found in serious distress, I heard that a concerted plot had broken out on the preceding day; that all the Government officials had been seized, he (da Nava), the Intendente and others being all confined to their houses; that the telegraph and the castle still held out, but would be attacked in a day or two; that the insurgents, consisting mostly of young men from the neighbouring towns and villages, had already marched into Reggio, and were hourly increasing in number; that on the opposite shore, Messina was also in full revolt; and that the future arrangements of the Government could only be known after time had been allowed for telegraphic communication between Reggio and Naples.

The Government officials are all naturally dejected, as nothing of their future fate is known, except so much as may be divined from the fact that no one has hitherto been maltreated. Thus, the agitation of the people at Montebello and Mélito; the suspicions of Don Tito and of the woodmen at Basilicò, and even those of the fat Baron Rivettini, were all fully explained and justified; for whether those persons were for or against the Government, the appearance of strangers on the very eve of a preconcerted revolt was enough to make them ask questions and put them all in a fuss.

I returned to the inn. As for what I should do, there seemed no will of my own in the matter; I might be arrested or exe-

cuted as either a rebel or a royalist – as things might turn out;
so there was nothing for it but to wait patiently.

He sat out the night and all the next morning in the hope of a boat
from Messina with news of events there and of Proby's likely fate, but
when none materialised he joined with others to persuade a 'very
reluctant' boatman to ferry them over the Strait,

> to a point about a mile from Messina, where we landed out of
> reach of the guns of the fort. Here I was glad at Nobile's Hotel
> to rejoin Proby, whose suspense had been equal to mine. The
> revolt at Messina has occasioned the death of fourteen or fif-
> teen men; but the Government has firm hold of the citadel.
> Distress and anxiety, stagnation and terror, have taken the
> place of activity, prosperity, security and peace. A steamer
> comes from Malta tomorrow, and I resolve to return to Naples
> thereby; for to resume travelling under the present circum-
> stances of Calabria would be absurd – probably impossible.

Their anxiety rose afresh the next morning when firing was heard
over the water from two men o' war sent to bombard Reggio, and
their relief when the Malta steamer duly arrived can be imagined.
They finally set sail just before dusk. As he watched the coastline
recede, Lear wrote:

> I leave the shores of Calabria with a grating feeling I cannot
> describe. The uncertainty of the fate of many kind and agree-
> able families – Da Nava, Scaglione, Marzano, &c. – it is not
> pleasant to reflect on. Gloom, gloom overshadows the mem-
> ory of a tour so agreeably begun.

Safely back at Naples, where the rebel forces had yet to stir, they
reaffirmed the decision to abandon Calabria. Lear resumed his
Journal a week later with a plan for a tour of Basilicata instead:

> To various towns in that province I have some good intro-
> ductory letters, from one of its greatest landed proprietors,
> and there is much [of] interest in that part of the Regno, par-
> ticularly in the country of Horace and some of the Norman
> castles of Apulia.

Their first objective was the Sanctuary of Monte Vergine, reached by the newly opened railway to Nocera and on by *caratella* to Avellino. From there,

> the path to the monastery is for more than three miles a very steep zig-zag, in overcoming which you are indulged with a fine view of Vesuvius rising from its velvet plain. Noble groups of chesnut-trees clothe the lower part of the mountain, and above their leafy heads is the craggy summit of the hill with the picturesque convent, which combine to make many a beautiful picture. This celebrated sanctuary, built on the site of a temple of Cybele, as several inscriptions and remains attest, was founded about 1100 A.D., and on account of its possessing a particularly miraculous image of the Virgin Mary (not to speak of the bones of Shadrach, Meshach and Abednego!) its sanctity is great.

Finding little to detain them there and discomfited by the sharp drop in temperature, they descended again apace. After another day spent sketching Avellino and its environs, they started out for their next goal, the volcanic lake of Mofette. Protracted negotiations ensued with the local *vetturini*, whose chicanery remained fresh in Lear's memory from his first visit to the Naples area nine years earlier, and when they finally settled on a fare it was only to find that the carriage road gave out well short of any point of habitation.

> Much search and earnest persuasion produced a half-witted old man with a donkey which might carry our small quantity of luggage, and after long hesitation he agreed to go with us to the Mofette, the way to which he knew, though he said he should not tempt Providence by going very near the spot. He also held out indistinct views of accompanying us all the way to Melfi if he were well paid. The more enlightened inhabitants of Grotta Minarda also said that we should have no difficulty in finding a delightful home at Frigento in the house of Don Gennaro Fiammarossa, who they declared was the wealthiest and most hospitable of living men – 'He is all money, and all heart; he owns Frigento, he owns everything.' So we set off, resolving to confide our destinies to the care of Don January Redflame.

Frigento itself turned out to be 'a miserable little town' with a single 'palpably disgusting' *osteria,* but they took heart from the appearance of the Don's mansion:

> We contemplated with pleasure the comfortable hall with crockery and barrels, and all kinds of neatness and luxury; and until Don Gennaro came, we were pressed to take a glass of wine by the steward and his very nice-looking wife.

> But lo! the great January arrived, and all our hopes were turned to chill despair! '<u>How</u> grieved he was not to be able to have the pleasure of receiving us, none but he could tell' – this he said with smiles and compliments, yet so it was. He was expecting an aunt, four cousins – nay, five – three old friends and four priests, who were to pass through Frigento on their way to a neighbouring town; they might come and they might not, but he dared not fill his house. But what of that? There was a capital inn at Frigento, one of the very best in Italy; he would take us there himself; it was time we should be sheltered for the night. And forthwith he led the way out into the street, overwhelming us with profuse expressions of compliment till, to our dismay and surprise, he stopped at the door of the very filthy osteria which we had ten minutes ago rejected with abhorrence as impracticable.

Once inside, they found civility but little else, and, after a supper of poached eggs, they finally took their rest 'in a granary on large heaps of grain, which had the advantage of cleanliness as well as novelty when considered as beds'.

Without even a cup of coffee to restore them, they were soon on their way again in the morning. Their route took them over a range of bare hills, which became 'ever drearier and less prepossessing till, as we neared a deep little valley, strong sulphureous odours warned us of our approach to the Mofette':

> The hollow basin in which lies this strange and ugly vapour bath is fringed on one side by a wood of oaks, behind which the mountain of Chiusano forms a fine background; but on the northern approach, or that from Frigento, the sloping hill is bare and terminates in a wide crust of sulphureous mud, cracked, dry and hollow at some little distance from

the pool, but soft and undulating like yeast at the brink of the little lake itself. The water, if water it be, is as black as ink and in appearance thick, bubbling and boiling up from a hundred springs which wrinkle its disastrous-looking surface; but when the liquid is taken out into any vessel, it is said – for we did not make the experiment – to be perfectly clear and cold. Whether or not birds can fly across or over the enchanted pool, I cannot tell, but as we found many stiff and dead on its brink – namely, two crows, four larks, three sparrows and eight yellow-hammers – it is but fair to conclude that the noxious vapours had something to do with stocking this well-filled ornithological necropolis; and as to ourselves, we found that to inhale the air within two or three feet of the water was a very unpleasing experiment, resulting in a catching or stupefying sensation, which in my own case did not entirely pass away for two or three days.

Possibly the strength and properties of this curious volcanic lake may differ at various seasons or states of the atmosphere; as for our guide, he implored us not to go near, and would not by any means be persuaded to go within a hundred yards of the 'accursed eccentricity', as he called it.

Lingering only for a quick drawing, they pressed on to the small town of St Angelo de Lombardi, arriving just as heavy rain set in:

We discovered a tolerable locanda and adapted ourselves to passing the rest of the day there. The hostess declared she had no food of any sort in the house, but the distinct odour of a roast fowl caused us to pay but little attention to her assertions; with the energy of hungry men we forced our way into the kitchen and laid violent hands on the detected viands, together with some eggs and anchovies – all intended for someone else.

They had less luck, however, with the accommodation, and the only warmth they could find to see them through the night was by sleeping fully clothed.

Although the rain had cleared by the morning, the landscape continued to offer little of interest:

The mountains on this part of the eastern side of Italy decrease by very slow gradations to the flat country near the shore... these undulating downs or plains grew sadly wearisome, and we were glad to spy the far-off top of a tower, which the foolish old man declared was the church of Bisaccia.

It was long, though, ere we arrived there, and when we did, in how odious a place did we find ourselves! So unwilling were the inhabitants to commit themselves by any attention to strangers that, for all the civility we met with, we might have had the plague. Most of the people loitering about to whom we spoke shrugged their shoulders and passed on, while a few indicated a very filthy osteria as the only place of accommodation – and which worse still, offered nothing to eat. Four priests gaze at us, with the shrug ignorant, as we again ask for food. A fifth says, 'It's a shame! Two well-heeled foreigners, and they don't know what to do, what to eat or where to lodge!' but his faint zeal is rebuked and extinguished by the others.

After a long hour of persuasion and quest, we are taken to another osteria, rather less filthy than No. 1, and here we unload our ass. But lo! to our additional dismay, the foolish old guide of Grotta Minarda suddenly vows he will go no further with us – 'How can I, with this little ass?' No animals or guide are to be procured here, Melfi is still eighteen miles off and there is the River Ofanto to be crossed in the way thither!

All sorts of evil seemed at once in array against us, so we took time to decide on future plans and, sending out for eggs and wine, we made a luncheon, to the best of our ability, among the half-naked children, dogs and dirt. All our endeavours of persuasion were now directed to induce the silly old man to go with us as far as the next town, Lacedogna, which, being a possession of Prince Doria (who had given me letters to his castle at Melfi), I thought promised some better chance of assistance on the journey than the forlorn place we were now halting in; and at length, by dint of bribes and appeals to his feelings, the old man relented, the last weight in the scale of our favour being a gift of three carp, which had been brought to us for sale and which we had innocently purchased, the same, on being boiled, proving highly odiferous. 'They're good for us, though not for you,' said the old gentleman on graciously accepting the present, and tying up two of the fish in his pocket-handkerchief for 'tomorrow' by way of waiting for the more perfect development of their flavour...

There we arrived about 2 or 3 p.m., and made instant inquiries for a horse. One, they said, was to be hired, so we engaged it hastily, for there was no time to be lost – Melfi is still twelve miles off. We sat in a wine-shop, unloaded the ass and paid the foolish man.

'Is the horse coming?' said we to the surrounding idlers.

'Yes, it is on the way: it will be here in half a minute.'

A quarter of an hour passes – half an hour – three quarters, and still no horse.

'Where is the horse?'

'Ah, signori, they are saddling it.'

It would soon be too late to start for Melfi, so we rushed to the stable indicated as containing the fabulous quadruped, and lo! there it was calmly lying down and evidently wholly guiltless of any attempt, passive or active, towards leaving Lacedogna. Moreover, a dark and surly woman said, 'It never was to be hired – it never was intended to go to Melfi – and it never shall.'

So, all our hopes vanishing, we were in a complete fix.

As they stood pondering their next move, a man appeared with a pair of mules, which they hired there and then for the vast sum of two ducats. When they finally reached their goal, it was

too dark to discern any of its beauties or failings. Yet the castle of Melfi, which we reach by a short ascent from the streets, is sufficiently imposing at this silent hour of night. There is a drawbridge, and sullen gates, and dismal courtyards, and massive towers, and seneschals with keys and fierce dogs – all the requisites of the feudal fortress of romance.

Signor Vittorio Manassei, the steward and agent of Prince Doria, received us most amiably and ushered us into magnificent halls, forming a strange contrast to our late sojourning places. Around were mirrors and gilded furniture in all the full splendour of Italian baronial style, and the perfect order and cleanliness of the establishment did high credit to the Roman agent's skill and taste.

Hardly believing their luck, Lear wrote the next day:

a delightful place of sojourn is Melfi, the first stronghold of Normans in Apulia. One of the towers of Roger de Hautville still exists, but the great hall, where Normans and Popes held councils in bygone days, is now a theatre. The present building dates from the sixteenth century, and the offices and other additions still later. The castle overlooks [or did, until brought low by an earthquake in 1851] the whole town of Melfi but no great extent of distant country, for one side of the horizon is wholly filled up by the near Monte Voltore, and the remainder by a range of low hills, so that the site of the town seems to have selected as much for concealment as for strength…

There is a formidable long gallery adjoining our room, full of old oak chests and older armour, and its windows are seized every now and then with terrible fits of rattling, so that one is apt to think old Andrea Doria's ghost may be walking about, if not that of some old Norman. We dined with the whole family today and found them very agreeable, particularly one of the daughters. Signora Manassei has, in speaking of the world of Melfi, that mixture of kindness and pity which characterises the true Roman manner. Then we loitered on vine terraces and under pergolate, and ate grapes in the large vineyards behind the castle; and, along with Signor Vittorio and his two merry daughters, examined all the older part of the building, the prisons, and the old hall used as a theatre in the last century… What a home one might make of the Castle of

Melfi, with its city below and its territory around – the beau
ideal of old feudal possession and magnificence.

After another day of this royal entertainment they took a reluctant
leave of the Manassei. Two horses were provided for them and a third
for the castle's factor, who was to act as their guide:

> Our large guardian, Don Sebastiano, was very obliging (he
> was extremely like Dr. Samuel Johnson seen through a mag-
> nifying glass and dressed in a tight blue jacket and trousers),
> but from having been Guardiano in the service of the king
> when he was staying at the Palazzo Doria and having then
> accompanied him in various hunting expeditions, the wor-
> thy man was so pompous, and so full of long stories of Royal
> doings, that his manner rather oppressed us, the more that
> being seventy-three years old, he seemed too venerable to be
> ordered hither and thither.

After some miles of rather unexciting terrain they decided to dis-
mount and

> proceeded to walk; but at this proceeding Don Sebastiano
> was horrified. The horses, he said, were not good, and he
> would return instantly to Melfi for others. In vain we assured
> him that Englishmen did occasionally walk as a matter of
> choice; this assertion he treated as wholly poetical.

In any event they reached Minervino, their stopover for the night,
in good time and received an equally warm welcome from their new
host, Don Vincenzino Todeschi. When they joined the family for
supper, he regaled them with

> statistics, commercial pursuits, railroads, and increasing facil-
> ities of communication, and other matters. 'Send any of your
> friends who come this way to me,' said he; 'to increase a con-
> nection all over the world should be the object of a liberal-
> minded man; knowledge and prosperity come by variety of
> acquaintance,' &c. &c. There were three sons also with their
> tutor, a gentlemanlike and well-informed abbate; and a very
> nice little girl, Teresa, who, her mother being dead, was evi-
> dently the family pet. The Fattore Don Sebastiano sat in

silence, though before supper he had been rather loquacious concerning the family Todeschi, who he looks down upon as nouveau riche [in] spite of the show drawing-room, chimney mirrors, carpets and tables full of nicknacks.

Their itinerary for the next day included both Canosa, the site of ancient Cannae and Hannibal's final battle with the Romans, and Castel del Monte, famous for the hunting palace of the medieval emperor Frederick Barbarossa. The two places were a good 15 miles apart, however, and as their timetable did not allow for both it was decided to split up for the day: Proby went to Canosa and Lear to Castel del Monte.

After five hours of hard riding over 'the dullest possible country', Lear was finally rewarded with the sight of his objective:

> It is built at the edge of these plains on one of the highest but gradually rising eminences, and looks over a prospect perfectly amazing as to its immense and singular character. One vast pale pink map, stretching to Monte Gargano and the plains of Foggia northward, is at your feet; southward, Terra di Bari and Terra di Otranto fade into the horizon; and eastward, the boundary of this extensive level is always the blue Adriatic, along which, or near its shore, you see, as in a chart, all the maritime towns of Puglia in succession, from Barletta southward towards Brindisi.

> The barren stony hill from which you behold all this extraordinary outspread of plain has upon it one solitary and remarkable building, the great hunting palace, called Castel del Monte, erected in the twelfth century by the Emperor Barbarossa or Frederick II. Its attractions at first sight are those of position and singularity of form, which is that of an octagon with a tower at each of the eight corners. But to an architect, the beautiful masonry and exquisite detail of the edifice (although it was never completed, and has been robbed of its fine carved-work for the purpose of ornamenting churches on the plain) render it an object of the highest curiosity and interest.

> The interior of this ancient building is also extremely strik-
> ing; the inner courtyard and great Gothic Hall invested with
> the sombre mystery of partial decay, the eight rooms above,
> the numerous windows, all would repay a long visit from
> anyone to whom the details of such architecture are wanting.

He had time for only a couple of detailed sketches and even then it
was past midnight before he got back to Minervino, but he considered the day well spent – as indeed did Proby, as Lear joked to
Fortescue: 'I believe he found one of Annibal's shoes or spurs – also a
pinchback snuffbox with a Braham lock belonging to a Roman genl.'

Although they were up again before dawn for some sketches of the
town, they then enjoyed another 'substantial' breakfast with their
host and so it was mid-morning before they were back on the road.

The 4,500-foot landmark of Monte Vulture pointed their way back
westwards and, although the day's ride was an easy one, they were still
some miles short of it when they stopped for the night at the old
Roman town of Venosa, the birthplace of Horace,

> which, both externally and internally a most picturesque
> place, stands on the brink of a wide and deep ravine, its
> cathedral and castle overlooking the whole area of habita-
> tions. Extremely lean streets paved from side to side with
> broad flags of stone like those in Naples, numerous bits of
> columns or capitals, medieval stone lions, and the machico-
> lated and turreted towers of the old castle, gave great hopes
> of great employ for the pencil.

> We easily found the house of Don Nicóla Rapolla, to whom
> Signor Manassei had addressed us, the principal proprietor
> of the place; it was an extremely large rambling mansion in a
> great courtyard, where granaries, stables and a profusion of
> pigeons and other domestic creatures indicated the wealthy
> man. Two ladies of considerable beauty, and graceful exteri-
> or and manners, informed us that Don Nicóla was from
> home, but his brothers, DD. Peppino and Domenico, hus-
> bands of the two ladies, soon joined and heartily welcomed
> us. Don Peppino, dressed in the extreme of Neapolitan fash-
> ion, and Donna Maria in a riding habit and hat, appeared to

our amazed senses as truly wonderful and unexpected objects in this land of Horace.

Presently Don Nicóla, a priest but head and eldest of the house and lord and master of all Venosa, came home, and renewed welcome followed; we were shown into very good rooms, containing four-post bedsteads, pier-glasses, wardrobes and other luxuries which Horatian ages knew not; and after a while we prepared ourselves in 'our best clothes' for supper, for our hosts are Neapolitan grandees of the first caste, and all their household arrangements exhibit good taste and order. As for the two ladies, they talk French as well as Italian and are infinitely agreeable...

In the morning they were taken on a tour of the 15th-century castle. Its features included a hall recently converted into a salon, replete with a grand piano; 'fearsome' dungeons, whose walls were scoured with the messages of desperate captives; stables equipped to hold 200 horses; and a deep moat surrounding the whole.

They returned at noon, only to find that lunch was still three hours away. It proved worth the wait, however:

the entertainment was excellent in all respects. The conversation is often on English literature – Shakespeare, Milton, &c., on whom there are various opinions; but all agree about 'quel Autore adorabile, Valter Scott!' The priest reads one of the novels once a month and the whole family delight in them, and are also equally conversant with other known English writers. The cuisine is of a much more recherché kind than is usually met with in the provinces, and we are particularly directed to taste this dish of seppia or cuttlefish, or to do justice to those mushrooms. The wines, moreover, are super-excellent, and the little black olives the best possible; and all things are well served and in good taste.

Coffee was then served in the library in the company of the town's other notables, followed by a four-hour soirée at the castle and a midnight supper back at the Casa Rapolla.

The next day was passed in similar style, beginning with a breakfast of coffee and hot buttered toast, the latter food being firmly believed by Neapolitans to be as much a part of English breakfast as roast beef is of dinner... Towards evening we walk out. The grandeur of these great men of Venosa is observable at every moment, in the obsequious demeanour of all the people we meet; as for the peasantry, they doff their hats a long way off and, crossing over to the opposite side of the street, stand like statues as we pass. After seeing the golden sun sink down behind Monte Vulture, we passed two or three hours in music, chess and drawing at Don Peppino's, returning to the evening meal at our host's.

It was 'with great regret' that they finally took their leave of the family and their erstwhile guide, but a still greater treat awaited them at Rio Nero:

If the provincial splendours of the Casa Rapolla had surprised us, what were they in comparison to the rich mansion of Don Pasqualuccio Catena, whither we had been directed by Signor Manassei, whom we found awaiting us with his son Pirrho. Here were halls and anterooms, and a whole suite of apartments for ourselves fitted up as well as those of any of the first palazzi of the capital.

When it came to lunch, however, there was one feature that they could have done without: 'the presence of a great Barbary ape, who made convulsive flings and bounces to his chain's length, and shrieked amain'.

They were then taken on a visit to the house of their host's brother, Don Tommas. It was 'a palazzo still finer than his own' – but without, they were relieved to find, a still larger ape.

Here were long galleries and large rooms, empty of all but a circle of sofas and glittering in all the novelty and magnificence of blue and gold papers, pedestals and busts, cornices and mirrors; and at the end of these apartments was one of still larger dimensions and supereminent splendour, where a grand pianoforte stood [in] the centre of the scene.

The lady of the house sang and played fifteen songs with terrible energy, and the master played four solos on the flute; after which they performed three extensive duets, till the night wore on and it was time to depart; but as it began to rain a little, these extremely obliging people ordered out their carriage and horses, and we were driven back to our host's two streets off. Such are the quasi-metropolitan 'finezze' of Rio Nero, a place full of thriving merchants and men of property, and rapidly rising as a commercial community by the production and manufacture of silk and other articles of luxury.

The next day they set off for the annual festa at the great monastery of San Michele, which they approached through magnificent beech woods:

> Soon through the branches of the tall trees we saw the sparkling Lake of Monticchio, and the Monastery of San Michele reflected in its waters. A more exquisite specimen of monastic solitude cannot be imagined. Built against great masses of rock which project over and seem to threaten the edifice, the convent (itself a picture) stands immediately above a steep slope of turf which, descending to the lake, is adorned by groups of immense walnut-trees. High over the rocks above the convent, the highest peak of Monte Voltore rises into the air, clad entirely with thick wood; dense wood also clothes the slopes of the hill, which spread as it were into wings on each side of the lakes. The larger sheet of water is not very unlike Nemi, on a small scale – only that the absence of any but the one solitary building, and the entire shutting out of all distance, makes the quiet romance of San Michele and its lake complete.

> Great numbers of peasants were arriving and encamping below the tall walnut-trees, forming a Fair, after the usual mode of Italians at their Feste; the costumes individually were not very striking, but the general effect of the scene, every part of it being clearly reflected in the water, was as perfectly beautiful as any I ever saw. We visited the chapel and the dark grotto of the patron saint (but the crowd of pilgrims in these cases makes this no pleasing part of Festa duty) and at noon, after drawing until rain began to fall, we came in to our two cells, which were already well cleaned out by the care of Don

Pasqualuccio Catena and arranged for our comfort with the
addition of a large dinner sent ready cooked from Rio Nero...

The long passage or gallery adjoining our rooms was full of
peasants sheltered from the weather by the monks of the
convent, and during half the night their jovial festivities were
very noisy, not to speak of the proximity to our chamber
door of asses and mules which frequently brayed and out-
noised the clamour of an improvisatore and four or five bagpipers in full practice, as well as some large choral parties
employed in singing, in a very terrestrial manner, spiritual
songs concerning the miracles of S. Michele.

This was to be the climax of their tour. Setting out again from Rio
Nero two days later, they were soon on the carriage way to Potenza,
'as ugly a town for form, detail and situation as one might wish to
avoid'. From there they took a caratella to Vietri di Basilicata, which
was, by contrast,

full of really fine scenery and material for good landscape,
and left a strong impression of beauty on our minds, though
every succeeding hour brought fresh charms to view. It is
hardly possible to find a more beautiful day's drive in any
part of the Regno di Napoli than this, the road passing
through a constant succession of lovely scenes to reach Eboli.

At Eboli they stayed at the inn that had been the scene of Lear's
comical misunderstanding over the bill nine years earlier, though
without incident this time.

The next morning they made a brief return to Paestum, before continuing on to the rail-head at Nocera and then, on 5 October, back
to Naples.

The *Journal* concluded:

Our tour is done. It has wanted the romance of Calabria, and
sometimes has it been too hurried; yet it has had its pleas-
ures, and has added many agreeable memories to an already
large store.[3]

Chapter Eleven
Florence and The Riviera (1848–64)

On his return to the Eternal City 10 days later, Lear reported to Fortescue that 'Rome is full of fuss and froth'.[1] This had less to do with the approach of the forces of revolution under the leadership of Garibaldi than with the onset of the social season. As he wrote again in February 1848, not only were the English again present in strength, but

> the variety of foreign society is delightful, particularly with long names: e.g., Madame <u>Pul-itz-neck-off</u>, and Count Bigenouff; Baron Polysuky, & Mons. Pig – I never heard such a list. I am afraid to stand near a door, lest the announced names should make me grin. Then there is a Lady Mary Ross and a most gigantic daughter – whom Italians wittily call 'the great Ross-child', and her mama 'Ross-antico'.

The recent loss of 'my oldest Roman friend, good kind Lady Susan Percy', was offset, he assured Fortescue, by

> your introduction to [Thomas] Baring: he is an extremely luminous & amiable brick, and I like him very much, & I suppose he likes me or he wouldn't take the trouble of knocking me up as he does, considering the lot of people he might take to instead.[2]

This was indeed the beginning of a lifelong relationship, as Baring, later Earl of Northbrook, became one of Lear's most loyal and generous patrons.

In a letter to his sister written on the same day, Lear reassured her that 'I am neither skinned nor robbed, but quite well.' Nevertheless, he once again firmly deterred her from joining him:

> My dear Ann, you must put quite from you all idea of coming abroad – or more especially here – for Italy is in a very uncertain state indeed. A man could find his way out of disturbances, but you could not easily do so. Nor, during the two years I may yet remain abroad, shall I be fixed – for my object being to gain materials for future home work, I shall be here & there continually.[3]

A month later he wrote more specifically of his future plans:

> I have a most advantageous invitation from Corfu – to come to stay there free of expense in April, & to see the Greek islands with all kinds of agreeable facilities. A friend (not a very old one) has a Govt. situation there, & would do anything to make me enjoy such a tour, & possibly would accompany me to some of the islands.[4]

This new connection, another introduction of Fortescue's, was George Bowen, then President of the University of Corfu and later Chief Secretary to the High Commissioner of the Ionian Islands, then a British protectorate. By March 1848 everything was fixed – and none too soon, as Ann was told:

> the political [news] is not agreeable, as all the north of Italy gets more & more disturbed, & Sicily, you perhaps know, has quite shaken off Naples – all but the Citadel of Messina, which the King's troops still hold.[5]

Lear had arranged to sail via Ancona and Trieste, but on the 28th he wrote again to say that, following 'the unexpected events in Vienna & Lombardy' – Austria's refusal to countenance requests for independence in the north, and the subsequent insurrection led by the King of Sardinia and Piedmont –

> I could not go up as I expected to Ancona – first, because the Trieste boats have ceased running at certain times; secondly, because the whole road there is full of troops & there is neither food nor conveyance.[6]

He eventually succeeded in booking a passage from Naples on a steamer to Malta. It was from the safety of Valletta, that he declared, not surprisingly: 'I was truly glad to leave Rome at the last.' His landlady there had not been so happy to see him to go:

> Every time poor old Giovanina came into the room she said she was bringing this or doing that for the last time, & went out in tears; poor old lady – she is a kind-hearted creature & very sorry to lose me – which after 10 years is not wonderful. On the Friday morning (March 31st) I left very early – & such a sobbing & crying never was! I sold her all my furniture at a mere nominal price, as she had been so good a landlady & I did not like to take much money from her.
>
> My journey down to Naples by diligence was most extremely pleasant – though naturally most unlike any previous one I had ever made. It would be quite impossible to make you understand how a few short months have changed all things & persons in Italy – for indeed, I can hardly believe what passes before my own eyes. Restraint & espionage has given universal place to open speaking & triumphant liberal opinions. One of my fellow passengers was a Neapolitan noble, exiled for 16 years; when he saw Vesuvius first, he sobbed so that I thought he would break his heart. Naples I found yet more unsettled & excited than I had left Rome. No one could tell what would happen from one hour to the next. The King still reigns, but I cannot think he will long do so... We left the harbour at noon on the 6th & truly glad was I to be out of Italy, I assure you – not from any fear of danger, but because the whole tone of the place is worry, worry, worry – & I am sick of it, having lived in it so long in quieter times.[7]

Contrary to Lear's expectations, the Bourbon King hung on to his southern throne for another 12 years and, although Garibaldi succeeded in taking Rome that November, the French soon intervened to restore the Pope to the Holy See. In the north the rebels were similarly crushed by the Austrians at the Battle of Novara, leaving the flame of the Risorgimento to be nurtured by Victor Emmanuele II, the successor to the Piedmontese throne, and his chief minister, Cavour.

Lear's return to Italy was likewise deferred and Corfu became his main base for the next 15 years from 1848 to 1864. During that time he made extensive tours of the eastern Mediterranean, visiting mainland Greece and Albania (out of which came another illustrated travelogue, *Journals of a Landscape Painter in Greece and Albania*), as well as Turkey, Syria, Lebanon, Palestine, Jordan and Egypt.

He also spent three years back in England before the climate finally got the better of him again. With the object of mastering the techniques of oil and, in particular, figure painting, he enrolled as a pupil in the Royal Academy Schools. However, he completed only one of the nine years of the full course. He had probably come to the conclusion that he had no prospect of maintaining himself over such a length of time, but he had also become attracted to the more naturalistic style of the Pre-Raphaelite Brotherhood, whose founding father, 'Daddy' Holman Hunt, adopted him as one of his personal protégés.

Another friendship that he struck up in London, with Alfred Tennyson, was to have an even larger influence on the future course of his life. He had long been a fervent admirer of the Poet Laureate's work, some of which he had set to music, and he now conceived the idea of producing an edition of Tennyson's verse incorporating 200 of his own illustrations, an ambition that increasingly preoccupied him over the remaining 35 years of his life. He also found in Tennyson's long-suffering wife, Emily, a kindred spirit on whom he could unload his own complex emotional burdens. She once wrote to him: 'I have a dim sad feeling we must help each other, those who at all understand each other & love each other.'[8]

On Corfu Lear forged two more intimate relationships. The first of these was with Franklin Lushington. As with Fortescue, Lear first met him as a good-looking young man fresh down from university, but, while the former's attraction had lain in their shared sense of spontaneous fun in each other's company, Lushington struck a somewhat deeper chord, albeit one that was never fully reciprocated. There is no evidence to support certain allegations that Lear ever saw the relationship as more than platonic: indeed, he expressed the hope to Emily Tennyson that 'were he [Lushington] married & settled here, such life would be his greatest blessing'.

As for his own marital hopes, which he had first spoken of to Gould in 1841, it was only now, in 1856, that he found someone in whom he could seriously nurture them. Helena Cortazzi's father was Italian and her mother was English (a relative of the Hornbys of Knowsley), but she herself had never been outside Corfu. Among her attractions Lear listed 'her complete knowledge of Italian, French & Greek, her poetry [including a verbatim knowledge of Tennyson] & magnificent music, but withal her simple & retiring quiet'.[9] However, when he returned to Corfu in November 1857, from the summer season of exhibitions in London (during which he sold a large oil of Corfu for £500) and an extended stay on Fortescue's Irish estates, it was to find that the Cortazzi family had left the island. 'If Helena Cortazzi had been here, it would have been useless to think of avoiding asking her to marry me,' he wrote to Fortescue.[10] Three months later he heard that they were moving to Russia and quoted Tennyson in his diary for 1858 (the first of the 30 that have survived): 'So sinks the setting sun.'[11]

During the summer Lushington resigned his post as a judge of the Supreme Court of the Ionian Islands, after a row with George Bowen. Lear went back to England with him, but William Clowes, an old friend from his Knowsley days, then suggested that they return to Rome together and Lear was soon caught up in an agony of indecision: 'To start at once for Rome with unfinished work? To go to Madeira? To try to complete the 5 paintings here?... I cannot fix any point, but meanwhile groan.'[12] He half wondered whether he ought not to set up home with his sister again, but concluded that 'our being together would not suit long... her being with one an ever increasing sadness: so good, & yet so unable to be a companion'.[13] In the end it was the weather – and Clowes's persistence – that made up his mind for him.

They arrived in the Eternal City on 1 December. Lear was at first anything but glad to be back, principally because, as he told Ann, 'everything is far more expensive than formerly, & no rooms suitable or comfortable to live in can be had under £65 or £70 [per annum], & even these are full of drawbacks'. He eventually settled for a 3-year lease on some rooms in the Via Condotti that were 'new & very good, but cost nearly £80 a year'. He was partially consoled by the number of old friends still there, notably James Uwins, Penry Williams and the Knights – he found Isabella 'now always confined to her bed, but if possible brighter & more lively than 20 years back'.[14] Yet it was not until the arrival on Christmas Eve of Giorgio Kokali, his Suliot servant and general factotum from Corfu, that he finally felt at home.

On 1 January 1859 Lear reported to Ann that: 'In many ways – the cleanness of the streets – goodness of shops – & new houses – Rome is certainly greatly improved, & altogether I begin to be a good deal reconciled, & happier.' The crate containing his unfinished oils followed with gratifying promptness. He was soon 'hard at work & making money' in his studio, while another room was set aside for displaying water colours and sketches to potential purchasers: 'One season will prove how far my chance of living comfortably is a good one, & then it will be a question whether it may not be the best plan to establish myself here entirely.'

The new arrangements began promisingly. In the first three months he attracted '7 or 800 people'; better still, 'the great difference between this & England, as to Art, is that everyone comes here with the express purpose to buy something'.[15] The high point came with the visit of the young Prince of Wales (the future Edward VII) on 29 March, which Lear described afterwards in his diary:

Nobody could have nicer & better manners than the young prince, who was generally intelligent & pleasing. I was afraid of telling or showing him too much, but I soon found he was interested in what he saw, both by his attentiveness & by his intelligent few remarx... when I said 'Please tell me to stop, Sir, if you are tired by so many,' he said, '<u>Oh dear no!</u>' in the naturalest way. Altogether I was much pleased with this hour...[16]

Once again, however, politics intervened. After a month of rumour and counter-rumour, war was finally declared again between Austria and the two allies, Piedmont and France. For Lear the news was particularly galling. As he told his sister:

this turn of affairs makes my having settled here at such great expense a very sad thing for me, as no English will come here if there is a continuance of war, & my only chance of getting away in summer-time would be to fill up my purse in winter. Moreover, I cannot give up these rooms – the rent of which must go on come what will – nor can I readily afford to move back all my pictures, etc. It is indeed a pretty mess.[17]

On 15 May he joined his compatriots on the steamer to Marseilles and then spent another summer in England, after dispatching Giorgio back to his family on Corfu. The news from Italy remained far from encouraging, until suddenly, in November, the French Emperor Napoleon III, without notice to his Piedmontese allies, signed the Treaty of Villafranca, which proposed to refer the whole matter of Italy's possible reunification to a Congress of European Powers.

Just before the New Year of 1860 Lear was back in Rome, where he was presently rejoined by the faithful Giorgio. 'Very few people are here, & no more will come now. The streets are literally empty, & very great poverty & consequently dissatisfaction prevails', he told Ann.

Worse still, everything is so <u>extremely uncertain</u> & disagreeable that I am not likely to remain here beyond the end of Feb. – when I think I shall return to Jerusalem. I am sorry to tell you Giorgio is not as happy & contented as he used to be... not but that he is always diligent & obedient, but that I find him crosser & more moping – not having a human being but myself to speak to [in Greek], & the rain, etc. preventing all going out. (For I must tell you it has rained, rained, rained, rained <u>continually</u>.)

There was another reason for Giorgio's discontent, as Lear now suddenly discovered:

> Mr. Giorgio Kokali is married & has 3 children! The fact of his never telling me this is one of the curious points of secretive character the Orientals always have. Fancy in nearly 5 years never saying a word of his wife and children!!! Yet the other night he told me all this, saying 'I had never asked him', so he thought it not right to tell me.'[18]

He could not then have guessed at the consequences of this revelation. In March the political situation deteriorated still further, culminating in a riot following a demonstration to mark Garibaldi's birthday. Lear wrote to Fortescue:

> It is impossible to give you an idea of the state the people are in. As many as 10 patrols in a body are placed at every other street end all down the Corso, so no movement is possible... I have become so fat from want of exercise that you would not know me, so I attach a portrait.[19]

Giorgio too was still evidently able to maintain a sense of humour:

> I said in fun, after the affair in the Corso of the 19th, 'George, if you go out, do not forget to take a basket with you, to put your head in if it happens to be cut off.' On which he said: 'No sir, I take soup tureen – hold him better.'[20]

Soon, however, Lear's patience was at an end: 'Oh God! Can any lousy place of lice & shit be like unto this pigstye of impostors!' he wrote in his diary on 11 April, with unwonted ferocity. By then, as he had told his sister in March, he had made up his mind to return to England for the summer, before heading for the Near East:

I am more & more inclined to leave here in 15 days or so & walk along the Corniche (& Riviera) from Pisa, taking G[iorgio] with me to Genoa, sending him thence to Marseilles & home. It cannot be right for me to keep him away from those he ought to be with, even if he wished it – & poor fellow, he is often pulled both ways. And, respecting the walk, altho' I leave much of my work unfinished, yet I gain more variety of subject for future illustration – so much the more if I write a journal. The sending my cumbrous boxes to England will be a great expense doubtless – & this house for a year to come – & much more – but all this has been inevitable for a long while past, & in no mode could Rome be possible for me.[21]

They finally left Rome on 8 May and sailed to Genoa, from where they took 'a very small & crowded steamer' to La Spezia, their new starting point, leaving the leg from Pisa until the following year. Although the mooted journal never materialised, Lear did keep a very full record of the walk in his diary, starting on 12 May, when in their hotel

there was a sort of table d'hôte – 2 French & 2 Anglais, the lady of which latter was a fierce Protestant, & although acknowledging the excellences of the people of these parts, could not allow they were different from those of Rome in reality – 'both are in darkness, & the glorious message of the Gospel truth has not yet reached the poor creatures.' She waxed very eloquent, & I wished her anywhere [else]. In the evening G. & I walked along the beach – very pleasantly – from 8 to 9. The day is lovely – but there are signs of change.

May 13th. Slept well. Rose at 5 1/2. As I expected, clouds. But, coffee had, we left at 6 – in a boat, with one old man, a simple soul, who said 'I am called really Francesco, but no one uses my name: they call me Gallina, & I always reply to

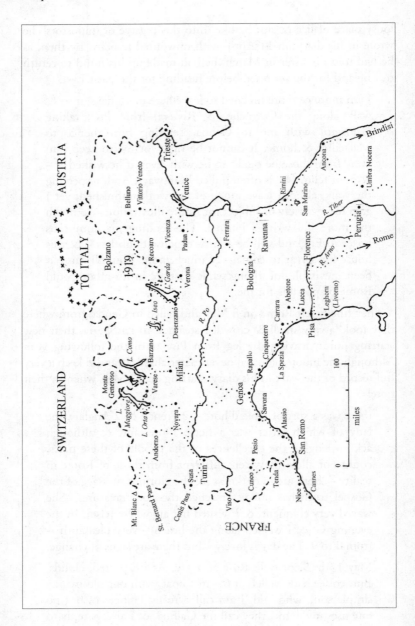

it.' The lake & gulf was very lovely, but the wind rose, & a swell, which made me miserable – so I was put on shore opposite P[orto] Venere, & sent back the boat. Here I & G. walked along dangerous paths, & I drew till 11 – when it rained, & all seemed dismal. Returning to a hole in the rox, we lunched, & when the rain ceased came fourth & went on to P. Venere. (The firing from the fort & the echoes were wonderful.) P.V. is very picturesque – its black & white striped marble church, etc., etc. – we also went up to the fort, & about the streets, where the people caught the rain in pans & spoke rapid dialex. Returning by the road, rain always; beautiful views – always like Corfu. School of marine youths. Polite & kindly people. Tho' wet, a pleasant walk. By 5 we were at S. Francesco, & soon [back] in the town – a garden of roses was a pleasant discovery. Dined at 7, the 2 French folk only. Illuminations afterwards, & short walk with G. & talk with landlord.

May 14th. Rained all day. Cookery here 'very fishy'... <u>food vile</u>.

May 15th. Every promise of a fine day. The giro of the gulf is pretty, & the views of La Spezia. Streams – bye & bye, a world of bog & slosh – & a nice woman who, having passed it, cocked her feet & legs amazing. She recommended a 'collo' – & so a lad came, who carried me over pick aback, & G. afterwards. Route along the shore & bye & bye leaving it, thru' gardens, & again bits of seaside. Thence, a long rise through a close-clinging valley & a sharp ascent ending in a lovely view of Lerici. Descent (& the courtesy of the people it is impossible to imagine) & so to the High Street of S. Terenzo, clean compared with southern towns in general. On the beach is the house of Byron & Shelley – sad looking; but the views are very glorious.

Hence by the rocks, & through a superb olive wood to Lerici, a large town. G. & I had some wine & ate our breakfast (we arrived at 9) in the osteria of a very political female ('Roma, città santa, populo curruto,' quoth she). All we observed in the town was pleasant & agreeable – such beautiful women & children! At 10 began to walk back & draw,

& so it was 1 before I got to S. Terenzo – & 3? before I had done the view above it. At 4 bathed. By 6 it was a little raining, & we got to the mud marsh, where after a time a strong peasant came to carry us over. But his foot striking on a stone, he stumbled & nearly threw me; after a time we righted & came off all right. The peasants beyond were 'deeply interested' by the scene, when I waved my hat, all shouted with laughter. Rainbow, as last night; arrived at 7. Hotel empty. Drank & ate. Communicative waiter. As pleasant a day as for years past.

May 16th. Rose early. Clouds – but calm. At 6 in Gallina's boat, & at 8 landed at Mr. Smith's in Palmária. A curious little snuggery, but shown by the most obliging & kindly master. After I had drawn 3 scraps (Byron's house is annually lived in now by a Captain Cross, who resides at Pisa), we left the good man & went up the new broad road. I not over-well, & George, poor fellow, very gloomy. At the top of the Island, about 11, we sat down to draw & lunch. I found that G. had taken a lot of onions out of Mr. S.'s garden, & as far as I could I showed him how that was wrong. But I could not in any way convince him it was so, & he was so irritable & glum I thought it right to say no more. A little later he set a lot of dry grass on fire with 'matches', & I thought all the hill would be alight.

By then – 12 – a thunderstorm had given warning, & we came to the shore & hailed a boat, & crossed to the other side by 1. Walking slowly, & drawing at times, brought us to Porto delle Grazie, where (X) [indicating an epileptic attack]... By degrees we went on, but a most violent storm rose over Lerici & obliged us to halt in a small cottage where was the master & sea captain & his family all preternaturally proper & kind. G.'s ways with the children are very nice. He was evidently thinking of the girl all morning, for he burst out about 'darlings' later. We were nearly wet through in one of the showers afterwards, but got home dry. The mountains came out most gloriously, with rainbows & all kinds of wonderments. Dinner is never good here. Garibaldi it seems has reached Marsala.

May 17th. Rose at daylight – all very lovely & bright. G. & I set off at 6 along the road – I drawing from time to time, anxious to secure the mountains. It is impossible to imagine any more 'Italian' hours, & scenes, than these: all the women going to mass, quiet & respectable; the soft loud bells sounding over the clear calm sea; the endless brightness of foliage, brusque original independent fig – dependent vine – tremulous olive. Drew incessantly – the mountains being like glass. It became hot, but we went on. One snake... Soon, by 12, to the rocks of Porto [delle] Grazie, where I finished my yesterday's sketch & then we went to a sort of osteria near the shore.

A day's sketching was then lost to thick mist, but by the next morning it had cleared sufficiently to allow them to set out for Riomaggiore, the first of the five towns known as the Cinqueterre,

a narrow town of one street, wholly ugly, women carrying immense slates... Ascend another tremendous staircase, like the side of a house, & rest at 9?; then more ascent, & corner bits not 8 inches broad, over the sea, so hideous that I funked – all the more that a steamer bumped below my feet. By 10 reached Manarola, the 2nd town – nearly as unpicturesque & at the very bottom of a stair.

The difficulty of getting a view persuaded Lear to abandon the coast for the higher path, which they eventually reached somewhere above Vernazza. From that height the village looked

like a small heap of dominoes against the sea, & all the landscape is gloomy & unpleasant. It would have been quite impossible to visit all the 5 towns, owing to the time taken up by crossing the steep abysses in between.

The path continued to rise dizzily, and at one point Lear slipped and tumbled 60 feet down the slope before being saved by a chestnut tree. Shortly afterwards he caught a glimpse of Monterosso, the last of the Cinqueterre, which 'appeared more picturesque than the others,' but by then he had thoughts only for a comfortable bed for the night, and pressed on to Levanto.

There he was woken by a caged blackbird at four, but his preparations for an early start were frustrated by the onset of rain and he hired a small vehicle drawn by a black pony. The driver did not take my fancy, being violent. Just out of the town a white ass was brought & tied on with ropes, but zigzagged more than my head could bear, considering the precipitous sides of the road. So I got out & walked – & walked on to the end of the day...

At the Hotel d'Europe in Sestri he retired to bed 'utterly sleepy'. The only incident he recorded there was an encounter with a man who informed him that 'I speek English, was twenty, yes, ten months in Birmingham, oui, in all your land toujours, and sounded one organ. Goodbye!'

After a day's rest for his weary legs, Lear was off again at five the next morning. The sun too was up, and he took the opportunity to make sketches of Lavagna and Chiavari before going on to Rapallo, a 'dirty & dull place':

Poste Hotel – ill-tempered hostess; particularly filthy room & nasty house. Ordered dinner & went out with G., but it rained, & I could hardly do anything. Bay of Rapallo dead & shut up. Women make lace. All is a contrast to the La Spezia province. Dinner not very bad. Then insisted on, & got, a better room, & came to bed at 8. No sleep; fleas, bugs, gnats, ants, noisy geese, fidgety sea, lightning all night, crying child, & all sorts of disturbances... I find the Portofino promontory can't be walked round, so I have ordered a car for tomorrow.

Finding nothing worth drawing on the final leg to Genoa, he arrived there in time for a late breakfast and took rooms in the Hotel Feder. After inquiring about a berth for Giorgio via Malta to Corfu, he returned to dine and found himself seated next to a Madame Buonoparte-Wise: 'a bouncing & tremenjus fat little female is this lady, but bears marks of great beauty – tho' the expression is not exactly likeable. After dinner walked out with G., & returned to bed at 9.35.'

When they went to buy Giorgio's ticket in the morning, they were informed that his passport required a visa from the British Consulate, which, for once, speedily obliged. Among those on the quay were the son of Charles Waterton, the eccentric whose exploits Lear had first learned of in Rome in 1841 (see Chapter 3), and a mutual friend, Richard Cholmondeley:

> At 8 we all breakfasted together, very pleasantly. Then they to my room. Then packed. At 12 paid G. his 25 Napoleons, & gave him his ticket... Good George – may you reach your mother & wife & children well! At 1 lunched with Waterton & C., much fun. W. bears a certain resemblance to his family. At 2 C. & I saw Waterton off in a boat. At 3.20 saw dear good George Kokali to a boat. He said one 'Grazie' in his own quiet way that was worth a heap of words. I have tried to do as well for him as I could, & trust he has gained by coming to me. A better human being I have not known.

> At 4.30 walked out with C. to the Acqua Sola, & to the Correrdi Cafè, where we had ices, etc. That street is assuredly beautiful. Then downwards, till at the A. Doria C[orso]. went back. I went on alone, beyond the lighthouse; so splendid a city hardly exists as Genoa! Returning, by the lower street, saw the Malta Steamer, with many boats round, just going off, & by my glasses I could see G. at the bowsprit, standing, calmly enough, & probably smoking. At the Hotel by 7.30, & dinner with C. at 8 – pleasant enough.

As they were both bound for England, they took the train together to Turin. This being his first visit to the city, Lear took time to

> walk 'all about the place', which greatly pleased me – nothing more than the Obelisk commemorating the downfall of Ecclesiastical supremacy. Then I went across the Po, & up to the Capuccini, whence the view is very grand, & returned by 6.30 or 7 by the public gardens. The whole morale & physique of Turin is refreshing after Rome.

The next morning he met up with Cholmondeley again, to take the train to the rail-head at Susa, the gateway to the Alpine pass of Mount Cenis:

> Arrived at 11.45. Very lovely morning & bright, cultivation, mulberry, etc. Very picturesque near Susa, but [a] high wind rose & became frightful. At the Hotel d'Avenue we got some

lunch. Tried to walk, but couldn't. C. seemed to wish to go on today, but it is not really possible. So we agree to go by Post tomorrow, & arrange accordingly…

May 28th. Clear & bright. Rose at 4. Coffee, & the carriage packed, started at 5. Walked up the steep ascent. Above a village (Giaglione?) the view over the valley of the Dora is most exquisite – a world of walnut foliage softened with light & distance, with snowy summits on each side. But beyond this, the views are dull & uninteresting; this only is one of the widest & loveliest of Alpine views. 7 1st Post (Molaretto?), Italy shut out. 7.45 short cut cuckoos – calves, cows & humans all going to Susa fair. 8 French artillery Capt. – & dog. 9 C. came up; snow. 9.30 road interesting, landscapingly; zigzags. 9.40 top of pass. 9.50 Barriera. 10.30 2nd post, M. Cenisio. Dreary lake of ice & snow – fog – fall of snow, rain, gloomy descent… Altogether the M. Cenis pass is not to be compared to the others for beauty & grandeur.[22]

Back in England, Lear decided to stay on for the winter in order to complete a major (nine-foot-wide) painting, 'The Cedars of Lebanon', which he hoped would finally establish his reputation in oils. Accordingly he took a room in the Oatlands Park Hotel near Weybridge, which boasted several large cedars in its grounds. Although the weather was unusually severe, he worked for the most part out of doors, but in March 1861 an event occurred that chilled him as bitterly as any frost: the death, after a brief illness, of Ann, his sister and surrogate mother. 'I am all at sea & do not know my way an hour ahead, ' he told Fortescue. 'I shall be so terribly alone. Wandering about may do some good perhaps.'[23]

It was in Italy again that he sought solace. Having completed 'The Cedars', and armed with a commission for two paintings of Florence from Lady Frances Waldegrave, a leading society belle of her day and Fortescue's long-standing love (she would eventually marry him the following year after the death of her elderly husband), he set out in the last week of May. The train to Folkestone was

> very shaking, & 2 darling little children, who with a nurse were in the carriage, were not frightened, but half-ill. So I

took the boy – 4 years old – on my knee & the girl in my arms, & told them my long name & all kinds of nonsense till they forgot the shaking bother... I <u>never</u> saw 2 sweeter & more intelligent children than those 2, & I <u>longed</u> to keep them both.[24]

His heart was similarly touched when the young Englishman with whom he found himself sharing a hotel room in Turin showed him a portrait of his fiancée which Lear found 'very nice, & not unlike Gussie Bethell':[25] the 23-year-old daughter of Lord Westbury, the Lord Chancellor and one of Lear's earliest patrons, she was already beginning to displace Helena Cortazzi in his affections.

Lear had arranged for Giorgio to meet him at Leghorn, but after three days of waiting in vain he despaired of his servant's appearance and took the train to Florence. 'Cavour is dead,' he noted in his diary. '"Dead" is a word – but Cavour does not die; yet this is a dreadful calamity for all Italy.'[26] The next day, 7 June, he received a letter from Giorgio explaining that he had not yet set out from Corfu because of the illness of one of his sons. The view from Petraija, as required by Lady Waldegrave, was another source of disappointment:

the foliage being meagre, & little at command... It does not seem possible to me to <u>paint</u> the Petraiji, but to go constantly in a carriage & <u>draw</u> all I can – I doubt painting here at all. Meanwhile poor George may not come for weeks...[27]

After a further fortnight of fruitless visits to the station, he was

pretty well resolved to write off to George at once, bidding him now <u>not</u> to come... when lo! at 11.15 – George Kokali! Just as if he had never been away! (The train had come to grief at Pisa, & he had hurt his face.)[28]

Lear's spirits revived accordingly. By 3 July the paintings were completed and he was able to write that 'the last two weeks at Florence, growing better as I was & constantly occupied, were of the happiest for a long time past'.[29]

They then set out, via Pistoia and Lucca, to complete the Pisa–La Spezia leg of their Riviera walk, held over from the previous year. Having booked in at the Hotel Vittoria in Pisa, they went out beyond the walls, along various hot roads, to find a place for a view. It was not hot, however, as the sun hardly shone at all. Drew, near the railway – vine festoons. Walk by various stagnant ditches. See great snake. Return at 10. The Pisa group of buildings are assuredly a wonder.

In Lucca Lear savoured

a vast charm about Lucchese life – so industrious & respectable are the peasants – so neat & quiet; oxen carts – large whitey-grey beasts with red bellrope tassels anti-fly about their eyes; barrows of pine cones; brook & no end of washing; endless hemp, which tho' lovely to the eye, is disgusting to the nose; women with plain triangle white or coloured shawls. All the Bagni di L[ucca] hills are in heavy cloud.

However, the drive on to Pietrasanta was

most lovely. What vines! from high abeles & willows, & crosswise, triple & quadruple festoons; reed-canes; mulberries; groves of tall thin olives, chesnut, acacia, abele, cypress, willow – more enchanting fertility it is impossible to see, with the great slopes of olive hills above, higher & higher.

Another day's climb brought them to the quarries of Carrara, 'very interesting & finely surrounded by mountains. Marbles is cheap, as the doors & windows show,' but Lear concluded that

I should not like to live in Carrara: apart from the fact of the mountain grandeur being all torn up continually & artificialized, everything is one great click-click rap-tap hammer-clamour chip-chipping of marble... cattle with Thessalian wheeled carts, ducks, & multitudinous calves seem a staple of Carrara besides marble, which breaks out in vases & busts, steps, window edges & ledges & all kinds of ways.

Even after a night at Sarzana the chipping & hammering was still ringing in his ears, and he was more than relieved to hear the sound of the sea breaking on the shore at La Spezia.

Walked with G. to the Lever's; all there, & made me stop to dine. Miss L. is a pretty warm-hearted nice girl, & even at my age I should not think myself safe if I saw much of her. Played & sang... Dinner at 3.30 (Lever in his boat & swimming). Talk with Julia L. Little old man singing to a guitar – Il Barbiere. Walk with Mr. & Miss L.; what a heavenly place is this gulf. Back to tea, & sang again. Kindly people. Met the Suliot near S. Vito; at Villa d'Odessa at 10. The steamers only go, it seems, Mondays & Fridays to Genoa – & carriage progress seems expensive & difficult.

July 15th. Rose at 5. Off with G. at 5.30 &, just above Marola, drew vines till 8.30. I can do no more. Doubtless La Spezia is perfectly lovely. Slept till 12. Dined nastily with flies... Made up my mind after some time – on my way to draw – to go tonight by the steamer, an irresolution which made G. laugh, being so unusual. So I came back, packed all, & then went to take leave of the Levers. Mr. & Julia L. walked back with me at 6. Took 2 places, & left at 7, coming on board. The sense of loneliness was most terrible, & it was strangely forced on me: no Ann now... & even the saying goodbye to Julia Lever was dreary. I sat some time on deck – more or less till 11. Porto Venere passed, & G. & I made out the 5 terre of last year. After leaving Levanto I lay down below.[30]

Having rested briefly at Genoa, they travelled by coach to Turin and then on up the Val d'Aosta to Courmayeur at its head. Lear found the view there of Mont Blanc 'very grand & vast, but destitute of all but immensity – graceless'. Worse still was the

perfect torture from flies which are horrible here. I resolve to go tomorrow. Life in Switzerland is harder work than in any place I know. I shall not waste time in going up the Cramont, & I don't respect or like Mt. Blanc enough to stay longer.[31]

They therefore hurried down again to Aosta, from where they set out the following day, 1 August, for England, over the St Bernard Pass.

In November Lear and Giorgio returned to Corfu, where Lear saw out the next three winters. He might well have settled there permanently if the British government had not decided, in 1864, to hand over the Ionian Islands to the jurisdiction of Greece. It was decided simultaneously to restore the Greek monarchy, which was offered to a number of outsiders, including Lord Derby. Lear joked with his banker, Edgar Drummond, that

> You may not have heard (it is not generally known) that I refused the throne of Greece – King Lear the First – on account of the conduct of Goneril & Regan my daughters, which has disturbed me too much to allow of my attention to governing.[32]

When the time came, on 4 April, to make his final departure, his mood was more sombre. He told Fortescue that 'I am now cut adrift' from Corfu, 'though I cannot write the name without a sort of pang.'[33]

After much deliberation Lear settled on Nice for his next winter quarters, and it was from there that he set out with Giorgio on 6 December for Genoa, thus completing his circuit of the Ligurian Riviera.

They crossed into Italy four days later at Ventimiglia, which Lear found 'wonderfully picturesque – torrents, broken bridge, old houses, &c. &c. Drew, tho' half frozen, till I could not hold my pencil.' At dinner in the new and imposing Hotel de Londres at San Remo he noted 'many English, & 2 Polish ladies who declared themselves hungry at the end of dinner & ordered a 2nd'.

After searching in vain the next morning for something worth drawing, he decided that 'S. Remo is an absolute failure' and that they should take the diligence on to Oneglia for the night. When it arrived, there was

> no end of fuss about places, I not caring what I had for 2? hours but the rest making a row, one brazen hussy being furious. She continued to annoy the Directeur for an hour: 'O Dio!' she howled out by fits, 'What heat! What torture! O! How I am suffering! O how I am sweating! I am sweating buckets! I cannot take any more!' &c, &c.

> The road seemed to me very uninteresting, & dreadfully horrid from long tracts of fallen earth in the last great rains – 40 days of it, they say. Obscure torrents, & unpleasant villages; roaring sea – but no peacock-hue bays nor any other pleasure.

There was no let-up in the rain and they were forced to spend two nights at Oneglia before it finally relented: ' I tire sadly of this Corniche – the lopsided views & blank grey sea – & the everlasting smash of railway cuttings & blowings up & knockings down,' Lear wrote. It was another two years before the line to Genoa was completed.

Nearing Diano, 'G.'s hat blew away, but stuck on a stone right over the sea; to which that Suliot, cat-like, crawled, & regained it.' On the other side of the village, however, there was 'a lovely view as far as Noli, & of Laiguelia & Alassio, perhaps the prettiest scene – next to the Mentone – I have yet seen in these diggings'. At Alassio the weather once again closed in, trapping them for a further two days. Lear's patience was now exhausted and on the first break in the rain they set off, leaving the luggage to come on by the next coach:

> About 9.15 descend towards Albenga & come to a marshy plain, olive-grown at intervals. Later, the ancient city itself, many-towered – whose towers I saw on Jan. 5 of this year [from the steamer]. It is very medieval & picturesque, & today being fine & the snow hills clear, a pleasure... Low, maize-cultivated fields lead on to Pietra – another large place, near which were very large orange & lemon gardens. Beyond, a long straight uphill road. Ever the growing railway aboundeth. Drew a bridge & river scene.

They reached Finale well before dark, but, after waiting up till nine for the luggage 'I succumb to circumstances & come to bed, to sleep in shirt & drawers'. When it still had not appeared in the morning, Lear sent Giorgio back to Alassio in a pony trap to fetch it and took advantage of a clear sky to do some sketching:

> Many pretty bits of scene are along the coast. Returned from the furthest point I went to at 2 & drew, & again at the town till 4.15. On going back to the Hotel, the Suliot was there with the luggage – a comfort. So having nothing more to do at Finale, I order dinner & the same trap for Savona tomorrow if fine.

It was – but not for long:

> I could not draw any part of Capo di Noli, which is certainly immensely grand as a rock & sea scene. Beyond is doubtless one of the finest views on all the Riviera, but all the dis-

tance was indistinct. Stopped – cold & wet – in a lull of rain to draw Noli & Speturno; the former is very picturesque – its curious towers. Fishers abound, & are passed outside the town. Along the beach to Speturno, a place of some pretension – as to large & painted houses with gardens, oranges, &c.

The rain then came on even harder, pursuing them all the way to Savona, but the dining room of the Hotel Reale held a welcome surprise:

Lo! no end of 'Mess' dinner – ossifers, & 2 ladies; 2 English Engineers – youngsters. The dinner became allegro, & no end of bottles of champagne were distributed & healths 'all' Inghilterra' & 'all' Italia' till we broke up. Then I, sitting with the 2 Engineers, had a bottle of Marsala & very pleasant company till past 8. G. came in, & I said, 'If it rains, don't call me.' Indeed, what to do? Cogoleto? Or Diligence to Genoa?[34]

They woke once more to the sound of rain, so to Genoa it was. Before they were even halfway, however, they found the road completely blocked by a landslide and were obliged to pass the night at Cogoleto after all, in the Gallo Locanda, which Lear found 'direful' and 'a very gallows place'. The following day they were more successful, although the weather was little better and he was forced to abandon his attempt to draw the city, returning to their hotel 'sad & disgusted'.

At last, however, the weather gradually improved on their return journey, and by the time they reached San Remo Lear was writing of the 'wonderful change of climate! The sunset (seen from an open window) is glorious. At 5 P.M. nothing could be more beautiful.'[35]

It was San Remo that Lear would choose as the site of his first permanent home and abode for the last 20 years of his life.

Chapter Twelve
Venice and The Lakes (1865–7)

Back in England once more for the summer of 1865, Lear began seriously to contemplate proposing to Gussie Bethell, whose mother had recently died, only to be assailed by doubts when the first opportunity arose: 'But how to decide? If her life is sad, united to mine would it be less so? Or rather, would it not be more so?'[1] He departed two days later still undecided, but when he saw her again in September his mind was made up that 'it would not do. Better suffer alone than cause sufferings in others.'[2]

Before wintering in Malta he returned to Italy on the strength of another commission from Lady Waldegrave, this time for a painting of Venice – a city, then still under Austrian rule, that was little known to him. His only previous sight of it, while en route between Corfu and England eight years earlier, had left him distinctly underwhelmed:

> Now, as you will ask me my impressions of Venice, I may as well shock you a good thumping shock at once by saying I don't care a bit for it & never wish to see it again... Canaletto's pictures please me far better, inasmuch as I cannot in them smell these most stinking canals. Ugh!

His opinion had sunk again with the letter that he dropped while disembarking from a gondola: 'Gondola, forsooth! Why can't they call them boats – rickety old boats?'[3]

Now he was to spend two weeks in the city and Giorgio was to travel from Corfu via Trieste to meet him. Lear learned at Milan that cholera had recently broken out in Trieste and the rumour among his fellow passengers was that a quarantine had been imposed. Accordingly, following their arrival on the evening of 8 November,

> we were all (perhaps 70 or 80) urged instantly into a room 'to be fumigated'. The porter who took charge of my smaller roba said '<u>all</u> must be perfumed – it's the order,' but advised me to go in last. The clouds of smoke & pungent chloride burning made me quite blind, as well as cough violently; one could only see that every article of luggage was taken out separately & smoked by dirty Austrian soldiers. So I gave in altogether, being quite knocked up & threatened with bad asthma – not to say apoplexy. All at once said the porter: 'Then come with me, & leave your big baggage till tomorrow,' when, nearly choked, I rushed with him to a gondola, & my 3 objects went all choleriferously into Venice – to my amazement – unopened!!
>
> Gloomy & cold was that gondola passage, notwithstanding that I could not but see how tremendously full of picturesqueness is every moment in Venetian canals.[4]

His temper was not improved when he found that his room at the Europa looked out on to nothing more than a blank wall and, worse still, the waiter informed him that Giorgio was probably being held in a quarantine camp at Trieste. A switch to Danieli's solved the former problem, but there was still no sign of Giorgio. When Lear discovered from the police that Giorgio was not at Trieste either, he wrote to Corfu telling him not to set out if he was still there, as indeed a letter received a few days later confirmed.

The fog finally lifted the following afternoon, to Lear's delight: 'O! O! What a sunset, & what a dream of wonderful beauty of Air & Architecture! "Earth & Heaven"!' On the 13th he hired a gondola for the day and

> first drew S. Marco by the Doge's Palace – then from the Iron Bridge – & then went to the Rialto, but it was awfully cold, & I came back to the bridge & walked to the Hotel. The gondolier says the canals are frequently all frozen for a long time; I had always thought Venice a warm & soppy climate. Got some lunch at Florian's, hoping to see Princess [a fellow

artist] – but he did not come. Afterwards, went again to the
Rialto, & lastly drew from the Iron Bridge & near the Doge's
Palace once more. I see no other way of getting through this
fortnight – nor indeed of compassing Lady W.'s picture – but
by constant hard work.

The cold eventually began to weaken his resolution, however:
'Standing continually close to the water or mud – for the last 3 or 4
days – all day long – chilled me thoroughly. A rather depressing state
of things.'[5]

His spirits were rapidly revived when, at breakfast on the 24th, he
saw in The Times the news that Fortescue had been appointed
Secretary of State for Ireland, as he described in a letter to Lady
Waldegrave:

> Being of an undiplomatic and demonstrative nature in matters
> that give me pleasure, I threw the paper up into the air and
> jumped aloft myself – ending by taking a small fried whiting
> out of the plate before me and waving it round my foolish head
> triumphantly till the tail came off and the body and head flew
> bounce over to the other side of the table d'hôte room. Then
> only did I perceive that I was not alone, but that a party was at
> breakfast in a recess. Happily for me they were not English, and
> when I made an apology saying I had suddenly seen some good
> news of a friend of mine, these amiable Italians said,
> 'Bravissimo, Signore! We too are delighted! If we had some lit-
> tle fish also, we would be throwing them all over the room with
> you!' – so we ended by all screaming with laughter.[6]

He was also cheered enough to write 'a longish letter to dear little
Gussie, whose voice – sweet to me – I often hear, as it were, near to me'.[7]

A week later the news was not so good. The ship that he was bank-
ing on to take him to Malta was several days overdue, and when it did
arrive he learned that it was going straight on to Gibraltar, leaving
him no alternative but to return to England overland. As he set out
on 3 December he wrote in his diary: 'Strange sad lagoons of Venice!!
<u>Against my will</u> no place has so impressed me – ever.'

The journey over the Mount Cenis Pass was more arduous this
time:

At top of Echelles by 7. Dim daylight & thick fog following. Began the descent; snow very deep, & constantly changing by wind. Horses unmanageable from depth of snow; violent wind. Tourmente; incredible ghastly glorious effects of snow-storm & Alp cloud. Diligence all but upset – all passengers out – ran on. 2 tumbles. Coach righted – all in again; descent to Lanslebourg by 8.50.[8]

Apart from a fleeting call at Trieste, he did not return to Italy for another 18 months, when on 1 May 1867, after a winter in Egypt and Palestine, he and Giorgio landed at Brindisi en route for England. That same morning he was back at work:

I having got out a large folio to draw, G. & I walk along the weedy forlorn port – beautiful tho' it be as a future. Old cas-tle – picturesque – & good view of town, but [a] sentinel warns me not to draw, & we flit. Try other points, but give it up, & I am too happy to be in Italy – & too tired – to com-plain. At 2 or 3 come to hotel & sleep – after a lunch – till 5. Bright fine day. (I had resolved to begin this new set of Italian drawings with 2 good ones of Brindisi, so my failure was disgusting.)

Continuing by train the next morning, Lear found the journey up the low-lying Adriatic coast pleasant but unremarkable: 'Poppies; green cultivation – corn – olives – figs. Almost flat. S. Vito station 7.50; olives & wheat... always a vast garden everywhere.' Their next stop, Bari, appeared to have done well out of the revolution, as the name of their hotel, the Risorgimento, implied:

A capital inn, good clean rooms above; drawback – polished mosaic floors, suggestive of leg-breaking. By 12 I & G. got a good lunch, & then walked broad fine streets of new Bari; good shops & well-to-do folks... The sprightly go-aheadness of this place – & its cleanliness! – remembering as I do the Apulia of 1847!

They embarked again in the evening with some misgivings at the prospect of a night on the train, but on arriving at Forli at midday Lear conceded that it had been

on the whole a very bearable velocity-journey. Here it suddenly struck me – would there be time to drive to Ravenna?
Yes, there was, so I got off at once in a good 2-horse carriage
for 12 (fr) & 2 to be for good performance. Start at 1, a rat-
tly pace along a good road, the river on one side, & pretty
farms & villas on the other standing low in greenery of corn
– flax – mulberry & all vivid luxury.

At Ravenna – invisible till close by – by 3. It <u>don't</u> look venerable or grievous at all, & seems very unantique to look at,
the streets being clean & the people – tho' few – apparently
decent. I had expected grass grown streets & millions of beggars – nobles in rags, &c. [Presumably because the city had
been one of the last redoubts of the Papal forces.]

He devoted the next morning to an examination of the famous
Byzantine mosaics:

Went first to S. Apollinare Nuovo – so called as being the 2nd
church of that name. A basilica like S. M[aria] Maggiore; roof
modern, but the series of mosaics above the columns are really wonderful & far finer than any I have ever seen: the procession of virgins to the V. & child, & that of saints to the
Christ. Next, passing the facade of palace of Theodora – a
mere scrap of ruin – went by very clean & broad streets, looking at the Tomb of Dante, & then to the Palazzo Guiccioli –
which moves me – al modo mio – more than the Poet of
Florence [&] his memories. When a little boy I knew nothing
of Dante, but was always thinking of Byron.

Then I saw S. Vitale, a most delightful edifice – like S. Sofia
of Constantinople, & built by the same Emperor. The
mosaics of the choir, altho' not so grand as a whole, are more
perfect as to preservation than those of S. Apollinare. The
portraits of Justinian & Theodora in 2 compartments are
absolutely astonishing – & rank with the works of Abydos on
Saccara Kalabike as to the exact resuscitation of past costumes & portraits of life. The dome & most of the church is
disgustingly modernized – O Art of the year 450 & 500,
compared with that of 1800! The mosaic tablets representing

the sacrifice of Isaac & the entertaining 3 angels by Abraham, & that of the death of Abel, are wonderful truly. Close to S. Vitale is the tomb of the Empress Gallina Placida – a most remarkable "antiquity", but as it was very dark, I couldn't see it well. I followed my leader to the walls, from which one sees nothing (as Ravenna stands in a sort of pit), & walked round them to the Tomb of Theodora – which don't delight me. There is no possible view of the city any-whence, & one's impressions – except from the mosaics – are all negative.

After lunch he hired a trap for a tour of the surrounding Pineto, including the modest hut

where Garibaldi was hidden, & close to where his wife died. They say that now, on that anniversary, crowds flock to the place; I suppose that in a hundred years, if it could add to their prestige, the hound-scoundrel priests would canonize him... Then we turned off, crossing marshy rice-ground & some lagoons, to the world of pines. This wood is really love-ly; I cannot say grand or magnificent, for the trees are not large, but the glades & green, & the underwood of bright foliage, makes the whole scene enchanting.

So struck was he indeed that he returned twice more to draw the wood and Garibaldi's hut, and even on the fourth day he 'half wished I had seen the north side of the Pineto' as he and Giorgio drove to rejoin the railway at Rimini. However, having booked into the Hotel Tré Ré and

lunched singularly well, on eggs well dressed – & a fried sole – cum strawberries & Parmesan cheese, it seems to me, being so far here, I had better go up tomorrow (at 5) to S. Marino, & come down again the day after to sleep here.

The next day dawned brilliantly, and Lear was able to capture sev-eral views of the little republic's fastness before the incline proved too steep even for the pair of oxen hitched to his carriage and he struck out for the summit on foot:

The view is wonderful for extent & variety – on the east to

sea; towards the west, undulations of Apennine, & the bed
of the broad white Marecchia, are beautiful, spite of the
shadowless hour of noon. But the distance is all too equal, &
with this few forms of remarkable shape or size to be very
drawable. Stiff walk up to city, the streets of which are very
steep – also clean. Palazzo Communale, where the government is carried on; several rooms of no large size, with portraits: 2 of Napoleon 2nd [&] the Empress, with a 3rd of the
Emperor; one of Napoleon 1st given by himself.

Making a wider sweep to the west on his return to Rimini the next
day, he crossed the Rubicon, but he was disappointed to find that his
guide knew the river only by its modern name of Uso. After another
night at the Tré Ré, he and Giorgio reboarded the train and arrived

at Bologna the high towered by 1 PM. Bus to the Hotel
Brun, a 'not good' hotel. At the Post got a letter from Daddy
[Holman Hunt] – his movements are quite uncertain, & I
shall not go to Florence as I might miss him there, but may
well see him in England. Poor fellow! his baby has been ill…
G. & I bkft with difficulty – the hotel is badly served.

Clearly despairing of anything better, he was soon back on the train
again and heading for Ferrara:

Bus to Stella d'Oro by 5.30. The effect of the old ducal castle is surprising, & of the picturesque streets – such as are
inhabited – & the others are wonderful as so deserted. Took
a guide; saw Cathedral – beautiful facade. Heard the 16
echoes in another church; saw the column of Ariosto & his
house; the prisons of Dante; the most magnificent Diamanti
palace, that of the Bentivogli, all, with many more, in those
wide gaunt empty streets – so broad & long!! A real desert,
& most impressive. At sunset bought a few photographs &
at 8 dined alone as usual. It is good to have seen Ferrara.

May 11th. Rose at 4. The dead giant red castle of the D'Este
is awful grim at sunrise. Fidgety to get off, & paid bill by 6.
Off by rail 7.40 – line new, & horribly shaky. Pass the great
river Po, & at 8.50, the Adige. A subaltern dilates on the horrors of the S. Italy brigandage, at Basilicata, Bari, &c., &c.

Monselice at 9.25. Very picturesque all the run thru' the Enganean hills; sycamores give place to willows as vine supporters.

Passing on through Padua, where they 'got excellent breakft. 2 fr. a head; Gattinara wine (2 fr.), soup, eggs, veal & artichokes,' Vicenza and Verona, they arrived by mid-afternoon at Desenzano, on the shores of Lake Garda, which Lear had made a note of on his way to Venice two years earlier. He enjoyed another 'excellent' meal at the Albergo Reale and was further delighted to find that the only other guest, a man from Canada, knew his cousin Caroline Jones and her husband, who was a member of the Canadian Senate.

After a day of cloud spent reconnoitring suitable vantage points, he and Giorgio set out the next morning on foot

> to the narrow neck of land leading to Sirmione, reaching the village by 7. The beautiful mulberry trees are all being despoiled of their leaves by individuals with sax, reducing the trees to a wintry look. The mountains, hitherto dark & grey, begin to light up rather hopefully. The fine old castle with 2 drawbridges made one think Sirmione a sort of city afar off, but it is only a poor village – 300 souls; & so far from there being sentinels or military, the quiet of decay was on all things. Went thru' the narrow streets, no one creature asking a single question – no beggars – no dogs – & worked our way to the higher part of the promontory, & thence to the northern end, where there are fine Roman substructions [including the remains of Catullus's villa], tho' coarse & not of fine red brick… As the day has gone on, the lake & hills have become more lovely than can be described or depicted – filmy lilac or all blue – the water as calm as glass.

The next day was again fine, and they took a steamer trip to the northern end of the lake, only to find that it lay over the Austrian border; being without their passports, they were obliged to disembark at Gargnano. From there they worked their way down the western shore of the lake to spend the night at Salò:

> Two or three points on the road were truly magnificent – one nearly above the town – but nearly all the way was between

very narrow & high walls – with astonishing pilasters for lemon cages built thereon – so that to have drawn from any points below was quite impossible, tho' from the height of the chaise one saw a peep now & then.

In the morning they visited

a novel & handsome cemetery: terrace walls on the side of the hill sloping north & in the walls arches for coffins, & inscribed slabs of stone or marble; altogether one of the neatest & best-looking burying places I ever saw. Saló is evidently an 'original' place – witness 1st the cemetery, 2nd the lemon-cages, 3rd the horseradish sauce, & 4th the tin or metal jugs & basins instead of porcelain. The cemetery is not finished: urns & stone steps are to be placed, where now but a very few are.

Returned to the town at 9.30, after drawing below various mulberry trees, & then tried the other side in hopes of a view, but it was impossible to get near the Lake or to see over the walls.

He solved the problem by hiring a boat for the afternoon, taking it up the shoreline as far as Molignano.

The weather broke overnight, and they took advantage of the cover of a coach to make a day return trip to Idro. The next morning dawned fine again, and they set off at 5 in a chaise for Gargnano, which Lear was determined to get a view of:

Walls – walls – & gardens. The inhabitants of the shores of L. di Garda are your true exclusives: you only rarely get a peep of the lake down a narrow alley – all else is wall, & such wall! Towards Maderno the walls are often 25 feet high – & then follow pilasters some 30 feet higher! Walking for miles between such is out of the question. Also one meets immense loaded hay carts, delays & bitterness resulting. Before reaching Maderno at 6.25, the omnibus [of] 3 horses abreast bothered our trap not a little.

Above Maderno the effect of the gigantic conservatories is very odd, like some sort of network for catching big birds.

Toscolano at 6.30. The women have nearly all pleasant &
pretty – if not beautiful – faces hereabouts. Several are exactly like Leonardo da Vinci's females. Alas! for the rattle &
bumping of the shay!

Having finally got his view of Gargnano and sampled the local delicacy of eels *in umido*, which Lear judged 'too fat', they continued
northwards, but when the rain clouds descended again they called it
a day and returned to base at Desenzano.

After another day there, during which Lear discovered the signature
of his youthful friend Daniel Fowler in the Reale's visitors' book, he
and Giorgio took the train to Brescia, which he found 'clean & cheerful'; more particularly, 'all the women are brilliant & pleasing & soft
in expression, & well & tastefully clad.' From Brescia they went on
by chaise to Iseo, but the next morning threatened more frustration:
'What to do if it goes on raining? The wretched little steamer – which
once went to the bottom – came at 6, bringing people for the Brescia
diligence.' However, the rain soon ceased and they took off in a trap
for a circuit of the lake, which Lear thought

very attractive from its varied character. The large & lofty
island is its most remarkable feature in the middle, & at the
upper end its very grand mountain forms. There are also
some really good olives, with lovely vine drapery. Mulberries
of course & corn – & figs, & on the hill – eastside – large
groves of chesnut. At the water's edge are several villages –
not particularly picturesque in themselves, but adding to the
whole picture – a moving diorama – great cheeriness & life.

He was pleased to find too that the road hugged the shore throughout, so that he had no need this time to take to the water in order to
get his views.

After another night at Iseo, they headed for the rail-head at
Coccaglio, where they 'consigned the luggage, then walked up Mt.
Orfano at 4.15 – a most glorious view from which I hope some day
to revisit. Certainly one does get an idea of Lombardy from this
place.' After an interesting supper of 'boiled meat & pickles, fried
eggs & roast kid,' they boarded the train for Milan, 'where before 11
I was housed in a capital room. Bed 11.30; the cleanliness & comfort

of this Hotel Cavour!' (It is still accorded four stars today.)

Two further days of rain prompted Lear to question 'if it is any use to go to the other lakes? or at once to London?' He pressed on, however, to Como,

> & in a storm on to the steamer – I having taken places to Cadenabbia, foolishly. But so great was the crowd on the small steamer, so bad the prospect of weather, & so unwell from suppressed waterworks my own self, that I suddenly resolved not to go on, whereon I came hastily off & giving my ticket to the most obliging Rlwy. people, who promised to extract my luggage & send it to the Inn, rushed to the Angelo Hotel...
>
> No sooner had I begun to arrange things in my room than I heard some row in the street, & saw everybody running to the quay – the whole town; whereon I also went down; by this time the Lake had become a sea, & high stormy waves with violent wind. A boat with 5 English people & 3 rowers had been upset, & tho' every help was sent from boats starting, one boatman was drowned & another is said to be dying. How thankful I was not to have gone in the steamer! Then I walked with G. round the Port, when lo! a violent gust, & down fell the top of a wall – perhaps 10 or 12 heavy stones – on a poor soldier, who was taken to the Hospital. I & G. voted Como a baddish place.

The morning dawned no better, so Lear ordered a trap to take them to Varese. After lunching at the Albergo Angelo, he set off on foot to climb the 3,000-foot Monte Sacro,

> a remarkable looking place. The growth of immense chesnut trees is gorgeous, & the delicate distance of Alp-snow, & Lombard plain, most exquisite. The 14 large chapels contain (gesso-?) painted figures representing the various Christ-life & death, &c. points. Some very well designed, & almost startling as to reality. From the sides of the hill, as one winds up it, the views are amazingly lovely. At the top by 4.20, & come down, drawing at times. By 7.30 reached the Hotel, where a capital dinner closed the day.

After giving over the next to a circuit of the lake, which unfortunately Lear found 'not interesting', they turned in early in order to catch the 8 a.m. bus back to Como. The lake had duly composed itself again in the interval, and they took the steamer up to Bellagio – only to be overtaken once more by rain and, worse still,

> a knot of Americans whose conversation was boring & odious... 'D'ye know Col. Pollimer, fresh looking man, dark eyes, dark hair, no whiskers, spots on his nose, married Miss Tobson-Lowndes who had 80,000 dollars, & their son is to be called Tobson-Lowndes dropping the Pollimer name quite?' (said one American lady to another) 'Lord! Lord! do I know Col. Pollimer! O Lord! he's my most intimate friend. But do you, Madam, know Mrs. Crewser-Stacklethwaite? Tell me that!' & so on incessantly.

An even more distasteful encounter awaited him on the return journey when the wife of a clergyman 'tried to put some odious tracts into my bag, but I snubbed her "severely". What bores are these fools!'

Although the weather on the lake remained fine, the surrounding mountains were still hidden in cloud, which led Lear to conclude

> that Como, from its many positions & ins & outs, & from its very variable climate, wants more time than do the other Lakes to draw thoroughly. To make a book of North Italy, I must come here again for 2 or 3 months.

A second tour of Lake Varese also forced him to amend his opinion of it:

> Those beautiful bright villas – those beautiful scenes, with the Lake below! And, spite of its small repute as an Italian Lake, Varese has some qualities wanting to all the rest: its endless delicate gradation of multiplicity of verdure – slopes of green – & far away bits of level mixed with shining water – long lines of distant blue plain – deep or faint, & grade beyond grade of more faintly delineated soft hills or more decided ridges, with Alpine snow above...the tall Lombard towers (their bells so fine in tone) – the rich green of the walnut, the almost yellow acacia – the grey willows, olives, poplars or aspens – the thick oak copses, where nightingales

sing always – the smooth undulations & declivities of turf –
the cheerful hayfields, the many winding paths – the glittering villages, & single silvery villas or cottages or chapels – the
winding bright streamlets – fig, almond, pomegranate, corn,
mulberry for foreground – who would not rejoice in the
landscape of Lake Varese?

They set out early next morning for Lake Maggiore and took a
steamer across to Baveno, causing another reshuffle in Lear's league
table of lakes: he now decided, 'This Lake is far lovelier & grander
than the others,' and the following day he wrote that 'the calm &
loveliness of this Lake is beyond mortle imagination'. He completed
his tour of it with a further day at Stresa.

Driving over on 1 June to the last and most westerly of the lakes,
Orta, he found that too

> really beautiful. The contrast of massive chesnuts, so decided
> in form & colour, with the blues & lilacs palenesses, & the
> very delicate & innumerable details of the distance! And
> somehow it has all at once become summer, & life becomes
> a pleasure simply as life among such beauty of sight, sound
> & scent.

He realised that the idyll could not last, however, and decided that
'as I am to go back to the terrible & shocking London life, let me go
at once'.[9]

Returning to Maggiore to rejoin the railway, he left Giorgio at
Novara to continue on to Corfu, while he himself turned west to
Turin and so to England. Although he regularly returned to the Lakes
during the last 20 years of his life, his mooted book about them never
materialised.

Chapter Thirteen

San Remo and the Italian Tyrol (1867–73)

Even before Lear set out for London Gussie was once more in the front of his mind, just as she had been on his return the previous summer in 1866, when he had put aside his earlier misgivings and written, after their second reunion, that

> the 'marriage' phantasy 'will not let me be' – yet seems an intangible myth. To think if it no more is to resolve on all the rest of life being passed thus – alone – & year by year getting more weary.[1]

When he had broached the matter to Lady Waldegrave her advice had been blunt: "'If she hasn't any money it will be one struggle more, & shall be the last feather & your back will be broken.'" Fortescue, on the other hand, had been more equivocal: 'His opinion of the possible marriage coincides with that of My Lady; but he rather advocates it if there are £300 a year' (there were currently only £200).[2] More confusingly still, Emma Parkyns, Gussie's sister, had been openly encouraging but on finding himself pushed again to the brink, Lear drew back, concluding that 'Emma's wishes & thoughts are not difficult to divine, but again I say it would not do'.[3] When Gussie herself had called on him shortly afterwards (perhaps to force the issue?), it had been 'a pain rather than a pleasure, & was so to her also; for the gulf is not to be passed'.[4]

Yet here he was, nine months later, confessing, on finishing Elizabeth Gaskell's novel *Wives and Daughters*, that 'Gussie & the old story come up to me on reading such books, & I even now hardly know what I may do'.[5] Although he corresponded regularly with her after his arrival, he seems deliberately to have stopped short of actually seeing her again. He wrote in his diary in August: 'Certainly, now & at this time I do not "make" sadness, but eschew it carefully. O Gussie! Gussie!'[6]

Two months later another letter from her 'puts me all no-how again,' and he determined to resolve the issue once and for all: 'Go to Hinton it seems I must.'[7] As he took the train down to Somerset to the country seat of her father, Lord Westbury, he mused:

> it is absurd to think that at 54 years old I am within a point
> of doing what will fix the rest of my life – be it short or long
> – in one groove – good or bad. I do not say I am decided to
> take the leap in the dark, but I say that I am nearer to doing
> so than I ever was before.[8]

Emma was again to act as the go-between, but when he talked to her the following morning, she at once made it clear that she had reversed her opinion of the previous year: she told him that he should now finally abandon his suit. As he reflected afterwards, 'after what she said a year ago, her "certainty that now A[ugusta] & I could not live together happily" seems strange.' One can only speculate on her reasons, but this entry in his diary two days later, referring to Lord Westbury's will, possibly provides a clue: 'E.P. says each of the girls is to have 20,000 – but for ten times that sum I would not marry where I now see there is small chance of happiness – even if I could do so.' (The conventions of the day severely frowned on a match between an heiress to such a sum and a penurious artist.) 'Anyhow, <u>it broke up a dream</u> rudely & sadly,' he wrote, crest-fallen.[9]

The prospect of wintering in England was now more intolerable than ever, but where was he to go? The news from Italy seemed to him to be 'shocking, the French & Papal troops defeating Garibaldi; no one can now forsee what is beyond'.[10] Worse still, 'The Cedars of Lebanon', the large oil on which he had pinned such high hopes and a price-tag of £750, had still failed to find a buyer and his horizons were thus uncomfortably restricted. He settled eventually on a return to the French Riviera, but it was not a success, as he told Emily Tennyson the following May:

I was so disgusted .with furnished lodgings last winter in Cannes that I resolved at length to have a settled place to come to for the winter, & thereupon hired a floor in a new house opposite the sea, & having purchased a sufficiency of pots & pans, &c., set up house for the present in the Maison Guichârd, Boulevard l'Imperatrice. How long I shall remain there remains to be seen.[11]

He finally accepted an offer of no more than £200 for 'The Cedars', but at least this allowed him to extend his lease for another two years and to undertake a tour of Corsica, out of which was to materialise his last *Journal of a Landscape Painter*. Another consolation was the return of the faithful Giorgio, 'who cooks, markets and keeps the house clean so systematically that I have no trouble whatsoever'.[12]

However, his hopes that he would also be able to support himself by the sale of drawings and watercolours to the burgeoning English colony on the Riviera proved badly misplaced. There was, he found, 'nobody of the faintest taste at Cannes' except 'Belgravian idlers, beastly aristocratic idiots who come here & think they are doing me a service by taking up my time!'[13] He wrote to Fortescue on New Year's Day 1870 mentioning that 'only £12 was expended on this child by strangers last year, and I forsee no greater luck this year'. He had also now come to the conclusion that

my floor, or flat, here is very unsatisfactory in some points, i.e. being in a house with three other floors full of people, noises abound; 2nd, I have no good painting room; 3rd, my bedroom is cold; 4th, the chimneys smoke... Could I get any suitable house here for £3000 it appears to me that such a step would be a wise one, for as that sum, all I have, produces only £90 a year [being invested in Consols 3%], I should gain by the move... Shall I build a house or not? There is a queer little orange garden opposite for £1000, if only one could ensure that no building could be placed opposite.[14]

Before he could make up his mind politics overtook him once again, this time in the shape of the Franco-Prussian War. Not only did this destabilise the French property market, but it also increased the attraction of an investment in Italy, for the return of the French garrison from Rome to the front allowed Garibaldi's forces to march into the Holy City unopposed and so, at last, to complete the country's reunification. There was also the additional incentive that land in Italy was then a good deal cheaper.

The first point over the border at which the English were present in any numbers was San Remo. The town had not particularly impressed Lear five years earlier (see Chapter 11), and his first reaction on seeing it again was that it 'strikes me as <u>bald</u>, & the olives are skimpy meagre'; but on the other hand, 'undoubtedly everything is cheaper here... for £1200 a capital house may be built.'[15] He was also encouraged by meeting an old acquaintance, Sir George Walker, who introduced him to an ex-schoolmaster, Walter Congreve, who had recently retired there, and 'whose house is a wonder for good arrangement & clever contrivance'.[16] Together they inspected several plots, but all of them were ruled out on one ground or another and Lear returned to France still in two minds about what to do next.

His disillusionment with Cannes continued to mount, however, and three weeks later he 'pretty well resolved to go to San Remo tomorrow, & to "buy & build"'.[17] In a rare rush of decision, within the space of the next three days he fixed on the plot to the west of Congreve's property, added to it two smaller adjoining parcels, engaged an architect and exchanged contracts.

Shortly afterwards he was able to acquire a third extra plot from Mr Bogge, the owner of the Hotel de Londres. 'And thus ends the "Great Land Question",' he wrote with undisguised satisfaction in his diary on 28 March, bringing his total outlay to £740.[18]

'What do you think as I have been & gone & done? I have bought a bit of ground at San Remo & am actually building a house there,' he informed Thomas Woolner, another member of the Pre-Raphaelite Brotherhood, enclosing this mock design:

1. *Dining-room*
2. *Drawing-room*
3. *Staircase window*
4. *Hall windows*
5. *Street door*
6 & 7. *Back & front*

It was to have been like this, only the architect wouldn't let me carry out my simple principles of art... & so I shall begin life again for the 5th & last time. As I have sold no drawings this winter & have no commissions ahead, I shall endeavour to live upon figs in summer-time, & on worms in the winter. I shall have 28 olive trees & a small bed of onions; & a stone terrace, with a grey parrot & 2 hedgehogs to walk up & down on it by day & night. Anyhow, I shall have a good painting room with an absolute north bells light, & no chance of its being spoiled...[19]

He took some rooms nearby so that he could keep an eye on the builders' progress, until the summer heat – 'both I & G. compare it to Wady Halfa & more' – drove him into the hills. His goal was the Certosa di Pesio, a hotel converted from a Carthusian monastery near Cuneo, which he planned to reach via San Dalmazzo di Tenda; however, he 'learned from old Bogge that going to Dalmazzo by road was absurd, [&] pretty well decided to go by Pigna'. He set out on 26 June, accompanied by Giorgio and Bernardino, a young gardener whom he had recently taken on, together with an ass called Roma. It was a 'lovely morning, & delightful shade all the way – or nearly – to S. Romolo, which by slow walking was reached at 7.30'. On descending the first ridge, however, Roma 'absolutely refused to stir,' obliging them to unload her and carry everything themselves until they reached Perinaldo, 'a large village' where they hoped to find a replacement; but their luck was out.

Leave Perinaldo by painfully slithery downward paths. Long descent to Apricale – awful. Bottom by 3.15; bridge, & very picturesque scene. Pass through Apricale – strange archy village – by 4; gloomy narrow streets, well behaved people. Another long & winding descent to Isola Buona; pass through it at 4.35. Then a very long & weary valley road, bad & stony, & an ascent to Pigna by 7.15. Populous close village. Carabinieri question me. Inn at Pigna 'for the general use'. Very unwell, & fearful of heart illness. Slept a bit. That good G., instead of resting, <u>will</u> make soup. Inn very seedy, slip-slop girl. Later a supper of rice soup, rabbit – tough – & really good potatoes. X.

Rising after a sleepless night, compounded by the epileptic seizure, feeling 'very far from well, & very fearful of heart agitation,' he at least succeeded in hiring a 'mule & quiet old man', before starting out again.

> Tremendous pull up curves of paved road. After the last vine-yards, bare hill, then scantily covered worm-eaten pine hill till 7 (2? hours out) when I, very unwell, rest for water. Ill enough able to bear the constant upward fatigue, but hold-ing on as well as I can, for it can't be helped – medically.

When he did consult a doctor on arrival at Pesio, he was told that

> I have the same complaint of heart as my father died of quite suddenly. I have had advice about it, & they say I may live any time if I don't run suddenly, or go quickly upstairs; but that if I do, I am pretty sure to drop dead. I don't know when I have suffered more,[20]

he complained again after negotiating a 'frightful series of sharp zigzags down a bare & shrubby almost perpendicular hillside of slip-pery shale into a deep gorge leading to the Roya.'
When they finally reached the river,

> G. goes to look after trout. B. says I want coraggio, & cuts a rosebush stick for G. – which G. characteristically throws away shortly – 'I'm not used to carrying these things' – to B.'s dis-gust. An ascent follows – of little interest – & Saorgio [Saorge], a largish town in the gorge of the Roya, is reached about 2.30. Long delay with French officials about the man's mule – they seem to give obstructive bother purposely. (plus ça change…)

Lear then decided to dispense with Bernardino's services and send him home; not surprisingly, 'B. seems pleased & goes back.'
After enjoying a much better night at a 'convent of small huddly rooms', Lear spent the next day drawing the impressive chestnut woods surrounding it, 'but badly, as it is a difficult subject, & the flies are "too" awful'. At dinner he found himself seated next to a German from Menton(e), 'one Dr. Müller, agreeable enough – wants to trans-late [my] "Corsica" [*Journal*], says 100 Germans go there this year'. If only he had made Majorca its subject!
His sleep was interrupted this time by 'nightingales close to the win-

dow,' but on venturing into the woods again they were redeemed by 'a lovely bird about the crags, like a creeper or woodpecker, with rose-coloured underwings he continually opened & shut – was he a kind of kingfisher? – like a butterfly, odd-mannered & grey-headed like some other people'. If this was an oblique reference to the flies rather than to himself, they quickly had their revenge, becoming 'beyond description horrible & intolerable' as soon as he produced his sketchbook:

> I am convinced they are so numerous here on account of the calves & eggs & fowls, &c. which momentarily pass by in carts, all of which are stopped & counted at the frontier Douane – not to speak of sheep – mules – oxen, &c, &c... Demoralization, & try another spot, but at 2.30 give it up & come away. Try the drawing again twice, but at 4.30 am forced to acknowledge myself dead beat...

> Dine at table d'hôte. Messrs. Müller, Murphy, Chambers, &c., &c., & afterwards play on piano to Mentone guinea-pig-pervert till 9.30. Bed, after a short walk out, when poor old Mrs. Vigors comes after me & we talk of N.A.V. (her late husband, who had been Secretary of the London Zoological Society when Lear made his drawings of parrots there.)

> ... Strange, to come to this out of the way place & find all this pumped up out of the depths of memory 40 years ago!! Fire flies! Dr. Müller of Mentone mentions <u>Härtel Breitkopf of Leipsig</u> as likely publishers for a German 'Corsica'.

Progress was then further slowed by an injury to Giorgio's foot, and it was not until after stopping overnight at Tenda that they gained the 4,500-foot pass of the same name – still accompanied by the persistent Dr Muller, who Lear acknowledged had 'translated some of the "Corsica" very well'. The view from the top was 'grand enough looking back, but nothing to scream about', for the Alps to the north were obscured by haze, with only Monte Viso, some 40 miles away, being visible.

After descending across the border again into Italy and stopping for lunch in Limone Piemonte, they went 'to the first hotel – dell' Europa – Miss E on a Bull sign. Very large rooms & apparently clean – no end of pictures, curtains ornaments.' Impressed, and deterred from exploring for alternatives by 'nasty dogs', Lear booked in for the night and was rewarded with a dinner of

> very decent rice soup; 2 surprising trout as to size & flavour; thin veal cutlets well fried with potatoes – all excellent. Afterwards, smiling landlady brings lots of variously-vanity-made dishes – liver & pease, boiled veal, stuffed marrows – but I send away all except cheese & cherries.

Later, as he debated whether to abandon the mule path for the carriageway, the landlady suggested, 'Why not stay here 30 days? Good air & water, what more can I want?', but in the end he and Giorgio opted for the carriageway.

It turned out to be 'a rattling good road' down to San Dalmazzo, taking them on to Cuneo, 'a large & very interesting place. Arcades – shops – silkworm cocoons for sale,' in time for lunch. Still making good speed, they arrived at

> Certosa by 6.30, the road being quite exquisite for beauty & extreme greenness. The chesnuts are taller & more beautifully grouped than any I almost ever saw. The whole valley is a wonder of fertile & magnificent vegetation, but the Certosa itself, though immensely large, is – or seems to be – hideous. The room given me is quiet, but with a wall of green opposite – very prison like.[21]

The monastery generally was a disappointment, as he told Lady Waldegrave and her husband:

> I have been walking over the Col di Tenda, which produced so to speak a Tenda-ness in my feet, and it will be Tenda one if I can get a shoe on, which keeps me on Tendahooks. For all I write cheerfully, I am as savage & black as 90000 bears. There is nobody in this place (an ex-Carthusian convent with 200 rooms) whom I know, & they feed at the beastliest hours – 10 & 5... I live the queerest solitary life here, in company of seventy people. They are, many of them, very nice, but their hours don't suit me, & I HATE LIFE unless I WORK ALWAYS.[22]

As usual, he found consolation among the children staying in the hotel, on one of whom he made a particular impression, as she recorded many years later under her married name of Mrs Winthrop Chandler:

One day there appeared at luncheon sitting opposite to us a rosy, grey-bearded, bald-headed, gold-bespectacled little old gentleman who captivated my attention. My mother must have met him before, for they each greeted each other as friendly acquaintances. Something seemed to bubble and sparkle in his talk and his eyes twinkled benignly behind the shining glasses. I had heard of uncles; mine were in America and I had never seen them. I whispered to my mother that I should like to have that gentleman opposite for an uncle. She smiled and did not keep my secret.

The delighted old gentleman, who was no other than Edward Lear, glowed, bubbled and twinkled more than ever; he seemed bathed in kindly effulgence. The adoption took place there and then; he became my sworn relative and devoted friend. He took me for walks in the chestnut forests; we kicked the chestnut burrs before us, 'yonghy bonghy bos', as we called them; he sang to me 'The Owl and the Pussycat' to a funny little crooning tune of his own composition.[23]

Back in San Remo he made a similar hit with Hubert, the elder of the two Congreve boys, who recalled their first meeting:

I ran down the steep path which led up to our house to meet my father; I found him accompanied by a tall, heavily-built gentleman, with a large curly beard and wearing well-made but unusually loosely fitting clothes, and what at the time struck me most of all, very large, round spectacles. He at once asked me if I knew who he was, and without waiting for a reply proceeded to tell me a long, nonsense name, compounded of all the languages he knew, and with which he was always quite pat. This completed my discomfiture, and made me feel very awkward and self-conscious. My new acquaintance seemed to perceive this at once, and laying his hand on my shoulder, said, 'I am also the Old Derry Down Derry, who loves to see little folk merry, and I hope we shall be good friends.' This was said with a wonderful charm of manner and voice and accompanied with such a genial, yet quizzical smile, as to put me at my ease at once.[24]

This new 'adoption' was a most timely one, for in October Mrs Congreve, the boys' stepmother, died of cancer. Lear began giving the two boys regular drawing lessons, but the pleasure that he derived from these was soon outweighed by his despair at the slow progress of the builders.

As winter drew on, the fits of 'the morbids' increased, until he was writing in his diary that 'Altogether, I am as about as depressed as I ever was in my life – & what to do ahead I cannot tell.'[25] More than once he was reduced to thoughts of abandoning San Remo for good and joining his two brothers in the United States, even complaining that 'this place is far less bracing in air than Cannes'.[26]

However, his spirits revived as the days began to lengthen again, and the work advanced to the stage where he was able to begin moving in his furniture and other 'impedimenta', and to plant out the garden with the New Zealand seeds sent him by his sister Sarah. On 1 March 1871 he wrote that 'it is difficult to fancy nicer loveliness & quiet than <u>might</u> be got at here,' and on the 26th he rejoiced that 'in exactly a year from the day I decided in buying the ground, I am living in the house built on it!'[27]

His new home was to be called the Villa Emily, officially in honour of Sarah's eldest daughter, although it was hardly a coincidence that this was also the name of his cherished soulmate Lady Tennyson. A month later he told the Fortescues that,

> Thanks to the excellent arrangement and care of my good
> old servant Giorgio, I have... been living as comfortably as if
> I had been here 20 years. Only I never before had such a

painting room 32 feet by 20 – with a light I can work by at all hours, and a clear view south over the sea. Below it is a room of the same size, which I now use as a gallery, and am 'at home' in once a week... Giorgio goes to town half a mile off twice or three times a week, & besides his other work takes to gardening of his own account. He finds he can manage all the indoor work, but I have a gardener as well... Letters are my principal delight, for tho' I like flowers and a garden, I don't like working in it.[28]

In July, having seen Giorgio on to a steamer at Genoa for his annual leave, Lear continued by train to the Eternal City, now once more the capital of a united Italy. 'Rome 1837 – 1859 – & now 1871! But it is walking on graves,' he told his diary. He found his old friend Penry Williams 'stouter, but seems well,' and together they did a round of his former haunts: 'S. M[aria] Maggiore, the Steps of S. Gio. Lateran – that wonderful view was dim by the great heat, yet still lovely. Quirinal hill greatly changed & improved.' Not so his friend's eating habits: 'Dined well – 3 fr. 50, with coffee included at a nasty filthy café, for P.W. still does the old Roman (stewed calves' heads, soup, a sole, Parmesan, fruit, Orvieto wine & ice & such water!).'

The next morning he took the train out to Frascati to call on the former Margaret Knight, now Duchess of Sermoneta, whose invalid sister Isabella, Lear's favourite, had died the previous July. They passed a pleasant day reminiscing:

These terraces <u>are</u> terraces indeed, & plain it is that in those days the magnificence of gardens was understood. The great ilex trees thread a beautiful broken shadow on the vast broad walks; beyond lies Rome, on the pale wide Campagna... These places are full of past memories for me – but they are literally of the past, and utterly without any link to the present or future – gone – broken – dead, & never to be renewed.

Another link was severed when, after boarding the train back, he 'discovered that my long-tried swordstick, companion of many years & travels, was left behind'. He returned two days later, but there was of course no trace of it.

He took the train north again on 27 July to stay for a night with the Prince and Princess Teano (he had known her originally as Ada Wilbraham), leaving Rome,

> as I have ever done, with no regret... it is, barring its memories, a dirty 3rd rate hole of a town. Off at 6. Campagna below Castel Giubelio very beautiful & interesting, & so all along the V[ia]. Salaria. Soracte exquisite. Very pleasant man, a Colonel of Ferrara, in the 1st Class compartment. Talk of present state of Rome. 7.30 below Soracte; all the valley of the Tiber is delightful & one sees M. Gennaro at the opening, as it were, endwise... All the Tiber valley by Soracte, Orte, Borghettanio, Narni, Terni, Spoleto full of beauty & interest. Trevi, a queer pyramidical town. Foligno, 11.30. Lunch.

Four hours later he reached his destination, Nocera Umbra, which he described as a 'trafficless, forlorn spot':

> I am wishing I had not come. 5 top of steep hill, & soon at the 'Bagni' – a most grievous & ridiculous sell, for of all ugly places one may call this the most so... Queer place – large rambling house – good water. Walk out with all the party – other princes & dukes beside. Fancy life here!! Ugh!... Certainly, <u>this</u> experiment for passing summer months in Italy has been a sumptuous failure!

He took a similarly jaundiced view of his journey on to Ancona – 'this line is extremely hideous hereabouts – frightful lumpy chalk, or sparsely spotted with green, are the hills'. Arriving in mid-afternoon, he adjourned to the beach to

> sit down on the sand in the shade of a bathing hut, close to the sea. Wish I had my glass: even without it can just discern the opposite Dalmatia. Alas! I forebode this small bit of disportment will be the most I shall see of southern climes in 1871 [as indeed it was].

Moving up the coast to Rimini for the night, he found that the Tré Ré had reopened nearer the station, although it was still under the 'same people, smaller house, very clean & civil. Capital supper & clean room.' It was thus in better spirits that he boarded the train to Bologna in the morning. He formed an altogether more benign opinion of the city than he had four years earlier:

> Got a good room for 3 fr at the Brun; dress & wash, & a
> good bkft. Later, walk out; no letters yet. Piazza, church of S.
> Petronius & other places. I am greatly surprised at the pic-
> turesqueness of Bologna – its beautiful effects of broad light
> & shade, its old buildings, & cheery bright hangings of pale
> orange & white.

Another surprise awaited him at dinner, in the form of gossip about
the celebrated 18th-century lady of letters, Ldy Mary Wortley
Montagu (who lived for many years at Brescia), from

> an Englishman who has come from Ischia &, as I understand
> him, passed 2 years (!!) at Lovere of Iseo, where he seems to
> have gathered a deal more about Lady M[ary] W[ortley]
> M[ontagu] than did her descendant Lady S. Percy.
> According to my informant, Lady M. lived with or loved a
> young man of the place, who for her money detained her
> after she wished to 'retire' – till finally the Venetn. Govt. had
> to send an armed party to bring her away by force!!

He stayed another two more days, which were 'filled up pretty
much by letter writing' apart from a visit to the Academia Gallery,
but 'I don't care for all the pictures there – fine as they be qua art'.

Arriving at Padua on the afternoon of 1 August, he 'went all about
town, Palazzo Ragione, Piazza di Signori, Sta. Giustina, &c., &c. –
very many strikingly beautiful bits… quaint old place; noble church
of Eremitani. Ice at Pedrocchi's. Bed at 9. No sleep – noises – & in
the morning, mosquitoes.' He then set out for the Italian Tyrol, then
still under Austrian rule, stopping for the night at Conegliano and
the next morning at Serravalle, which had been united with its twin
Cenada and renamed Vittorio di Veneto:

> Mark of place beautiful cattle – much from me who hates
> cows. Inn, by 9. Small Vienna man, with wife & lame child,
> come here to consult 'Regina di Cin', a name I have seen
> about the place, & photographs of her house. She seems a
> peasant, but very successful practitioner in cases of bone set-
> ting – malformed feet, &c. The Viennese say over 50 people
> were there when they called…

This place seems a bustling halt from the upper country & the plains: charcoal, oxen, wood, &c. At 4 went out, about & up to castle. Some bits are <u>exactly</u> like portions of Titian's paintings – form & colour. The colour of all the scenery is quite different from that of Piedmont – greens but golder & browner, & less positive, being intermixed with moss & grey rocks – "brown pink", with orange greys, & long slices of cloud over the very blue & grey hills close by. The plain – from the castle – stretches away finely, but not so much as in many parts of N. Italy.

Lear went on to report that at dinner

[the] waiting damsel discourses about the doctress. Her Christian name is Regina; a peasant, but has had from childhood a passion & knack of setting bones of fowls, cats, dogs – later sheep, cows, & horses; became noticed for it, so did more & more, & at length practiced on children. Remarkable for great strength of wrist & fingers, & flexibility; is now 52. Was imprecated for a quack; has one son, a priest, who also operates. At first all doctors her enemies, now obliged to confess her skill. Takes no money from poor, makes no charge. 4 lame sisters of Padua – ages 20, 18, 16, 12 – all recently cured. She cannot operate on the little German girl – says nerve is too far gone wrong. People come to her from all parts ('now she even writes in the gazettes'!!).

After a night in Belluno he threaded his way through the mountains to Bolzano (labelled Bozen by its Austrian rulers).

The Dolomites – such as one sees from here – do not appear nearly as fine as the crags of Bavella, because their surroundings are so wanting in detail, & so extravagantly large. O! these bells & the hammering of workmen adjoining!!... Walked out intending to 'climb' no end of hills over the Calvarien. Christ is dressed in pink & blue in one of the compartments, & Pontius Pilate in green squeezing a fat belly with his hands; singularly vulgar & ridiculous horrors.[29]

The weather too began to deteriorate and, although he stayed on for 10 more days, it was only for the purpose of working on his projected Riviera *Journal*, bells and workmen notwithstanding.

He found everything in order back in San Remo, except that the heat was 'tremendous' and the mosquitoes 'unbearable'. The garden was

> a great delight, & looking beautiful. Mice are plentiful & so are green caterpillars; I think of experimenting on both these as objects of culinary attraction... My elth is tolerable, but I am 60 next May, & feel growing old. Going up & downstairs worries me, & I think of marrying some domestic henbird & then of building a nest in one of my own olive trees, where I should only descend at remote intervals during the rest of my life...[30]

His only requirement now was for company. The Congreve family had moved to a cottage in the hills above the town and, although he still saw them at regular intervals, it was to his friends in England that he now turned. In September he appealed to the Fortescues:

> If you come here directly, I can give you 3 figs & 2 bunches of grapes; but if later, I can only offer you 4 small potatoes, some olives, 5 tomatoes & a lot of castor oil berries. These, if mashed up with some crickets who have spongetaneously come to life in my cellar, may make a novel, if not nice or nutritious, jam or jelley.[31]

He wrote to them again in February 1873:

> If you come, I'll show you the Infant School, & the Municipality, & a lemon valley, & an oil press, & a railway station, & a sanctuary, & several poodles – not to speak of my cat who has no end of a tail, because it has been cut off.[32]

This was the celebrated Foss. He was not the first or even the second of his kind to be installed in the Villa Emily to address the problem of 'mice, & as a "distraction" for good Giorgio'.[33] The first cat had not stayed even long enough to acquire a name and his successor, Potiphar, had vanished in Corfu, where Giorgio had taken him when Lear returned to England for the summer of 1872. Giorgio was taking no chances this time and, mindful of the tradition (mentioned in Chapter 1) that a cat would never abandon the house in which it had lost its tail, promptly docked it. This drastic action seems to have been justified, for Foss stayed on as Lear's constant and much-loved companion almost to the very end of his life.

Chapter Fourteen
San Remo, Monte Generoso and other mountain retreats (1873–88)

A month before the arrival of Foss Lear had started out for India, only to turn back at Suez (the Canal had been opened two years earlier) after an altercation with a customs official. The invitation to go there, with all expenses paid - had come from Lord Northbrook, the recently appointed Viceroy. Lear had thought long and hard before accepting it:

> The Himalayas, Darjeeling, Delhi, Ceylon, &c., &c., are what I have always wished to see; but on the other hand, here I have a new house, and to flee away from it as soon as it is well finished seems a kind of giddiness which it rather humiliates me to think of practising.[1]

This about-turn was followed by a relapse in his health, which

> entailed eight or nine days in bed, and with a long & slow recovery... I have, I am thankful to say, become far better in health than I have been for a year past. One thing however is certain: a sedentary life, after moving about as I have done since I was twenty-four years old, will infallibly finish me off <u>suddingly</u>. And although I may be finished off equally suddingly if I move about, yet I incline to think a thorough change will affect me for better rather than for wusse.[2]

He was energised too by the prospect of losing the £1,000 in commissions that he had garnered in advance. There was also another, more negative factor that was beginning to weigh on him: 'The Shuttleworths [plot] below me is all let to Germans for six years, a

Hotel and a Pension; and the ground is all bescattered with horrid Germen, Gerwomen & Gerchildren.'[3] Little did he know just how crushing it would become.

He had still not quite made up his mind when, in September 1873, he received a letter from Gussie bearing the 'terrible' news that she was to marry one Adamson Parker. Not only was her fiancé even older than himself, but, even more gallingly – in view of the fact that it was Lear's epilepsy that had been (for him) the greatest barrier to their marrying – he was an almost total invalid. 'There is now no hope of any but a dark & lonely life. I must leave this place,'[4] Lear wrote in his diary, and to Fortescue a little later:

> You know how I have always had this dream – i.e., for a good
> many years now – & just as the time came when I meant to
> let the decision of my proposal yes or no determine my plan
> as to India, the question suddenly resolved itself without my
> having pain of a refusal.[5]

Having made a new will, sorted out letters from no fewer than 444 correspondents for safekeeping, handed over Foss into the care of the Congreve family and shut up the Villa Emily, he boarded the S.S. *India* at Genoa on 24 October. Giorgio rejoined him at Naples and together they ranged over the length and breadth of the subcontinent for more than a year, ending in Ceylon (now Sri Lanka), where, in a reversal of roles, Lear had to nurse his servant through a serious attack of dysentery. As they prepared to re-embark at Bombay, Giorgio received another blow, in the shape of news of the death of his wife, and when they reached Italy again he hurried off to Corfu to attend to his family.

Lear was thus alone once more when he finally got back to San

Remo in January 1875. He was delighted to find that the Villa Emily's garden was 'beautiful with oranges!!' and that Foss 'somehow seems to know me dreamily'. He also remarked on the 'scores of new villas' and, more ominously, 'what crowds of Germans! Simply clouds.'[6]

It was not long before the combination of cold and loneliness began to dispirit him: 'The horrible depression & deadly melancholy I suffer is not to be told, & as I am at present, I can hardly compel myself to remain on here.'[7] To Fortescue, who had meanwhile been elevated to the peerage with the title Lord Carlingford, he complained of '42 thousand 857 colds in the head'.[8] As usual, he sought relief in work, settling down to pen out the thousand and more drawings that he had brought back from India. Giorgio presently returned to restore everything to rights, although it took a little more time before Foss was persuaded to resume the old order: on the last day of February he 'just before dinner time, rushed out, & – we supposed – fled away up to the Villa Congreve. But he soon came back again, repentant.'[9]

The arrival of spring also helped to revive Lear's spirits, the sight of his garden in full bloom giving him special pleasure. At the beginning of June he wrote:

> Garden wonderfully lovely – as one flower, e.g., roses, goes away, others – e.g., passionflowers, carnations & Guernsey lilies & hollyhocks – come on; a surprising variety of beauty... very much like Paradise, only Adam hath no Eve.[10]

His sense of isolation increased when he heard Walter Congreve, whose relationship with his housekeeper had become a source of local gossip, talk of taking himself and his sons off to Tasmania, and he decided to return to his friends in England for the summer.

He took with him a selection of his finished Indian sketches to cover his expenses, and his best hopes were fulfilled when both Lady Ashburton, (the purchaser of 'The Cedars of Lebanon') and Lord Aberdare, who, as Henry Bruce, had been one of his early friends in Rome, commissioned large oils of Mount Kanchenjunga. He told the latter delightedly that:

> I intend that the 'Kanchenjunga' shall be so good a picture that nobody will ever be able – if it is hung in your dining room – to eat any dinner along of contemplating it, so that

the painting will not only be desirable, but a highly eco-
nomical object. And I shall fully trust that all future grandchildren of yours & Lady Aberdare will be christened
Kanchenjunga as an additional appellative.[11]

During this visit to England he also completed *Laughable Lyrics*,
the last *Book of Nonsense* to be published in his lifetime.

When he got back to San Remo, Giorgio was ready and waiting,
accompanied this time by his second son, Lambi. The Suliot's aged
mother and the last of his brothers had both meanwhile died, and to
console him Lear had agreed to lodge the boy in return for the occasional
helping hand. He was relieved to find that the Congreve family were also
still in place. Hubert later recalled frequently going with him on

> sketching expeditions together, Lear plodding slowly along, old
> George following behind laden with lunch and drawing mate-
> rials. When we came to a good subject, Lear would sit down,
> and taking his block from George, would lift his spectacles, and
> gaze for several minutes at the scene through a monocular glass
> he always carried; then, laying down the glass and adjusting his
> spectacles, he would put on paper the view before us, mountain
> range, villages and foreground, with a rapidity and accuracy
> that inspired me with awestruck admiration.[12]

It was not only Lear's pace that was now faltering. In March 1877
he reported to Fortescue that:

> My dear good servant & friend George Kokali, who during
> nearly twenty-two years has attended me & served me &
> nursed me in illness with a faithfulness which better masters
> than I have had few chances of obtaining, has been growing
> weaker & weaker for months past. Two weeks ago he told me
> that he could work no more, but would like to go to Corfu
> to see his other two children. I had no doubt as to my duty...
> The journey from Ancona to Brindisi was terrible – one long
> snowstorm, such as has never been known so far south. At
> Brindisi, two feet of snow![13]

During the night the weather grew still wilder, and Lear was reluc-
tantly persuaded by Hubert Congreve, who had accompanied him, to
turn back and allow Giorgio and Lambi to go on to Corfu without him.

He and Hubert now set off for Naples, arriving in brilliant sunshine. His spirits quickly recovered, the more so for becoming embroiled in a struggle for his luggage with a crowd of hotel touts at the station. Hubert took up the story:

> Before I could intervene my old friend had tumbled into the wrong bus, out of which nothing would move him, and so we were driven off to an hotel at which we had had no intention of staying, Lear, on the way there, giving me a long lecture on the care I must take while we were in Naples, as the Neapolitans were the greatest scoundrels he had ever met!

After revisiting Pompeii, which Lear found 'a far more wonderful sight than in 1847 when I saw it last, so much more of the site having been excavated,'[14] they went on to tour the sights of Rome, in a week that Hubert described as 'one of the fullest and happiest we ever spent together'.[15] For Lear, however, the memories of the past weighed even more heavily than they had in 1871: out of the legion of his former friends he found only Penry Williams left, and he was hobbled by rheumatism. 'If the dreams of the past are gone, & if those of the present are fading, what is there left? Nothing, I think,' Lear lamented, worse still 'in a few days I must face the unknown dark – <u>alone</u>!'[16] In fact, the future was darker than even he could then guess.

Back at San Remo he resumed tutoring Hubert and his brother Arnold, but they (and Foss) provided his only regular company. Not only had their father now become still more deeply involved with the housekeeper, getting her pregnant and declaring his intention of marrying her, but he also gave the appearance of being ready to shed all his responsibilities towards them. He deputed Lear to break the disagreeable news to Hubert and was even prepared to consider lodging the boy at the Villa Emily, with a view to his becoming a professional artist. Lear could hardly contain his disgust at this turn in his friend's character: 'It is difficult to imagine anything more cold & unfriendly than this man's conduct – a bad & heartless neighbour, & though a violent egotist, indifferent apparently to everything either for his own life or those of others.' he raged.[17]

However, Congreve then decided that 'Hubert is not the least cut out for a professional artist.'[18] Lear had already reached the same conclusion himself, and he began to think that he should wash his hands of the whole relationship: 'If soon finished, perhaps better; for I think no light can ever brighten the dark gloom now nearer at hand than ever.'[19] This sentiment was strengthened still further by the news in April, of his brother Henry's death in Texas, half a century after their last meeting. 'Strange as it may seem', the news 'upsets me terribly,' Lear wrote. 'Most miserable, & nearly resolving to shut up all at once & discontinue the lessons, & to try to get to England as fast as possible.'[20]

He set out towards the end of May. On his arrival in London he warned the Fortescues that all these events had reduced him to such a state of shock 'that I have nearly lost all ideas about my own identity, & if anybody should ask me suddenly if I am Lady Jane Grey, the Apostle Paul, Julius Caesar or Theodore Hook, I should say yes to every question'.[21] He found his last surviving sister, Eleanor Newsom, deaf, blind and in the final stages of her dotage, and it took a visit to the Tennysons to revive him. 'Emily T. – instead of being aged & altered as I looked for – appears younger, & handsomer, & diviner than ever', he rejoiced, and even Alfred he found 'more genial than of old, though of course he had his growl about his publishers after dinner.'[22] The relief was not to last long, however, for in the last week of July Walter Congreve's brother called with the shock news that Hubert had been entered for a degree course in civil engineering at King's College, London, in the autumn. 'I was never nearer to utter & total madness than now,' Lear wrote on 2 August. 'Yet, I don't mean to give way, & shall stave off worse things if I can.'[23]

Worse was to come, for a month later he received a letter from Corfu indicating that Giorgio's decline was accelerating. Lear hurried out there for the last rites and found Giorgio 'very thin & altered, & feeble – yet not so much as I had feared... If he recovers, he may yet come back to me...'[24] It seemed a forlorn hope, yet just over a year later, in October 1878, Lear was writing to Fortescue to thank him 'for your congratulations about George's return':

> It is really almost unreal, his recovery... His doctor wrote to me that a sea voyage & completely new air might possibly restore him. So in June I sent for him to come by sea to Genoa; & he got there, a mere skeleton & unable to walk. But I thought I would run the risk, & took him straight up to Monte Generoso.[25]

At nearly 5,500 feet above Lake Lugano it was 'no end of a pull up' and, on dismounting from his mule, Giorgio 'had one of his giddy fits & fell down senseless'. A few days later he began 'suffering immensely from a bad tooth',[26] but once that had been extracted by the hotel's versatile proprietor, one Dr Pasta, he rapidly regained his strength in the invigorating mountain atmosphere.

They stayed there for the best part of two months. Lear found the company in the hotel 'a screaming bore' for the most part, but otherwise the wonderfully clear air provided him with a rich field of fresh material, extending from the whole range of the Oberland Alps in the north to Milan in the south: 'You could see the flies walking up the Cathedral any afternoon.' he told Fortescue. [27] It also inspired him to launch himself again into working up his Tennyson illustrations; their projected number had risen to 200 and their completion had become such an obsession with him that he now referred to them as his 'Tyrants'.

'I was very sorry to leave that beautiful Monte Generoso, as well as Dr. Pasta & everybody there,' he wrote when the time came to depart. 'I have never known – for years – such a place to look back on with nearly unmixed feelings of pleasure.'[28] Even better, Giorgio now

> was able to sleep, eat and walk as he had not done for three years. Before we left in September, he walked about Como, carrying my folios, &c., as he used to do twenty-four years ago. And now he is here and just the same orderly good active man as ever... So you see we are just now as before the fathers fell asleep, George, Lambi [who had recently rejoined them], myself, and the excellent Foss now eight years old.[29]

Lear may well have felt that at last he was set to see out the evening of his days in the tranquillity that he thought he had bought for himself with the Villa Emily. He was very soon to be disabused.

On 24 October he noted in his diary that

> all the trees, or nearly all, below my ground [on the Hanbury-Shuttleworth land] are cut down – & I heard today that the Hotel is to be the very largest in San Remo. It is possible that it will hide all my sea-view. But I do not allow myself to think of this ugly affair...[30]

However, it was not long before 'the dreadful annoyance from the blasting & building below' allowed him to think of little else and he began to inspect other building plots available in the vicinity. Returning to Monte Generoso again for the summer of 1879, he even viewed some sites for sale at Sacro Monte near Varese, in the area that had so impressed him a decade earlier. However, he found that even the cheapest would cost him a full thousand pounds more than the one he favoured at San Remo and the shocking news of the sudden death of Lady Waldegrave only served to increase his depression and indecision. Yet another source of distraction was the behaviour of Lambi, who was discovered to have contracted both gonorrhoea and a mass of debts. Lear told his American publisher, James Fields, that:

> Having but an income of £110 a year, the destruction of my Artist life is miserable enough, & as I have not a chance of buying other land here (now since 1869 greatly advanced in price) I suppose I shall have to flee away & be heard of no more. It is however better to be sinned against than to sin, & I would rather be as I am at 68 than be the Druggist Hanbury or Miss Shuttleworth who have worked me this misery. I cannot help laughing at one bit of advice suggested to me – that I should stump all Europe & America & wherever the English Language is spoken, as the Writer of the Book of Nonsense, with a view to collect innumerable sixpences so as to raise 7 or 8 thousand pounds to buy new land & build another house!! So look out for me & my cat some fine day – by a Boston Steamer, on my way to San Francisco...[31]

Fortescue wrote cautioning him against any hasty move and half-promising to visit shortly, and a 'wonderfully kind letter' arrived from

Lord Northbrook, 'offering to lend me £2000 with no interest till I rebuild a house – & earnestly urging me to do so'.[32] For his part, Lord Derby (the 15th Earl, who had succeeded his father in 1870) offered to commission £500-worth of watercolours rather than provide a loan, which he considered would be 'a mistake' in the light of Lear's previous mismanagement of his finances.

Still Lear could not make up his mind. 'It seems a dreadful folly to build again & resettle, but there seems no alternative,' he conceded in his diary, yet two days later he veered towards the counter-argument that he should 'send all resettling to the wind'.[33] The New Year of 1880 found him 'unable to apply to work in the half-dark room', but, 'on the other hand, the thought of mortgages, new purchase & new building & moving, all tend to drive me insane...'[34] When he did manage to gear himself up sufficiently to view some other plots for sale, it was only to find that they each suffered from some insuperable disadvantage: one was too exposed to the east wind, another was too far out of the town, still another too hemmed in by other properties.

It seems that it took the prospect of Fortescue's imminent arrival to push Lear into making a decision, and a week later he paid a deposit of £1,000 on a plot which, he told Emily Tennyson, 'has only the road and the railway between it & the sea, so unless the fishes begin to build, or Noah's Ark comes to an anchor below the site, the new Villa Edouardo cannot be spoiled'.[35] No sooner had he paid the remaining £1,800 when he received an offer for a section of the plot from a neighbour who planned to replace his house with a 'palazzo'. Lear's immediate reaction was 'a distinct NO', but he reflected later that if he could obtain £4,000 for it 'I might do worse than accept that offer.'[36] However, such a figure was hopelessly optimistic – as was the price-tag of £7,000 that an agent persuaded him to put on the Villa Emily – and nothing came of it.

The new house was to be an exact replica of the old, except that, because of the configuration of the ground, it was the other way round. The builder's estimate amounted to £2,000, and to pay for it Lear decided to hold one more exhibition of his work in London during the summer of 1880. It would be his last visit to his native land and he found life in the capital more distasteful than ever, being 'horribly exasperated by the quantity of respirators or refrigerators or percolators or perambulators or whatever those vehicles are called that bump your legs with babies' heads'.[37] Two events provided him with more than sufficient consolation, however. The first was the sight of Hubert mounting the rostrum no less than 11 times during prize-giving at King's College; the second was a reunion with Gussie. 'Adamson Parker's gentleness under complete privation is beautiful, & so is Gussie's constant care of him. What would life not have been with that woman!!'[38] he wrote afterwards. The exhibition also went well, but its success was offset by the bankruptcy of his publisher, who still owed him royalties on the last *Book of Nonsense*.

Giorgio had written to tell him that 'the new House he go on like one Tortoise'.[39] When Lear returned at the end of August, he was therefore pleasantly surprised to find the ground floor almost complete, although he was constrained to describe it in his diary as 'a work of doubtful happiness. Nevertheless, I think of Gussie ahead...'[40] Another discovery was the presence of his servant's youngest son, Dimitri, who had been drafted in to replace the errant Lambi. When, a few days later, Giorgio's eldest son, Nicola, telegraphed from Corfu that he was about to be conscripted into the Greek army, Lear packed Giorgio and Lambi off to make their farewells and retired with Dimitri to the Italian Lakes in order to escape from the noise of the builders.

They stayed a week at Sacro Monte before moving on again to Monte Generoso, where they were joined by Hubert, but a week after returning to San Remo he and Lear parted for the last time.

Having finally 'made an honest woman' of his housekeeper, who, according to local gossip, had already borne him one other illegitimate child, Walter Congreve now sold up all his interests in San Remo and decamped. Grieved though he was at this loss, Lear was not left quite alone, for he had befriended the family of William Bevan, the new British Vice-Consul; it was with the help of the eldest daughter that he composed the verses that were to become his epitaph, 'How Pleasant to Know Mister Lear'.[41] Other recent arrivals who became regular companions were Hugh de Freyllenberg Montgomery and his wife; he in particular commended himself to Lear as being the godson of Lady Byron and having 'long lived with her as a boy'.[42]

By the end of October the roof was on the new house, which was now named, unambiguously, Villa Tennyson, and Lear threw himself enthusiastically into a new series of 300 Tennyson illustrations:

> When the 300 drawings are done, I shall sell them for
> £18000; with which I shall buy a chocolate coloured carriage
> speckled with gold, & driven by a coachman in green vest-
> ments and silver spectacles – wherein, sitting on a lofty cush-
> ion composed of muffins & volumes of the Apocryfa, I shall
> disport myself all about the London parks, to the general sat-
> isfaction of all pious people.[43]

On another front, however, his hopes of a speedy return to his former regimen were being seriously undermined. Far from being safely
employed in the army, Nicola was still at Corfu and looking to Lear
to relieve him of the debts that he was now running up with Lambi's
help. After receiving yet another begging letter Lear concluded:

> I see no way out of all this bother, but either that George
> goes & settles at Brindisi – which is fatal for the poor old
> man – or that he sends his sons to America – which is equal-
> ly shocking, since the poor good father would then break
> down utterly. It seems strange, at a time when I want money
> more than at any previous period, everything conspires as it
> were to prevent my working.[44]

In the end he decided to compromise by establishing the two sons
in a trattoria at Brindisi while retaining their father at San Remo.

He was thankful at least not to be in London, which was experienc-
ing its worst winter of the century. He read newspaper reports of Oxford
Circus being buried under 15 feet of snow with 'feelings of horror. With
such wretchedness existing, why am I in such luxury?' He sent a cheque
for £5 to Frank Lushington for his Thames district poor:

> Of course one 'can't afford' this, but if one is only to relieve
> others from one's superfluities, that can't be right. I have
> every comfort at present in all sorts of ways, & ought to help
> those who are wretched.[45]

The lease that he had taken on in Brindisi for Nicola and Lambi
fell through at the last moment, and he set out himself to secure
another for them there. However, the British Consul warned him
bluntly that 'trattorias are set up by the score here, & fail every week...

To set them up here would be madness. Rather advises near Genoa or Savona.'[46] He headed home again convinced that his journey had been a 'feeble, futile, foolish failure'. At Genoa, however, he found consolation in a friendly hotelier who 'to my extreme delight not only offers to look out for a small house somewhere on the coast, but to get a room for the 2 Cocali to come before June 1st [1881].'[47] and who afterwards even took them both on as waiters.

A week after his return from this journey, Lear dined at the Villa Emily for the last time, feeling 'sad enough', and the following week he spent his first night in the Villa Tennyson:

> I cajoled Foss into a general examination of all the rooms, &
> Foss seemed gratified till all at once the animal disappeared,
> & no search of mine nor of Erasmo [the new gardener] could
> find it... presently Foss rushed out of a chimney, amid gen-
> eral applause.[48]

The relief that he must have felt now that the move was at last completed was soon overtaken by the realisation that a great deal of work remained to be done on the new house and that most of the £3,000 bill was still to be paid. A fortnight later he wrote:

> Somehow it is difficult to see one's way to being ever com-
> fortable here, & were it not for the dislike I have to break up
> all my life-diary-sketches, I would certainly sell all & go
> hence. What folly it all seems! this fuss – on the mere chance
> of my being able to make use of this new house![49]

Getting away to the Lakes again for the summer allowed him to write that:

> I have not felt so well or so cheery for a long, long time. The
> calm & brightness of the view, & the lovely sweetness of the
> air, bring back infinite days & years of outdoor delight, & I
> am thankful for this blessing – though it can only last a few
> minutes.[50]

On his return to San Remo however, his problems once again threatened to overwhelm him:

> Knowing the immense difficulties I may drift into if the Villa
> Emily does not sell, & considering that my expenses keep

growing greater with constantly less means to meet them, uncertain both as to having energy & health to complete some & commence other work; & – if it could ever be finished – whether it could meet with sale; all these doubts afflict me terribly, the more that I am so utterly lonely & unable to consult anyone... sometimes I think I will dismiss Giorgio & his sons at once, shut up the house & let it & go to Rome. But how then could I commence a new life at my age & ill as I am? God help me.[51]

Once again he sought solace in his work and in the preparations for the opening of his new gallery:

After a good deal of indecision I ordered a matting for all the gallery – some £7 or more expense, but as I had worked so much for these gallery drawings – 150 in number – it appears absurd not to give them a chance of sale – & that can only be done by making a fair gallery for showing them in... These are tranquil & by no means unhappy days, which I had not thought could occur again, & for which God make me thankful.[52]

In March 1882 Fortescue rejoined the Cabinet as Lord Privy Seal. Lear was delighted at the prospect that his friend's return to high office would distract him from his continuing grief over his wife's death, and he derived some amusement for himself from the news:

I have never had a clear idea of what the Privy Seal's work really is, & my last notion is that you have continually to superintend seal-catching all round the Scotch & English coasts, in order to secure a Government monopoly of seal skins & calves.

In the same month Queen Victoria arrived at nearby Menton to take the Mediterranean air, and the appearance of Lord Spencer, the Lord President of the Council, at the house of her former drawing master caused crowds to gather at Lear's gate in anticipation. He told Fortescue:

I hope if H.M. does come, I shall be told of the future event before it comes to pass, as it would not be pretty to be caught in old slippers & shirt sleeves. I dislike contact with Royalty, as you know, being a dirty landscape painter apt only to speak his thoughts & not to conceal them. The other day

when someone said, 'Why do you keep your garden locked?'
says I: 'To keep out beastly German bands, & odious wandering Germans in general.' Says my friend: 'If the Q. comes
to your gallery, you had better not say that sort of thing.'
Says I: 'I won't if I can help it.'[53]

It was thus just as well, perhaps, that she did not come after all.
However, Lear, back at Monte Generoso for the summer, was at
lunch one day when 'a little lady came & looked at me through the
glass door of the Ristorante; as she continued looking, I observed her
to be like the Queen'. It was not Victoria but her eldest daughter, the
Princess Royal, who then sent in her husband, Prince Frederick of
Prussia, to tell him that 'my wife wishes to know if you are Mister
Lear, & she would be glad to make your acquaintance again'. After
the reintroductions the Princess accepted Lear's suggestion that he be
allowed to accompany her on an afternoon walk to show her the
views, causing him to describe her in his diary, as he had her mother,
as 'the most absolute duck imaginable'.[54]

The following year he received a visitor more important to him
than any queen. It was during that same summer that he had learned
of the death of Adamson Parker and speculated, 'What will now happen, who can tell?'[55] Three weeks later he had written to Fortescue: 'I
wish I were not so "dam old", but I think 71–72 will perhaps be a little too advanced.'[56] Nevertheless, in February (1883) he took heart
again and wrote to Gussie to persuade her to come out to San Remo:

> My garden is now admirably beautiful, & were it not for the
> Slugs & Snails would be inimitable. But these melancholy
> mucilaginous Molluscs have eaten up all my Higher-cynths
> & also my Lower-cynths, & I have only just now found a
> mode of getting rid of these enemies – which is by flattering
> their vanity in taking them friendly walks up & down the
> garden, a ploy which blinds them to ulterior consequences.
> And thus (they being of a monstrous size as you may see by
> the sketch below), when I get them near the cistern, I pitch
> them into the water, where they justly expiate their unpleas-
> ant & greedy sins. Please write again soon.[57]

She responded almost at once, arriving on 17 March chaperoned, as

the rules of the day dictated, by two nieces. They saw each other almost every day for the next fortnight and Lear was reduced once again to an agony of indecision. After their second meeting he wrote: 'I – at times – am miserably undecided as to what to do ahead'; gradually, however, his old pessimism reasserted itself: 'Alas! Alas! Alas! It cannot be... As a dream is a dream, it is better to treat it as such... It is for the last time, & the end & loneliness till that end comes is all now left to me.'

On the last day of her visit he

> got as good & large a nosegay as I could for dear Gussie, & 2 others for the nieces, and, having made them up in parcels, took them up to the Royal [Hotel], where I saw <u>& took leave</u> of Gussie. So ends the very last possible chance of a change of life. Many causes occasion this – my age the least among them; the knowledge of all my misery – physical & psychical – now & of late quite clear to me & unescapable from – among the greatest. It was a hard effort at the last, & I could only not burst into tears before I left – when I did...[58]

'I miss her horridly,' he told Fortescue a few days later.[59]

The Villa Emily still could not find a buyer, in spite of the price being brought down progressively to £3,000. In desperation Lear considered reducing it even further:

> It is becoming a question whether I had not better sell it for £2000 rather than keep it. My former income of over £100 a year from £3500 in the 3 per Cents is now gone, & the worry of getting money to pay weekly bills is not pleasant at 70 aet, when one had thought to be high & dry above all bother of that kind.

In order to replace the lost income he eventually let the house 'for some sort of a collegiate concatenation'.[60]

An even greater source of worry was another rapid decline in Giorgio's health. Genoa had soon proved no solution for Nicola and Lambi, obliging Lear to take both of them in again under his own roof. Far from bringing their father comfort, however, their disruptive presence had merely driven him to drink and, eventually, off the premises altogether: he was found several days later wandering around Toulon, totally destitute. 'I hardly think poor George can again thoroughly recover, and should he ever drink again, he is doubtless lost, for all his life,' Lear had written. Worse still, Lambi was caught stealing wine from the cellar, giving Lear little option but to dispatch him back to Corfu where, like his father before him, he was found to have a family whose existence he had hitherto concealed. The one consolation was that Dimitri continued to earn his keep: 'So after all, one has much to be thankful for, as the Centipede said when the Rat bit off ninety-seven of his hundred legs,' Lear joked to Fortescue.'[61]

Retreating again to Monte Generoso for the summer, Lear sent Giorgio on ahead with Dimitri in the hope that the mountain air would work its restorative magic, but when he got there himself it was to find that his old servant's 'bronchitis has returned & he can hardly speak, & his cough is incessant & terrible. He must leave off smoking, or worse will happen...'[62] The decline was now irreversible, however: a month later Giorgio was dead. Lear vowed that he would 'never, never more return here,' feeling that 'the only thing that can mitigate this sorrow, & give a thorough change to the direction of my thoughts, will be to try the novelty of some place hitherto unvisited, say Madeira, or S. America, or Japan, or Java...'[63] He appealed to Fortescue, 'Please write to me'[64] and in a letter to Emily Tennyson he quoted some verses from Alfred's 'In Memoriam'.

Burying Giorgio at Mendrisio, the nearest town, Lear then set off with Dimitri on what was to be his last tour of his adopted homeland, leaving Nicola in charge of the Villa Tennyson.

His eye for a pretty face remained undimmed, for he recorded that the train journey to Bologna was made

> very interesting owing to a singularly nice girl – one Miss Florence Elliott – & her mother. She was born in Australia,

& knows it all as well as New Z... [and] all Tennyson, & is altogether well informed, besides being good-looking & well-mannered.[65]

After a fortnight's recuperation in the Tuscan mountain resorts of Abetone and San Marcello, he retraced old ground in Lucca and Florence before going on to Perugia, Assisi and the Etruscan tombs at Ponte San Giovanni, which, however, were 'too dark for me, so I sent Dimitri in alone'.[66]

Stopping to make some fresh sketches of Pisa, he found that he had almost run out of drawing paper and, worse still, that Dimitri had mislaid the pencil; however,

> Thanx to the memory of George & his great patience, I was not angry at all, but as it was now too late to send for more paper, I came on slowly, drawing twice more by the way. Only 4 more pieces of the new paper now being left, I came at 11 to the Gombo, & walked with Dimitri to the sea, where I drew the coastline – being near to where Shelley's body must have been found. The whole scene seems before me as I write as it did 22 years ago.[67]

At La Spezia he did not at all approve of the alterations that had taken place in the interval:

> Any place so changed for the worse – picturesquely speaking – it is not possible to imagine. The old Croce di Malta stands in a street of houses, & the place we were at, now 'Locanda di Odessa', is only just to be recognised – among new garden squares & streets, with a vast arsenal & endless warships to fill up the Gulf of Confusion.[68]

The Gulf had become, as it still is, the main base of the Italian Navy. It was thus a relief to get back to San Remo and find that Nicola had the Villa Tennyson in perfect order. Things were not so happy at the Villa Emily, however, as he told Fortescue;

> Last autumn it was let to people for a school, but they, having furnished and inhabiting it, declare their utter inability to pay a farthing of rent! As the villa was mortgaged for £2000 to our dear good kind Northbrook three years back, when there was

every prospect of its sale for £5000 or £6000, & when no one could have foreseen so brutal an increase of wicked injury, you may suppose how miserable I am about it...[69]

Even worse was to follow, as he wrote again at the beginning of 1884:

The people who took Villa Emily for a school have come to utter grief & have absconded, paying me £4 only out of the £100 due, & having had all their furniture seized & carried off by the tradesmen of San Remo who supplied it. One of the partners sends the key of the Villa to the agent, & begs that I may be informed that any effort to be repaid is useless on my part, as they have no money whatsoever.

A month later the burden was off his shoulders at last, for the derisory sum of £1,600:

I considered the matter thoroughly, & finally came to the conclusion that a great & serious present loss is more easily to be endured than an infinitely greater one in the future, aggravated meanwhile by constant necessities of tax & repair payings.[70]

Not surprisingly the whole tortuous business took a toll on his health, and a few days after the completion of the sale he fell seriously ill with pleurisy. By mid-May he

was just able to get away from here on my journey of discovery; I was frightfully pulled down by my illness – with swollen feet, & unable to walk; but George's youngest son, Dimitri, continually pulled me into & out of railway carriages like a sack of hay. So by dint of pluck & patience I got to Vicenza & to Recoaro, where I have taken rooms for eight or ten weeks... Generally speaking I have latterly resembled this...[71]

He told Fortescue that some of the company at this new choice of mountain resort was not altogether to his taste:

You would have been edified by the society of several Americans at Recoaro. One, a well-bred & educated family, electrified me by their opinion on 'Slave Emancipation': 'It [the Civil War] had nothing to do with a hatred of slavery, though hatred of slavery was used as a factor in the matter. It was wholly in substance a political move against the Southern States. Not one of us, nor of thousands in America, would sit at table with a black man or woman!' 'But,' said I to one of the sons, 'you would sit in a room with your dog?' 'Dog? Yes, Sir! But you can't compare an inferior creature such as a negro is with a dog.'[72]

He soon had another 'shocking matter' to report: he had caught Dimitri stealing and felt no option but to dismiss him. This left him only with Nicola who, it became apparent as the winter drew on, was gradually dying of tuberculosis; the only consolation was that Luigi Rusconi, the servant who was taken on to replace him, 'seems a jewel'. For all Lear's attention, Nicola continued to sink and on 4 March 1885 he died. Two weeks later Lear lost the last link to his own family with the death of his sister Eleanor.

With the arrival of summer his health picked up again and his latest choice of a retreat, Barzano, in the hills to the east of Como, proved a great success:

> In all the 50 years I have more or less lived in Italy, I have never met with such a perfect climate as this of the Brianza district – nor any summer place so everlastingly green & lovely. The view of the Lecco mountains from my windows is enough to make a blacking-brush squeak with delight...[73]

'I never passed three months so tranquilly & comfortably, that I can remember, <u>anywhere</u>,'[74] he wrote on his return to San Remo. He even felt able to joke with his doctor's wife:

> I did not say all I might have said to Dr. H[assall] about my health, thinking he might upbraid (or down-braid) me for doing more than I ought to do at my age, & considering how feeble I am, consequently – though I tell you in confidence – I did not tell him that I had climbed to the top of the tallest Eucalyptus tree in my garden & jumped thence into the Hotel Royal grounds nor that I had leaped straight over the outer V. Tennyson wall from the highroad – nor that I had run a race with my cat from here to Ventimiglia, having beaten Foss by 8 feet & a half. Those facts you can impart to Dr. Hassall or knot as you like.[75]

In December, following the defeat of Gladstone's Liberals in the recent general election, Fortescue was at last able to accept his old friend's long-standing invitation to visit. Lear wrote delightedly on his arrival:

> I do not know if the Phoca Privata [Privy Seal] has a permanent place, or if he is changed with a change of government, but if you have brought him with you, please give him to Luigi, who will put him into the cistern and give him a piece of bread & ham.[76]

Within a few days, however, Fortescue was taken seriously ill as a result of a chill and Lear promptly went down himself in sympathy. The two men rose from their respective sick-beds to dine with each other on Christmas Day, when Fortescue recorded that 'Lear said he felt as if he were dying. He was the better for his dinner, & we had a great deal of talk.'[77] Lear returned to his bed and remained there for the duration of the winter. It was now that he completed his final nonsense verses, 'Incidents in the Life of My Uncle Arly', which seem to have been intended as his own obituary.

Happily it was premature, for by May 1886 he had recovered sufficiently to return to Barzano and Mendrisio, and later he even made a foray into Switzerland, as far as Lucerne. In November Frank Lushington came out to see him, but the visit was not a great success: like Fortescue, he was caught out by the sudden drop in the temperature in the late afternoon and succumbed likewise. 'You can well understand that the depression & sadness of my life in these days was not much relieved by Frank, who you know is often silent for days together,'[78] Lear confided to Emily Tennyson.

An even greater disappointment was in store for him. In the hope of finding a way of reproducing his Tennyson illustrations 'by which I can eventually multiply my 200 designs by photograph or autograph, or sneezigraph or any other graph,'[79] he had sent them to the Autotype Company, who now reported that they had

> failed to do any good, & their suggestion that at my age I should execute all the 200 drawings afresh is of course too absurd to think of. But I fear this labour of fifty years must be given up altogether.[80]

(After Lear's death the Tennysons published a limited number of the illustrations in a private edition.)

The promise of further visitors from England served to see him through another winter. First came Lord Northbrook and his wife, and then, even more importantly, Gussie. She arrived on 1 April 1887, seeming to Lear 'more nice & charming than ever'. She sat with him in his bedroom for the next four days, and on the last he wrote in his diary:

> Pondering – more or less perplexed as to if I shall or shall not ask Gussie to marry me. Once or twice the crisis nearly came off, yet she went at 5 & nothing occurred beyond her very decidedly showing me how much she cared for me... This, I think, was the day of the death of all hope.[81]

In May he received a visit from an American publisher, a Mr Estes, who was considering an edition of Tennyson's poems and wrote:

> I found Mr. Lear sitting up for the first time for several weeks, and he insisted on showing Mrs. Estes & I not only all the Tennyson drawings, but all his other paintings & drawings, one of which I bought, to his evident satisfaction. He assured us that our call had enlivened him and done him a world of good.[82]

This would indeed appear to be the case, for the following month Lear reported to Fortescue:

> I am <u>considerably better</u>. At 7 A.M. today I walked nearly all round the garden, which for flowers in bloom is now a glorious sight. Also the ten pigeons are a great diversion, though beginning to be rather impudent & aggressive. Their punctuality as to their sitting on their eggs and vice versa I never knew of before. The males & females take their turns EXACTLY <u>every two hours</u>. Guiseppe [who had replaced Luigi] believes they have little watches under their wings, & that they wind them up at sunset – 8 P.M. – standing on one foot & holding the watch in the other.[83]

By July he was even fit enough to make his usual journey into the hills, this time to Andorno at the entrance to the Val d'Aosta. He did not enjoy it as much as previous retreats, however, complaining that 'the tremendous heat (even up here) and the incessant labour of knocking away flies worries me sadly...'[84]

After his return to San Remo he suffered two blows from which he was never to recover. The first was the sudden death in New Zealand of 'my dear good nephew, Charles Street'; the second, following shortly afterwards, was that of Foss:

> Whoever has known me for 30 years has known that for all that time my cat Foss has been part of my solitary life. Foss is dead, & I am glad to say did not suffer at all – having become quite paralyzed on all one side of him. So he was placed in a box yesterday & buried below the Fig-tree at the end of the Orange Walk... All those friends who have known my life will understand that I grieve over this loss.[85] (In his grief Lear exaggerated Foss's age: he had arrived as a kitten in 1872 and was therefore 15 when he died.)

Three months later, on 29 January 1888 Lear himself was dead. He was buried beside Nicola in the English cemetery. His tombstone is inscribed to the memory of 'Edward Lear, landscape painter in many lands', who was 'dear for his many gifts to many souls', and carries the following quotation from Tennyson's poem to him:

> all things fair,
> With such a pencil such a pen,
> You shadow'd forth to distant men.
> I read and felt that I was there.

Gussie Parker remained alone for another two years before marrying Thomas Nash (an uncle of the painter Paul Nash). She died, a widow once more, in 1931, at the grand age of 93.

Chapter Notes

The following abbreviations are used in these notes:

CF   Chichester Fortescue

D   Edward Lear's Diaries

EL   (letter from) Edward Lear

LEL   *Letters of Edward Lear*

LLEL   *Later Letters of Edward Lear*

SL   *Edward Lear: Selected Letters*

VN   Vivien Noakes, *Edward Lear: The Life of a Wanderer* (new edition 2004, except as shown).

Further details on these and other items mentioned below can be found in the Bibliography.

Introduction

1 *The Complete Nonsense of Edward Lear*, p. 27.

2 *Pall Mall Magazine*, 15 February 1886.

3 *The Times*, 4 October 2001.

4 *LEL*, p. xiii.

5 *Indian Journal*, 13 January 1874; VN, p. 6.

6 D, 17 January 1865.

7 Angus Davidson, *Edward Lear*, p. 4.

8 D, 14 February 1880.

9 D, 24 March 1877.

10 EL to Ann Lear, 10 February 1856.

11 D, 18 September 1861.

12 D, 10 September 1863.

13 EL to C. Empson, 1 October 1831; *SL*, p.14.

14 'By Way of Preface', *Nonsense Songs and Stories*; Angus Davidson, *Edward Lear*, p. 12.

15 Daniel Fowler, *Autobiography*, pp. 103–4; VN, p. 15.

16 EL to Fanny Coombe, undated [July 1832]; VN, p. 12.

17 Peter Levi, *Edward Lear*, p. 19.

18 EL to C. Empson, 1 October 1831; *SL*, p. 16.

19 W. Swainson to EL, 26 November 1831; Brian Reade, *Edward Lear's Parrots*, p. 16.

20 EL to C. Empson, 1 October 1831; *SL*, p. 14.

21 D, 7 February 1881.

22 EL to Sir John Lubbock, 3 November 1883; *LLEL*, p. 366.

23 EL to George Coombe, 24 June 1835; VN, p. 30.

24 Daniel Fowler, *Autobiography*, p.104; VN (third edition, 1985), p. 33.

25 *The Diary of Frances, Lady Shelley, 1787–1817*, p. 13; VN, p. 28.

26 EL to George Coombe, 24 July 1835; VN, p. 32.

27 Introduction, *More Nonsense, Pictures, Rhymes, Botany, etc.*

28 EL to John Gould, 31 October 1836; *SL*, pp. 23–24.

Chapter One

1 EL to Ann Lear, 3 November 1837.
2 EL to Lord Derby, 14 February 1838.
3 EL to Ann, 3 November 1837.
4 EL to Ann, 4 November 1837.
5 EL to Lord Derby, 14 February 1838.
6 EL to Ann, 14 December 1837.
7 EL to Ann, 27 January 1838.
8 EL to Ann, 14 December 1837.
9 EL to Ann, 27 January 1838.
10 EL to Lord Derby, 14 February 1838.
11 EL to Ann, 29 March 1838.
12 EL to Ann, 3 May 1838.

Chapter Two

1 EL to Ann Lear, 11 May 1838.
2 EL to Ann, 21 May 1838.
3 EL to Ann, 28 May 1838.
4 EL to Ann, 10 June 1838.
5 EL to John Gould, 17 October 1839; *SL*, p. 47.
6 EL to Ann, 26 September 1838.

Chapter Three

1 EL to John Gould, 17 October 1839; *SL*, p. 48.
2 EL to Ann Lear, 26 September 1838.
3 EL to Ann, 11 October 1838.
4 EL to Ann, 29 October 1838.
5 EL to John Gould, 17 October 1839; *SL*, p. 47.
6 EL to Fanny Coombe, 27 October 1841; VN, p. 48.
7 EL to Ann, 29 October 1838.
8 EL to John Gould, 17 October 1839; *SL*, p. 48.
9 *The Letters of Samuel Palmer*, Vol. 1, p. 156; VN, p. 275.
10 D, 16 January 1867.
11 D, 20 April 1862.
12 EL to John Gould, 17 October 1839; *SL*, p. 50.
13 *SL*, p. 293.
14 EL to Lady Susan Percy, 22 December

1840.
15 EL to John Gould, 27 February 1841; *SL*, pp. 51–2.
16 EL to John Gould, 28 August 1841; *SL*, p. 53.
17 *Murray's Handbook of Travellers in Central Italy*, p. 459; VN, p. 51.
18 EL to Lord Derby, 5 June 1842; *SL*, p. 54.
19 EL to Lady Susan Percy, 28 February 1842.
20 EL to Lord Derby, 5 June 1842; *SL*, pp. 54–9.

Chapter Four

1 EL to Ann, 6 February 1847.
2 EL to John Gould, 12 August 1844; *SL*, p. 61.
3 *Illustrated Excursions in Italy*, Vol. I.

Chapter Five

1 All quotations in this chapter are from *Illustrated Excursions in Italy*, Vol. II.

Chapter Six

1 *Illustrated Excursions in Italy*, Vol. I, pp. 126–7.
2 EL to Ann Lear, 27 August 1844.
3 EL to Ann, 24 September 1844.
4 EL to Lady Susan Percy, 29 March 1844.
5 Diary of CF, 14 April to 12 May 1845; *LEL*, p. xxiii.
6 EL to CF, 11 October 1845; VN's private collection.
7 Queen Victoria's diary, 15 July 1846; VN, p. 61.
8 *LEL*, pp. xx–xxi.
9 EL to CF, 21 January 1884; *LEL*, p. 300.
10 *LEL*, p. xiii.
11 EL to Ann, 22 December 1846.
12 EL to Ann, 8 January 1847.
13 EL to Ann, 16 January 1847.
14 EL to Ann, 24 January 1847.
15 EL to Ann, 6 February 1847.
16 EL to Ann, 25 February 1847.
17 EL to Ann, 27 March 1847.
18 EL to Ann, 11 April 1847.

Chapter Seven
1 EL to Ann Lear, 29 April 1847.
2 EL to Ann, 4 May 1847.
3 T.D.H. Battersby, quoted in *Lear in Sicily*, p. 16.
4 EL to Ann, 23 May 1847.
5 EL to CF, 16 October 1847; *LEL*, p. 3.
6 EL to Ann, 23 May 1847.
7 EL to Ann, 17 June 1847.
8 EL to CF, 16 October 1847; *LEL*, pp. 3–4.
9 EL to Ann, 17 June 1847.
10 EL to Ann, 11 July 1847.
11 EL to Ann, 24 July 1847.
12 EL to CF, 16 October 1847; *LEL*, p. 4.
13 EL to Ann, 24 July 1847.
14 EL to Ann, 29 August 1847.

Chapter Eight
1 EL to Ann Lear, 24 July 1847.
2 EL to CF, 16 October 1847; *LEL*, p. 4.
3 *Journal of a Landscape Painter in Southern Calabria* (JLPSA), 25 July to 12 August 1847.

Chapter Nine
1 All quotations in this chapter are from JLPSA, 12 to 28 August 1847.

Chapter Ten
1 JLPSA, 29 August 1847.
2 EL to Ann Lear, 31 August 1847.
3 JLPSA, 29 August to 4 October 1847.

Chapter Eleven
1 EL to CF, 16 October 1847; *LEL*, p. 5.
2 EL to CF, 12 February 1848; *LE*, pp. 6–7.
3 EL to Ann Lear, 16 October 1847.
4 EL to Ann, 15 November 1847.
5 EL to Ann, 9 April 1848.
6 EL to Ann, 28 March 1848.
7 EL to Ann, 9 April 1848.
8 Emily Tennyson to EL, 17 August 1855; VN, p. 111.
9 EL to Emily Tennyson, 9 October 1856; *SL*, p. 142.

10 EL to CF, 6 October 1857; *LEL*, p. 68.
11 D, 2 February 1858.
12 D, 12 October 1858.
13 D, 22 to 25 September 1858.
14 EL to Ann, 4 December 1858.
15 EL to Ann, 1 January 1859.
16 D, 29 March 1859.
17 EL to Ann, 29 April 1859.
18 EL to Ann, 27 January 1860.
19 EL to Ann, 16 February 1860.
20 EL to FC, 22 March 1860; *LEL*, pp. 171–2.
21 EL to Ann, 27 March 1860.
22 D, 11, 15 April 1860.
23 D, 11 to 28 May 1860.
24 D, 27 May 1861.
25 D, 1 June 1861.
26 D, 6 June 1861.
27 D, 7 June 1861.
28 D, 20 June 1861.
29 D, 3 July 1861.
30 D, 9 to 15 July 1861.
31 D, 28 to 30 July 1861.
32 EL to E. Drummond, 23 March 1863; *SL*, pp. 181–2.
33 EL to CF, 8 April 1864; LEL, p.308.
34 D, 10 to 18 December 1864.
35 D, 29 December 1864.

Chapter Twelve
1 D, 8 July 1865.
2 D, 23 September 1865.
3 D, 23 May 1857.
4 D, 8 November 1865.
5 D, 13 November 1865.
6 EL to Lady Waldegrave, 24 November 1865; *LLEL*, p. 64.
7 D, 28 November 1865.
8 D, 29 November to 4 December 1865.
9 D, 1 May to 4 June 1867.

Chapter Thirteen
1 D, 2 June 1866.
2 D, 8 and 10 June 1866.
3 D, 23 August 1866.
4 D, 14 September 1866.
5 D, 30 May 1867.

6 D, 21 August 1867.

7 D, 21 October 1867.

8 D, 2 November 1867.

9 D, 3 and 5 November 1867.

10 D, 5 November 1867.

11 EL to Emily Tennyson, 6 May 1868; *SL*, p. 211.

12 EL to Lady Waldegrave, 9 January 1868; *LLEL*, p. 91.

13 EL to Lady Wyatt, 15 January 1879; *VN*, p. 209.

14 EL to CF, 1 January 1870; LLEL, pp.110-2.

15 D, 26 February 1870.

16 D, 27 February 1870.

17 D, 24 March 1870.

18 D, 28 March 1870.

19 EL to Thomas Woolner, 1 May 1870; *SL*, pp. 216–17.

20 EL to CF, 31 July 1870; LLEL, p.123.

21 D, 26 June to 2 July 1870.

22 EL to Lady Waldegrave, 6 July 1870; EL to CF, 31 July 1870; *LLEL*, pp. 117, 122.

23 Mrs Winthrop Chandler, *Roman Spring*, pp. 29–30; *VN*, p. 211.

24 Hubert Congreve, *LLEL*, pp. 17–18.

25 D, 12 October 1870.

26 D, 17 October 1870.

27 D, 1 and 26 March 1870.

28 EL to Lady Waldegrave/CF, 24 April 1871; *LLEL*, pp. 132–5.

29 D, 21 July to 9 August 1871.

30 EL to CF, 25 December 1871; *LLEL*, pp. 141–2.

31 EL to CF, 13 September 1871; *LLEL*, p. 139.

32 EL to CF, 28 February 1872; LLEL, p.145.

33 D, 30 April 1872.

Chapter Fourteen

1 EL to CF, 26 May 1872; *LLEL*, p. 149.

2 EL to Lady Waldegrave, 6 July 1873; *LLEL*, pp. 153–4.

3 EL to CF, 12 September 1873; *LLEL*, p. 159.

4 D, 20 September 1873.

5 EL to CF, 15 October 1873; VN, p. 225.

6 D, 30 January 1875.

7 D, 7 February 1875.

8 EL to CF, 28 March 1875; VN, p. 233.

9 D, 28 February 1875.

10 D, 5 to 6 June 1875.

11 EL to Lord Aberdare, 26 September 1875; *SL*, p. 248.

12 Hubert Congreve, *LLEL*, p. 23.

13 EL to CF, 15 March 1877; *LLEL*, pp. 199–200.

14 D, 5 March 1877.

15 Hubert Congreve, *LLEL*, pp. 29–30.

16 D, 8 March 1877.

17 D, 21 March 1877.

18 D, 27 March 1877.

19 D, 20 April 1877.

20 D, 21 April 1877.

21 EL to CF, 28 May 1877; *LLEL*, p. 204.

22 D, 7 July 1877.

23 D, 2 August 1877.

24 D, 15 September 1877.

25 EL to CF, 28 October 1878; *LLEL*, p. 210.

26 D, 2 to 11 July 1878.

27 EL to CF, 28 October 1878; *LLEL*, p. 212.

28 D, 16 August 1878.

29 EL to CF, 28 October 1878; *LLEL*, p. 210.

30 D, 24 October 1878.

31 EL to James Fields, 15 October 1879; *SL*, p. 254.

32 D, 19 October 1879.

33 D, 18 and 20 October 1879.

34 D, 2 January 1880.

35 EL to Emily Tennyson, 16 February 1880; VN, p. 245.

36 D, 17 February 1880.

37 EL to CF, 27 June 1880; *LLEL*, p. 234.

38 D, 22 and 26 June 1880.

39 EL to CF, 27 June 1880; *LLEL*, p. 234.

40 D, 28 August 1880.

41 VN, p. 240.

42 D, 17 February 1879.

43 EL to CF, 14 April 1881; *LLEL*, p. 239.

44 D, 14 November 1880 and 21 January 1881.

45 D, 23 to 24 January 1881.

46 D, 18 May 1881.

47 D, 22 May 1881.

48 D, 5 June 1881.

49 D, 19 and 23 June 1881.

50 D, 8 August 1881.

51 D, 9 October 1881.

52 D, 16 December 1881.

53 EL to FC, 30 March 1882; *LLEL*, pp. 258–9.

54 D, 2 August 1882.

55 D, 5 August 1882.

56 EL to CF, 31 August 1882; *LLEL*, p. 269.

57 EL to Augusta Bethell, 19 February 1883; *SL*, p. 263.

58 D, 18 to 28 March 1883.

59 EL to CF, 8 April 1883; *LLEL*, p. 284.

60 EL to CF, 30 March 1882 and 2 August 1883; *LLEL*, pp. 258, 287.

61 EL to CF, 2 July 1882; *LLEL*, pp. 264–5.

62 D, 10 July 1883.

63 D, 12 August 1883.

64 EL to CF, 8 August 1883; *LLEL*, p. 288.

65 D, 12 August 1883.

66 D, 6 September 1883.

67 D, 9 September 1883.

68 D, 11 September 1883.

69 EL to CF, 23 December 1883; *LLEL*, p. 294.

70 EL to CF, 27 January 1884; *LLEL*, p. 302.

71 EL to CF, 4 June 1884; *LLEL*, pp. 309–10.

72 EL to CF, 8 September 1884; *LLEL*, p. 315.

73 EL to F.T. Underhill, 19 August 1885; *SL*, p. 271.

74 EL to CF, 17 September 1885; *LLEL*, p. 340.

75 EL to Mrs Hassall, 21 October 1885; *SL*, p. 275.

76 EL to CF, 11 November 1885; *LLEL*, p. 342.

77 CF, Diary, 25 December 1885; VN, p. 258.

78 EL to Emily Tennyson, 7 December 1886; *SL*, p. 281.

79 Hubert Congreve, *LLEL*, p. 25.

80 D, 27 November 1886.

81 D, 2 to 4 April 1887.

82 Mr Estes to H. Tennyson, 8 May 1887; VN, p. 262.

83 EL to CF, 18 June 1887; *LLEL*, pp. 354–5.

84 D, 31 July 1887.

85 EL to Lord Aberdare, 29 November 1887; *SL*, pp. 282–3.

Acknowledgements

I would like to express my gratitude first and foremost to Dr. David Michell for the loan of his copy of Lear's letters to his sister Ann, which, after his published travelogues, are my most important source for the years up to her death in 1861, and more generally to the part which his family, as descendants of another sister, Sarah, played in preserving these for posterity. For the subsequent years I have drawn most frequently from Lear's Diaries (1858-1887) which are held by the Houghton Library, Harvard, and I have to thank the present Curator, Leslie A. Morris, and her predecessor, Rodney G. Dennis, for their permission to do so; I am similarly grateful to the Earl of Derby for permission to quote from the letters of the 13th Earl; to the Somerset Record Office, Taunton, the holders of Lear's letters to Chichester Fortescue and Lady Waldegrave; and to the Henry E. Huntington Library, San Marino, California, the holders of the letter to James Fields. I am indebted also to Vivien Noakes, universally recognised as the leading authority on Lear, both for her consent to reproduce material from her (recently enlarged and updated) biography and her *Selected Letters*, and for her generous assistance and encouragement over the years.

For sources outside Lear's own writings, both published and unpublished, I am most grateful for the permission of Her Majesty Queen Elizabeth II to quote from Queen Victoria's diary; to Macmillan General Books from *Edward Lear* by the late Peter Levi; and to Sotheby's Holdings Inc. for supplying copies of Lear's letters to Lady Susan Percy. For the illustrations, I have drawn extensively on the copies of Ann's letters held by Dr. Michell and those reproduced by Vivien Noakes in her publications, but I also wish to thank Sandra Powlette of the British Library Permissions Department for permission to reproduce the cartoons (held under BL shelfmark CARTOONS BY EDWARD LEAR, 1843) which accompanied Lear's tour of the Abruzzi; Sir William Proby for those published in *Lear in Sicily*; and Messrs. Agnew's for the photograph of Lear's oil of Venice reproduced on the front cover (it has unfortunately not been possible to trace the current owner).

My final thanks go to my editor, Sarah Such, for her help and encouragement in condensing the original manuscript to a size acceptable to the general reader.

Bibliography

(Published in London unless otherwise stated)

Quoted works by Edward Lear
Views in Rome and its Environs: Thomas McLean, 1841
Illustrated Excursions in Italy, Vol.s I and II: Thomas McLean, 1846
Journals of a Landscape Painter in Southern Calabria, etc: Richard Bentley, 1852
A Book of Nonsense, by 'Derry down Derry': Thomas McLean, 1846
More Nonsense, Pictures, Rhymes, Botany, etc.: Robert Bush, 1872

Quoted editions of works by Edward Lear
Nonsense Songs and Stories, 6th Edition: Frederick Warne, 1895
Lear In Sicily, Drawings selected by Granville Proby: Duckworth, 1938
Edward Lear's Parrots ed. Brian Reade: Duckworth, 1949

Other works by Edward Lear
Gleanings from the Menagerie at Knowsley Hall, ed. J.E. Gray (privately, 1846)
Journals of a Landscape Painter in Albania, &c.: Richard Bentley, 1851
Journals of a Landscape Painter in Corsica: Robert Bush, 1870
Laughable Lyrics, A Fourth Book of Nonsense Poems, Songs, Botany, Music, &c.: Robert Bush, 1877
A series of cartoons accompanying *Illustrated Excursions in Italy,* held by The British Library

Other edited works by Edward Lear
Fowler, Rowena, *Edward Lear: The Cretan Journal*: D. Harvey, Athens/Dedham, 1984
Hyman, Susan, *Edward Lear in the Levant*: John Murray, 1988
Murphy, Ray, *Edward Lear's Indian Journal*: Jarrolds, 1953
Sherard, Philip, *Edward Lear: The Corfu Years*: D. Harvey, Athens/Dedham, 1988

Diaries
Edward Lear's Diaries 1858-1887, held by the Houghton Library, Harvard, USA (call no. MS Eng 797.3)
HRH Queen Victoria's Diary, The Royal Archives, Windsor Castle, UK

Letters
Edward Lear: Selected Letters ed. Vivien Noakes: Oxford University Press, 1988
Letters of Edward Lear, ed. Lady Strachey: Fisher Unwin, 1907
Later Letters of Edward Lear, ed. Lady Strachey: Fisher Unwin, 1911
Letters to his sister Ann, copies held by Dr. David Michell
Letters to Lady Susan Percy, Lots 110-2 Sotheby's sale, 5 May 1982

Biographies
Chitty, Susan, *That Singular Person Called Lear*: Weidenfeld & Nicolson, 1988
Davidson, Angus, *Edward Lear*: John Murray, 1938
Hofer, Philip, *Edward Lear as a Landscape Draughtsman*: Oxford University Press, 1968
Lehmann, John, *Edward Lear and his World*: Thames & Hudson, 1977
Levi, Peter *Edward Lear*: Macmillan, 1995
Noakes, Vivien, *The Life of a Wanderer*: first published by Wm. Collins & Co., 1968
revised edition by Fontana Publishing, 1979
revised again by Ariel Publishing (BBC) 1985
new edition by Sutton Publishing Co. 2004

Articles about Edward Lear
Indian Journal, 13 January 1874
Pall Mall Magazine, 15 February 1886
The Times, 4 October 2001

Articles and books referring to Edward Lear
Chandler, Mrs Winthrop, *Roman Spring*: Williams & Norgate, London 1935
Edgecumbe, Richard (ed.), *The Diary of Frances, Lady Shelley 1787-1817* (1912)
Fowler, Daniel, *Autobiography,*1979
Hyman, Susan, *Edward Lear's Birds*: The Wellfleet Press, 1980
John Murray's *Handbook for Travellers in Central Italy including the Papal States, Rome and the Cities of Etruria*: John Murray, 1842
Palmer, Samuel, *The Letters of Samuel Palmer*, ed. Raymond Lister: Cambridge University Press, 1974
Royal Academy of Arts, *Edward Lear*, exhibition catalogue, London: Royal Academy, 1985

Books on Italian history
Holt, Edgar, *Risorgimento: The Making of Italy*: Macmillan, 1970
Mack Smith, Denis, *Making of Italy 1796-1866*: Holmes & Meier, New York 1988

An up-to-date bibliography, edited by Marco Graziosi, is available on the Edward Lear website, www.nonsenselit.org/Lear